The
PEOPLE
in
the ATTIC

Doretta Johnson
with *Jim Henderson*

The
PEOPLE
ATTIC
in
the

The Haunting of Doretta Johnson

St. Martin's Press
New York

Library of Congress Cataloging-in-Publication Data
Johnson, Doretta.
    The people in the attic :   the haunting of Doretta Johnson / Doretta
Johnson with Jim Henderson.—1st ed.
        p.   cm.
    ISBN 0-312-13583-1
    1. Johnson, Doretta. 2. Psychics—Indiana—Madison—Case studies.
3. Adult child abuse victims—Indiana—Madison—Case studies.
I. Henderson, Jim. II. Title.
BF1517.U6J64   1995
133.1'12977213—dc20   95-23287
                                                                  CIP

First Edition: October 1995

10 9 8 7 6 5 4 3 2 1

For my loving and courageous children,
Steven Scott and Elizabeth Ashley Johnson.
And in memory of my big brother,
Patrick Denise Carrow.
My guardian angel.

Acknowledgments

Many people deserve my thanks but none more than those friends and family who loved and supported me and my family through the darkest of times.

My love and appreciation to Jenny and Paul Geary. To Kellie Sloan for being a true friend. Thanks to Kevin Bradley and Rich Geglin for your friendship and encouragement. My heartfelt thanks to Father Jeff and Father John for all their love and prayers. To Patty Folgerson for all her love, courage, and honesty, and for helping me to unlock the crates. Also thanks to the Jefferies family for their support and kindness.

Forever thanks to Dr. William G. Roll for his lifelong commitment to the study and understanding of parapsychology and for helping me to take my life back and unlock the doors to a happy future. Also a special thanks to Patricia Hayes, and all the wonderful people at her Delphi School of Inner Sense Development in McCaysville, Georgia, for guiding me into the light.

Special thanks to Laken Mitchell for his outstanding guidance and loyal commitment to me first, the book second. To Fred Morris for all his hard work, his positive attitude, and for taking a chance. To Betty Carder and Joe Tackett for their professional guidance and loving support.

A very gracious thank you to Jim Henderson, coauthor of this book, for sharing his knowledge and talent to help me tell my story. Also thanks to Mel Berger, our literary agent, and to Keith Kahla, our editor.

Your adversary the devil, as a roaring lion, walketh about, seeking whom he may devour.

— 1 PETER 5:8

The mind is its own place, and in itself
Can make a Heav'n of Hell, a Hell of Heav'n.

— MILTON

The
PEOPLE
in
the ATTIC

Chapter 1

It is well past midnight and until an hour ago, the house was mostly calm. The occasional disturbances of late have been so innocuous that no one in the family is bothered by them. Still, I am never certain that the battle is over, never certain that whatever we've been fighting has not merely retreated to the crevices and crannies of this house and lies there, waiting.

Although it is late, I have decided to write in my journal. It has become a valuable exercise to help me make even a dram of sense out of everything that has happened. Occasionally, the writing triggers memories of the sort that may, one day, reveal all the answers. Or perhaps not, but the ephemeral medicinal effect, a kind of spiritual balm, makes the effort worthwhile. The writing, the thinking, help give order to the mental jumble, and I want desperately to believe that each discovery leads me closer to the truth.

Something crawled out of hell and into our lives and no one in this family will ever be quite the same. *It*, whatever it is, left a trail of death and pain and emotional mayhem, and the scars will twist around our memories for as long as we live. The gruesome image of Ashley, my six-year-old daughter, hanging from a tree by a slender cord wrapped purposefully around her neck, the memory of Steven, my sixteen-year-old son, on a hospital gurney just down the hall from the grieving family of another young man who *didn't* survive the crash—those are moments that will never fade completely from our minds.

Something a counselor once told me has been rattling around in my head tonight. *When you have sorted this thing out, you will find that it parallels your own life in many ways.*

The suggestion was as cryptic as it was repugnant. What in my life could be kindred to the curse that has followed us the past five years, the noises that thundered in the crawl spaces and shrieked in the attic, the doors that slammed in the night, and the apparitions that paced the corridors of this house and followed us wherever we fled?

Recollections of my childhood exist only in fragments. Too many of those years were packed into crates and stored in a warehouse with no address. Over time, I have seen the contents of those crates in flashbacks that flitted past like subliminal messages embedded in videotape—a face or a sensation that I could not connect to anything in conscious memory.

Two years ago, I began in earnest trying to retrieve the missing pieces, and have succeeded to some extent. My search for those secrets has given me a degree of control over myself and my surroundings—enough command to hold at bay the horrors I may never fully understand. But the grip is fragile and the control may be more tenuous than I know.

For nearly four hours tonight I talked on the telephone with Danny Daines, pumping him for clues. Danny is just one in a string of stepfathers who passed through my life during the brief times that I lived with my mother. She had an affinity for losers, thieves, idlers, drunks, and toughs who enjoyed beating her and her children. Danny beat us, too, but he may have been the best of the lot. For a few fleeting years he also provided the only real home my brothers and sisters and I ever knew.

What I remember most about him is that he took a regular job in a Ford plant and our lives had some semblance of order and normalcy. Danny seemed to enjoy spending time with us. We had holiday dinners and birthday parties. He gave me haircuts, took me to parks to play, and saw to it, when the time came, that I was baptized in the Catholic Church and enrolled in Catholic school.

But he was by no means an exemplary father figure. He had grown up in children's homes and reform schools and had a taste for fast, easy money, even if it meant tempting the law. By the time I was five or six, I was a regular at the pool halls in Gary, Indiana, where Danny and I often spent time while my mother worked. I used to sit on a billiard table, rolling the balls or playing with dice while Danny hustled money from the other patrons. Afterward, we'd stop at a store for his favorite snack—sardines, crackers, and beer—which he shared with me when we got home. In deference to my tender years, he always poured my beer in a glass much smaller than his.

Danny had a violent temper on a short fuse. He beat my mother and whipped her children with abusive fury. But otherwise my memories of him were not all bad. For a time he had reunited me with my brothers and sisters and given us a home. The beatings I accepted. Because I had never known anything else, I simply thought all families lived that way.

Danny and my mother had one child, a daughter they named Nancy, and then they divorced. I did not stay in close touch with Danny and had not heard from him in several years when he called two months ago. He had just been released from federal prison and was living in New Orleans. One of the first things he asked me was "How the fuck old are you now?" I sighed and thought, *So much for father-daughter chats.* We talked for an hour or so that night, and I didn't ask him much about my childhood.

Tonight, the need to do so was more acute.

Over the past two years, I have been told by experts that the safety of my family and my own sanity may depend on this journey of personal discovery. My control is not yet complete. The evil that dwelled here may be in hibernation but this house is not free of its scourge. The little girl is still here and she mystifies us. She is growing older, just as Ashley does. Sometimes we see her and other times we only hear her footsteps or sense her presence, which is like a floral scent borne on a puff of cool air passing through the room. In the past she seemed tormented, but now that the other energies— there is no other satisfactory term for them—are largely dormant, she is almost carefree.

We don't know who she is. Dr. William G. Roll, a parapsychologist, thinks she is me, or some part of me, a spectral remnant of my own subconscious clinging to this household, grasping at the childhood I never knew. My husband, Ron, thinks she is Ashley's twin, the misshapen, undeveloped fetus taken from my womb moments after Ashley was born, then disposed of and never shown to us or discussed with us. As yet, I refrain from an opinion. She is simply a child energy, something that is present to remind us that our ordeal is not yet done.

Danny called about nine and at first I was not in a talkative mood. It was an evening made for solitude. Alternating bursts of sunshine and summer showers had made the day warm and sticky with the sort of gray, doleful air that clings to the skin and seeps into the heart. But after talking with him for a few minutes I felt energized by curiosity.

"Danny," I said, "tell me about the time when you were married to my mother. There are things I'm trying to figure out. Anything you remember would help."

"Well, I was about nineteen when I met her," he said. "She was several years older. You know she was pretty heavy into drugs and alcohol."

Yes, I knew. Booze and dope were as much a part of her life as food and water. "I know you used to beat her," I said. "I remember that much. Why did you do that?"

"Oh, she needed it. She wanted me to beat her," he said. "She hated herself for the life she chose to live. She wanted to be punished. She had this split personality, a good side and a bad side. When the bad side took over, she would do crazy stuff, mean things to people. After a good beating, she was as good as gold for a couple of weeks.

"Hell, she didn't have to stay with me. I beat her real bad one time, knocked all the teeth out of her mouth and put her in the hospital. Your aunt Mary called your grandmother and she came to get her. Your mother wouldn't go with her and she didn't file criminal charges against me. She told everybody, 'Hey, I love him and I'm not going to leave him.' "

"Danny," I said, knowing the answer in my heart before I asked the question, "was my mother a prostitute?"

There was a pause and I could hear him taking a deep breath. "Yeah . . . she was a prostitute when I met her and she worked while we were married . . . and after we divorced, as far as I know."

He not only knew she was a prostitute and accepted it, but he participated in her profession. People who knew him called him a *drugstore pimp*, he said without shame or remorse. "That's just the way things were," he said. "I didn't pimp for her but I took care of her . . . protected her from her johns . . . but I never took her money."

His admission neither astonished nor disturbed me. From what I could recall about my mother, her profession was not the worst of her failings. In truth, I wanted to know more about myself, specific things my grandmother and grandfather could have told me but didn't, knowledge I now needed desperately, knowledge they chose to take to their graves.

"What do you remember about me?" I asked him.

"Well, kid, you and I hit it off real well," he said. "I remember the first time I took you out to play in the snow. You were this little bitty, pale half-pint standing with your nose pressed against the window watching the other kids playing outside. Well, I put your coat on you and away we went. I took you to Goldblatt's and bought you a hat, mittens, and a pair of snow boots. Then we hit the toy department. I bought you a sled. When your mother found us, we were rolling around in the snow in the park. She started screaming that I was going to kill you. They still had you on heart medicine. I told your mother that playing might kill you but not playing would kill you a lot quicker. I told her, 'This baby is going to die laughing.' She didn't think it was a bit funny."

"You weren't around when I had the heart surgery," I said.

"No, that was before I came along. Your mother was still married to Jimmy Mikos then," he said. Jimmy Mikos. The name made me queasy.

"Did she ever tell you anything about it . . . anything that happened while I was in the hospital?"

"Just that you were always puny and sick until you had heart surgery."

"Nothing about a stuffed animal . . . or her getting angry at me for some reason . . . taking me out of the bed and shaking me?"

"Nah, I don't remember that. Why?"

"Nothing, really. Just something I've been trying to recall. I was only three at the time, you know."

Midnight came and went. I had been sitting on a hard kitchen chair for hours but did not feel tired or restless. A few more gaps were being filled, a few more cracks puttied up. The conversation was mildly liberating. Even knowing the truth, finally, about my mother was not as painful as I had expected. *That's just the way things were.* I not only had to uncover my past, but I had to make peace with it.

Just before we hung up, Danny asked me to come to New Orleans and visit him.

"I can't," I said. "I've got a lot of things going on here and I can't leave right now."

He snapped back at me, as if I were still his ward, "You're going to forget what you're doing and get on a plane and come down here."

My muscles tightened and my brain flooded with memories of his brutality, one especially painful memory of him catching me at Gordon's Grocery Store, where he had forbade me to go—he had some kind of feud with the owner—and beating me with his shoe all the way home. He dragged me into the basement, threw me across a bed, and grabbed a strap from the wall. Each time he swung the lash another welt bubbled up on my skin. My mother stood beside him, as passive as a lamppost. She had sent me to the store to buy soft drinks but now that I was being punished for it, she said nothing. I begged her for help with my eyes, but she only stood there watching the beating. At that moment, I hated her more than Danny. He was only wounding the flesh. She was betraying me.

Never had I talked harshly to Danny or stood up to him in any way, but I was no longer a child, no longer frightened by him, and his pushiness now inflamed me. *Who the hell does he think he is?* Suddenly, the house felt warm and the air was like syrup.

"No," I said. "You are not telling me what to do."

Gripping the phone nearly hard enough to break it, I struggled to stifle the rest of what I wanted to say. *Harness your emotions, Doretta, lest your demons smell blood.* I told Danny I was tired and ended the conversation with that.

I sat for a long time staring down at the table. Weariness had crept up on me and I felt too drained to stand up and make my way to bed. The house was so quiet that I was aware of a clock ticking in the other room and the sound of my own breathing. A few minutes ago, I opened my journal and stared at a blank page. I was annoyed by Danny's belligerence but embittered more by the necessity of this troublesome rummaging through my yesteryears in search of . . . what? I didn't even know that much. The bitterness Danny provoked lingered like cigar smoke in an old poolroom, bitterness for the things that had happened to my children and to my marriage and to the life we had hoped to find in this beautiful little town on the banks of the Ohio River.

Calm yourself, Doretta. This "thing" feeds on anger. It knows your emotions and your thoughts and you give it life.

Through the darkened window beside me, I could see the moonlit trees, moist and glistening and motionless. Light from the kitchen spilled across the rear entry of the house and faded onto the wing that had once been a motel. We had high hopes for putting those five rooms to profitable use, but they remain almost as we found them. This house defeated our schemes and our labors, and as the resentment and frustration churned inside me, I began to write in my journal:

I curse the day Ron found this old motel. . . .

A new wave of warmth rushed into the room and I heard faint creaking noises like those made by an old house settling onto its piers, but it wasn't my house settling. Setting my thoughts free on paper often stirred something in this house and the beasts came, like carrion birds to a fish kill, to feed on my anger. The back door slammed and a curtain fluttered as if touched by a zealous breeze.

To hell with them. I'm going to finish this entry. Looking up from my journal, I let my eyes scan the house and half expected the old man to show himself again. I caught a whiff of men's cologne and I knew he was there. Socrates, my cat, snapped awake from his armchair nap and scurried under the table.

"Go ahead, you bastard," I whispered defiantly. "I know all your tricks."

This old house. God, how thrilled we were to have it. To Ron, it was a chance to build his own business. To me, it represented the permanence and stability I craved. I remember the day he came home, excited as a kid on a Ferris wheel, with a real-estate magazine.

"Look at this," he said, shoving the publication toward me. He pointed to the picture of a house that was anything but my dream home. The driveway was unpaved, the lawn seriously neglected, and a wing with five doors jutted out from the stone facade of the main structure. It was not entirely unattractive, just unusual, and I could easily imagine how beautiful it could be with a little love and a lot of hard work. It was the latter that concerned me.

"It used to be a motel," Ron said.

The small print described it as two acres of land, a 4,100-square-foot dwelling, prime location on Clifty Drive, a highway that arches north and east along the outer edge of town where most of the commercial development was taking place. The asking price was $59,900.

"That's a bargain," Ron assured me. "Everything east has been overdeveloped. New growth will have to come this way."

For a year or two Ron had been talking seriously about starting his own business, and to him this property was an ideal opportunity. The large main house could provide us a home and the motel wing could be converted into a day-care center, something that was in short supply in Madison, Indiana. Marge, his mother, had experience in child day care, and he figured her knowledge could smooth out some of the bumps of getting the business started.

"It's perfect." My husband beamed with enthusiasm. "We can live there while we get a business going. Besides, the real-estate market is bound to go back up sooner or later. If someone wants that land for a motel or something in a few years, we can sell it at a nice profit."

"Let's go take a look," I said.

*   *   *

We had moved to Madison from Louisville a year earlier, in 1986, partly to be closer to Ron's job at the Kentucky Utilities plant in Ghent, twenty miles upriver, and partly to escape family problems. Ron's mother had not approved of our marriage, and the tension between her and me had spilled over to my relationship with Ron. Not only would the move put a sixty-mile buffer zone between our past and our future, but new surroundings might help mend the tear in our marriage.

We rented a house on Allen Street and immediately fell in love with Madison. It is a small town of sublime beauty—budding trees and wild lilies lining the riverbanks; rolling farmlands generous with soybeans, corn, and tobacco; winding roads cut through steep, craggy hillsides; nights so hushed you can almost hear the invisible clouds float by. *Norman Rockwellville,* I began calling it soon after we arrived. There is a restful, bucolic tempo to life here, and I wanted that for my children as well as for myself. I could run to the grocery store without bothering to fortify the house against burglars or cross a darkened parking lot without looking over my shoulder for muggers. Ron's twenty-mile commute to work was as easy as circling a block in downtown Cincinnati. Most important, it was the perfect environment for raising my children—in all, a blessedly benign family habitat.

Ashley was three months old when we came here and Steven was eleven . . . eleven years going on twenty. In Louisville, he had been growing up too fast, being swept along by fads—hip clothing, funky haircuts, earrings—and heading into his teen years on streets awash with the usual urban temptations of drugs, alcohol, and crime.

I had seen what those streets had done to my brothers and sisters, and to me. Patrick, three years my senior, was shot to death in the backseat of a car. Larry and Billy, who are older than Patrick, bounced back and forth between drugs and jail cells. My baby sister, Nancy, barely out of her teens and the mother of a young daughter, was facing sentencing for drug trafficking about the time we left Louisville. As a teenager, I had my own flirtations with drugs, and had it not been for my grandmother, I might have fallen all the way into that pit.

Small towns have their temptations, too, but in our new surroundings, it did not appear that vice had reached critical mass.

We had been in Madison a short time when two boys walked by the house carrying fishing poles. They were about Steven's age and they invited him to go along. As they walked away, I saw one of them point to the ring in his ear and ask, "What is that, man?" That air of innocence was as sweet as a breeze from an alfalfa field. Yes, this was where I wanted my children to grow up.

The first few months here were close to idyllic. Steven had no trouble adapting to his new school, and I made a couple of close friends: Barbara Summers, who had six children, the youngest being close to Ashley's age, and Kellie Sloan, who had two daughters who would become Ashley's best friends. Almost effortlessly, my family had geared down and merged into the slower pace of life.

Much of the recent turmoil in my life—the emotional strain of losing my grandmother, the troublesome pregnancy with Ashley, the steady in-law friction—was fading into the distance. As the spring of 1987 arrived, I felt more relaxed than I had in years. Even the notice that we were being evicted from our rented house had little effect on my mood.

My biggest concern was Nancy. She was convicted of the drug charge and was being sent to Pewee Valley Women's Correctional Institute for six years. If not for her, then for her daughter, I felt a responsibility to try one more time to help her get her life straightened out.

"This is it," Ron said, turning off of Clifty Drive and parking in front of the motel wing of the old house. My first impression bordered on gloom. The place was sadly unkempt. The grounds were overgrown with weeds and untended bushes. The house had a haggard, forsaken look, and the dusty windows were sad eyes staring out at us.

Ron got out, cupped his hands around his face, and leaned against a kitchen window.

"Well, it needs some work," he said.

The interior was illuminated only by light filtering through the dusty windows, but I could see well enough to measure the degree of my husband's understatement. We made our way across the front and down the other side, past three bedrooms and two bathrooms, and around the corner to a screened-in porch in back. We peered into the three vacant motel rooms and walked around the large backyard.

Another house, also old and in not much better repair, sat 150 feet or so behind and slightly to the north. A man came out and ambled casually toward us.

"Can I help you folks?" he said. "I'm Benny Cyrus . . . sort of the caretaker around here."

"We're just looking around," Ron said. "We saw this place advertised for sale."

Benny told us the property was owned by a man named Jerry Freeman, who bought it as an investment a couple of years before. Cyrus and his family had lived in the house and managed the motel before it closed. After that, Freeman offered to let them move into the smaller house out back.

"We just couldn't handle it here anymore," he said. I assumed he was referring to the upkeep on such a large, old dwelling.

Whatever commercial plans the owner had for the place apparently were abandoned when construction on the Marble Hill nuclear power plant was suspended and Madison was thrown into a kind of economic withdrawal, one symptom of which was depressed real-estate prices. Freeman put the place up for sale, Benny Cyrus said, but had found no takers in two years.

"You're welcome to look around all you want," he said, walking away without offering to show us the inside.

Driving home, Ron said, "I'm going to call the realtor."

"Shouldn't we think about it for a while?" I wondered.

We had not started out looking for real estate with commercial potential. A couple of months earlier we had been notified that the owner of our rental house had sold it and the buyers were eager to take occupancy. Since we had to move anyway, buying was the prudent option, but this place needed a lot of work and we were not flush with money. The $59,900 asking price may have been reasonable, but when you're broke everything seems out of reach. Ron, though, was like a man with a fever. He talked incessantly about the potential of the property and I couldn't have restrained him with logging chains.

Although this house was not the castle of my fantasies, I wasn't difficult to persuade. Running a business from our home was an appealing prospect. I had not worked since before Ashley's birth, and we certainly needed a second income. A day-care center would allow me to be with my children and at the same time contribute to the family's financial health.

"There may never be a better time to buy," Ron said, and I had to agree.

*   *   *

Unfortunately, I had to leave most of the house hunting and negotiating to my husband. That spring I was distracted by the predicament of my baby sister, and my involvement in her problems began to open up my own past to me in painful, awkward ways.

Nancy was only five years younger than I, but had been more like a daughter to me. When we were growing up, I dressed her and took her to school and tried to steer her from the paths our older siblings had taken. In the latter effort, I had failed, but now she had a daughter, not yet four years old, who needed her. Nancy's ex-husband, Tim, had joint custody of the child but single-parenting was an enormous struggle for him.

As soon as I learned that Nancy had been sent to prison, I began making phone calls and writing letters trying to find some grounds for getting her released. I had bailed her out of jail before, but this wasn't so easy. Her offense was serious, but I argued to the parole officials that she needed psychiatric help more than incarceration. I offered to take responsibility for her.

Eventually, a judge was persuaded to grant Nancy a shock parole. She was released to me on the condition that she enter Madison State Hospital for psychiatric evaluation and treatment for drug addiction. I visited her often, and, initially, her presence in Madison was no burden to me. I was just happy to have her out of prison and on her way to another chance in life. At least, that was the case until I received a call from the hospital requesting that I come in for a talk with one of Nancy's therapists.

"I wonder if I'll ever get her raised," I said to my husband.

"You're going to have to let go of her sometime." He shrugged.

"She hasn't had it easy," I said, a primal defensiveness welling up in my chest. Ron grew up in a normal, middle-class family. How could he even begin to comprehend the things Nancy had been through?

At the hospital, the psychiatrist was courteous but wasted no time in explaining why I had been summoned.

"We need a little background information on her," he said.

"I'll try," I said, suddenly uncertain that I really knew, or could remember, everything.

"I'd like to discuss your family with you," he said. "I'd like to discuss your and your sister's sexual activity with your mother."

"WHAT?" I was floored. My face crimsoned and I gripped the arms of the chair. "Are you crazy?"

Some question to throw at a shrink.

He sat calmly and kept his eyes fixed on mine. I took a deep breath and tried to compose myself.

"What has she told you?" I said.

"Nancy has talked about when the two of you were young, about being in bed with your mother and her men friends. She's told us both of you took part in the things that went on."

"Are you nuts?" I asked him again. "Nothing like that ever happened."

For the next few days, that conversation stuck in my head like an old tune. I resented my sister's attempts to include me in her therapeutic sessions and having my personal life probed because of her problems. Ron tried to talk to me about the house on Clifty Drive, but I was preoccupied with the things Nancy was telling her doctors about our childhoods. I tried hard to remember those years and it made me feel lousy, like a scavenger prowling through a garbage dump looking for salvageable junk.

The apartment is small, untidy, and sparsely furnished. I am eight years old, maybe nine. Patrick is there. Nancy, too. Mother has been drinking hard. Vodka. I know what it does to her and cringe at the sight of that bottle. She puts us in a small room and locks the door. "I've got a friend coming over and you're not my fuckin' kids," she warns us. "I'm your baby-sitter, you fuckin' understand? If one of you motherfuckers calls me Mom, I'm killing you." She slams the door shut and we hear the lock turn. There are no windows and the room is hot and stifling. Nancy curls up in a corner and cries. Patrick and I sit on the floor, afraid to speak, afraid that Mom will hear Nancy crying and punish us all. We sit and we wait for her to let us out.

Mother was a scary person. She was rough and she did crazy, mean things. But the story Nancy told the psychiatrist was too bizarre. I began to wake up during the night, sweating and gasping from bad dreams. I tried to put Nancy's problems out of my mind and concentrate on finding a new house, but sometimes, when driving or cleaning house or pushing a grocery cart through the aisle of a supermarket, an image would scamper through my mind and vanish before I could seize it. It was like an old black-and-white photograph of four people in a bed—two little girls, perhaps seven and two years old, a young woman, and a man. I recognized my mother, Nancy, and myself, but the man's face was faded and blurred. It is an instant locked in time. Nothing is happening. Nothing.

*   *   *

June Nighbert, the realtor who listed the property, was pleasant and helpful, but when I saw the interior of the house, I wanted to run. It was in far worse shape than I had ever imagined. At first glance we could see that whoever bought this place was in for a long siege of Sheetrocking, plumbing, wiring, painting, caulking, patching, carpeting, and Lord knows what else.

Ron did not seem discouraged by the condition of the house. He chattered away about what could be done with one room or the other, how walls could be removed in the motel wing, about the playground potential of the large backyard.

Mrs. Nighbert had been forthright about the house's shortcomings and she didn't give us the hard sell. In fact, after observing Ron's enthusiasm, she asked a question that could not have come from a salesmanship textbook: "Do you know what you'd be getting yourself into here?"

Peculiar question, I thought. *Is she trying to discourage us from buying it?*

"Why has it been vacant so long?" I asked her.

"Oh, a rumor had gone around town that the floor joists were bad. It wasn't true but nobody will even look at it now," she said.

I literally had to drag Ron out of the house. Bad joists or no, he was not ready to retreat.

"Thanks for your help," I said to Mrs. Nighbert.

"We'll be in touch," Ron said.

Oh, yeah? I thought.

We were. Ron knows a lot about carpentry and fixing things up. He was convinced that he could do most of the repair work himself. Over the next several days, he kept calling Mrs. Neibert and going back to the house. He pestered her so much that she gave us our own set of keys so we could visit the house at will. Ron measured nearly every inch of the place trying to estimate what the materials and other rehabilitation costs would be. He even called his mother in Louisville to see if she would lend us the money for a down payment.

"I'm going to make him an offer," he said when he was satisfied that he knew all he needed to know about the house. "Twenty-four thousand dollars."

I laughed. "He'll never take it. That's less than half what he's asking."

"Won't hurt to try," he said.

Mrs. Nighbert's reaction was similar to mine. "I don't know if I should insult him with that offer," she said. "I doubt that he's ever going to go that low."

"Let's see," Ron insisted.

The realtor shook her head with amusement. "Okay," she said, "but don't hold your breath."

Ron handled all the haggling from that point. Jerry Freeman turned down his offer and countered with a compromise of some kind. Ron stood his ground, and the dialogue went back and forth for a few days. When Mrs. Nighbert called him with the owner's latest offer, he hung up the phone, grinned at me, and said, "We got it for twenty-four five."

On July 2, 1987, we took possession of the property. We were so excited that we didn't think to ask ourselves why the owner would settle for $24,500—$35,400 less than his original price. Sure, real-estate prices had tumbled. But that much? We didn't ask ourselves why Benny Cyrus and his family had moved into the smaller house in back. We didn't ask why the realtor raised the question of what we would be *getting into*. We asked nothing about the house or the land on which it sat. Why would we? It was just a house, wood and stone. How many homebuyers truly know the history of the house they purchase?

Chapter 3

Most of our spare time that summer was spent trying to repair a few rooms of the new house so we could at least partially move in. We hadn't expected it to be a piece of cake but we weren't quite prepared for the impediments we faced at every turn. Not only was the house uninhabitable, it seemed to resist all of our efforts to rehabilitate it. Even simple tasks, such as painting and wallpapering, turned into monumental challenges.

Our first priority was to have the house rewired (I had a terrible fear of fires) and new heating and air-conditioning installed to replace the old baseboard heaters. One bathroom also had to be quickly put in order. The toilets wouldn't flush and we couldn't bathe because the water pipes and drainpipes were in such poor condition.

Nothing went smoothly. The electrician kept hitting snags that delayed the rewiring. His tools would disappear and the new parts that he ordered—switches, fuse boxes, and the like—would arrive so damaged that they couldn't be used.

The man from the phone company had just as much trouble. He installed the lines, hooked up the phones—and they didn't work. He would tinker with them for a while, try again, and get nothing. Finally, he got one phone to work a little. The line would cut in and out, and even when it was open the static was so bad that communication was impossible.

"We can do it," he said, exasperated by the effort, "but it's going to take a lot of work. We'll have to charge you forty dollars an hour."

Getting television cable installed was even worse. The first man who came out stayed only a short time before he threw the cable down at my feet and said, "Good luck. They don't pay me enough to go into your attic." He left with no explanation, and I merely assumed he was lazy or had an attitude problem. Another contractor eventually did the job, but only after numerous delays.

Well, it's an old house, I reasoned, *and a few glitches are to be expected.*

Our plan was to first fix up one bathroom, the kitchen, and the large middle bedroom, which could be shared by the whole family until the other bedrooms were in order. That bedroom would soon become Ashley's. Steven laid claim to the front bedroom. The back bedroom was small but had several lovely windows and seemed ideal for Ron and me. The living room, the screened-in porch (which we planned to enclose into a sunroom), and the second bathroom would have to wait.

Ron's mother, sister, and brother-in-law drove up from Louisville to help us paint. We needed every hand we could recruit. Ron was busy repairing the bathroom floor and sealing off the door that led to the adjoining bathroom.

As we tackled the bedroom, we began to understand the frustrations of the electrician and telephone installer. The house refused to cooperate. We spread the paint with rollers but it bubbled and ran down the walls. We smoothed it again, and again it blistered and ran.

"I think we got some bad paint," Ron said. He took it back to the store, where it was tested and he was assured there was nothing wrong with it.

"There may be some moisture in the Sheetrock," the salesman said. "Try it again and if it doesn't hold, call me."

It didn't hold and the paint store sent a man out to check the walls. He could find no moisture, no reason why the paint should not coat. After a few more attempts, the paint held.

The house also rejected our initial efforts to paper the living room. We put the paper on at night, and when we checked the next morning, it was on the floor—not crumpled as though it had slid down the walls, but carefully laid out across the carpet. That happened a couple of times before the paper finally held.

In spite of the obstacles, enough of the house was habitable by the end of summer that we began moving in, taking just the bare essentials and storing the rest of our belongings. We had no way of knowing then that it would take a full year to completely settle into our new home.

For every foot of progress we made, we seemed to lose a yard. One morning we got up and found a wall in the sunroom sopping wet. There was no water source in the attic and we could find no evidence that the roof leaked. In fact, it had not rained in several days. Lights would flicker on and off, but an inspection of the wiring never revealed a cause. Appliances shorted out, lightbulbs exploded, and even our cars seemed jinxed. A couple of weeks after we moved in, one of them blew an engine. We could never overtake the backlog of malfunctions.

Nothing puzzled us more than the fireplace. Its beautiful sandstone face was marred by a long, crescent stain just above the opening. It had bugged me from the beginning and I tried, off and on, to remove the stain, first with household cleaners and then with stronger chemicals, but with no success.

"We could try a sandblaster," Ron suggested when everything else had failed.

It is a messy procedure, but the fireplace is the centerpiece of the living room and I didn't want to live with that stain. We rented the sandblaster, hung plastic over the walls, and sealed everything off.

It worked marvelously. The stain was gone and the blanched surface of the stone was smooth and flawless. Within a few days, though, the blemish began to reappear, faint at first, but deepening each day until it was exactly as it was when we bought the house.

It was as if this place had a mind of its own and did not want us tampering with its appearance. We planted flowers and bushes and they died. Nearly new lawn mowers quit working. We installed new window glass and it cracked. If I had been inclined to believe in ghosts, I might have believed that this property had spirits hell-bent on keeping it for themselves.

As the weeks passed, the setbacks shifted from the annoying to the inexplicable.

Lying under the covers in a half-waking state, I heard scratching noises in the attic. I stiffened and stared at the ceiling. Several minutes passed, and just when I had convinced myself that I had imagined it, the scratching resumed.

I shook my husband awake. "There's something in the attic," I said.

He listened and heard nothing. He scowled, gave me a you're-losing-it look, and went back to sleep. A few nights later, it happened again. But that time, the scratching was loud enough to wake Ron up without my prodding.

"A bird may have gotten in there somehow," he grumbled.

That was hardly reassuring. As a child I had heard people say that a bird entering a house was a bad omen, a harbinger of death. While I was never superstitious, I was not one to trifle with the Fates. Given a choice, I would prefer that birds stay outside. And, if that was a bird in the attic, it had to be something larger than a turkey to have made the noise that had awakened us.

"That was too loud to be a bird," I protested.

"Well"—he yawned and closed his eyes—"it was some kind of animal. Go back to sleep."

What else could it have been? Certainly not a rat or a squirrel. I imagined all manner of beasts that could have infiltrated our attic, and those thoughts made me feel silly.

The next morning, I had nearly finished making the bed when a feather fluttered down from the ceiling and landed on a sheet in front of me. I looked up at the air-vent cover and felt foolish. It was a bird after all. *Doretta, this place is getting to you.*

Fighting the house five or six days a week was oppressive, and we fell into a routine of trying to get away as much as possible on weekends. One Saturday morning, we drove to Louisville to visit Ron's mother and do some shopping. We returned the next day and found the inside of the house splattered with blood and membrane and dead birds lying on the floor. Somehow, they had gotten into the house and bashed their brains out flying into the walls. One was barely alive but still slamming into a wall when we walked in. Yet, the windows and doors were all closed and locked and the glass shield across the fireplace was intact.

How the birds got in was a mystery we had little time to pursue. We had to repaint and clean the blood from the carpets, and by the time that was done, another crisis presented itself. We came home on a Sunday evening and found water standing in the kitchen, laundry room, and back porch.

The source was a gash in a washing-machine water hose Ron had replaced less than a month earlier. When those hoses leak it usually is at the end, where the rubber joins the brass fitting. This, however, was a break in the middle of the hose, a break clean enough to be a cut.

"Damn the luck," Ron said. "Sometimes I wonder if somebody is out to get us."

Kellie stopped by to see how things were going and over coffee I confided in her. Ron and I were both exhausted from struggling with the house, and the health of the entire family seemed to be affected. I was having constant headaches. Steven got a poison-ivy rash that defied medication and nearly ate his leg off before the doctors could find a way to control it. Ron developed allergies that he had never had before, and his passion for this house was waning.

"I'm ready for some good news," I told her. "Every day is another problem, something else to fix, something else to cope with."

Our friends had begun to kid us about the house and the steady stream of complications and bad luck. Kellie was not exactly jovial that day. She listened to my tales of woe and nodded in sympathy.

I got up and walked to the living room and straightened a large painting that hung on the far wall.

"That picture always looks crooked," I laughed. "I think this house is lopsided or something."

"To tell you the truth, D. J., something about this house has always bothered me," Kellie said. "Every time I walk by those doors to the old motel rooms I get the creeps."

A pang of resentment shot through me. This house was eccentric and it might have been more than we bargained for, but it was my home and that meant a lot to me.

"There's nothing wrong with the house," I protested. "We've just had some rotten luck."

Unlike the rest of us, Ashley was not having health problems, but her behavior took a strange turn—nothing frightening, just peculiar. Ron and I had moved into our bedroom, and she and Steven continued to share the middle bedroom. During the night, we would hear her giggling and jabbering as though she were playing with someone. A few times, I went in to check on her and saw her sitting up in her bed, laughing, her arms stretched forward as if reaching for something that wasn't there. I wasn't concerned about her nocturnal escapades until the incident with the knife.

Ron was working late and I was sitting up watching television, waiting for him to come home. About two o'clock, I heard a knock at the door. From the street, this place still looked like a motel, and a few times since we moved in, people had come to the door to inquire about a room.

I opened the door and no one was there, so I went back to watching television. A few minutes later, I heard the knock again. I didn't get up immediately, and the knocking became louder and the door shook as though someone were pulling on the knob to force it open. I went to a window with a view of the entrance and saw no one there. The pounding stopped but I could hear leaves crunching and ruffling outside.

I stepped quietly to the phone to call the police. The line was dead. Someone was trying to break into the house and I couldn't call out. There was no gun in the house, so I took a butcher knife from a drawer and went back to the window to watch the front yard.

Time passed in slow motion. Then I saw a woman and two boys walking from the road toward my house. As they got closer, I recognized Barbara Summers and her sons and let them in.

"We were just driving home," she said, "We turned down Clifty Drive and the car died right in front of your house. Everything went completely dead, like the battery had been removed."

I told her what had happened to me earlier and she accompanied me outside to look around. We found no signs of a prowler.

"I need to call my husband," she said.

"Well, the phone's not working," I said, following her back inside.

She picked up the phone and said, "I got a dial tone. Guess it's okay now."

Her husband drove up a few minutes later, got in her car, and turned the ignition. The engine roared to life.

"It's been a crazy night," I sighed.

Steven had awakened earlier, complaining of pain in his lower abdomen, so I decided to sleep in the bedroom with him and Ashley. Besides, I was still a little shaken by the prospect of a prowler in the area. If he returned, I wanted to be near the children.

Leaving the kitchen, I picked up the butcher knife, took it into the bedroom, and slid it between the mattress and springs with the handle protruding for easy access.

My head ached and my eyes felt as heavy as bowling balls and I fell into a hard, deep sleep; it had lasted no more than a couple of hours when an extreme pressure on my jaw jolted me awake. Through hazy, stinging eyes, I saw Ashley standing over me, astride my neck, holding the handle of the knife in both her tiny hands, pushing the tip of the blade into my mouth. If the knife had not caught on the metal braces I wore on my teeth, it would have gone into my throat.

Ashley was a year and a half old and still wearing diapers, but she was balanced firmly on the mattress and her hand had a tight grip on the knife. Her eyes were wide and pale and she seemed to be looking past me. I grabbed the knife and she fell backward, screaming the screams of a terrible fright. I picked her up and held her until she was calm. I put her back to bed and took the knife into the kitchen.

Dawn was breaking and I was too frazzled to go back to sleep. I made a pot of coffee and waited until it was time to get Steven off to school.

Ashley's behavior didn't really bother me. I had become accustomed to her nighttime capers. But I blamed myself for leaving the knife where she could get to it. Her screams had awakened Steven, so he was aware of what happened. For weeks, he referred to his baby sister as Lizzie Borden.

Throughout the fall, we continued making a little progress fixing up the house, but it was expensive. After Christmas, our finances were in shambles and I decided to go back to work. Small factories provide most of the jobs in Madison, and work was not hard to find if you were not fussy about the hours. I took a third-shift job at Key Manufacturing but found the hours intolerable. I got to bed about the time the rest of the family was getting up. After a few weeks, I quit and went to work for the Coach House Restaurant. At least I was home by midnight.

One night after work I drove up to the house and found the screen door wide open. It had been pushed so far back that it was wedged tightly against the concrete porch floor. The kitchen door was not only unlocked, but was also standing open. Ron never left the doors open like that, especially not on a freezing winter night, and I was almost afraid to go inside.

Once inside, I woke Ron up and scolded him for leaving the door open.

"I checked it before I went to bed," he insisted. "It was closed and locked. I remember checking all the doors."

Of course, I believed him, but that meant I also had to believe that someone had unlocked and opened the door after he went to bed. Nothing was missing from the house. If someone had broken in, burglary wasn't the motive.

Before going to bed, I fixed something to eat and sat down at the table near a window facing the driveway. I had been there only a couple of minutes when I heard a car door slam. I got up, pushed the curtain aside, and saw the silhouette of what appeared to be a man sitting in my car. My first thought was to get Ron out of bed, but before I could move, a car came around the bend in Clifty Drive and its headlights shone through the windows of my car. The silhouette was gone. *You're seeing things, Doretta. Time for bed.*

Chapter 4

As much as the growing burden of this house, the stress of dealing with Nancy had put me in a fragile mental state. She had been released from Madison State Hospital and was living in Louisville again, but I had been called upon—"coerced" may be a better word—to attend therapy sessions with her while she was here. Those were unpleasant times. We relived our childhoods and tried to sort out memories and experiences. Some we had repressed and some we had exaggerated, but all were traumatic for me.

I have always dealt with the past by shutting it out of my mind. When an unhappy memory came calling, I slammed the door on it. When situations became unbearable, I turned away from them, became somebody else, and pretended they never happened. Denial was an integral part of my nature, but in helping Nancy wrestle with her demons, a few of my own were unleashed. Yes, our mother was a wretched soul who flung us into the world with heavier memories than we should be expected to carry, and I hated her for it. But I wanted to leave that behind, leave it interred in the grave I had dug for it.

Because of the way I grew up, I've always tried to be attuned to my moods and mental quirks, fearful that the violence that had always been around me would worm its way into my nature. The abuse and rejection, I feared, could have left hairline cracks in the emotional dike that impounds madness. If I was going to go crazy, I wanted to see it coming for the sake of my children.

More and more, as 1988 dragged on, I was certain I could see it coming. First the man, the silhouette, in my car. Then the woman in the bathtub.

Ashley was only about two years old and still required my constant attention, especially when bathing. She liked to make a game of her bath, and that day she was standing in the tub, drawing on the tile wall with her soap crayon. I sat on the side of the tub, gazing absently at her handiwork. From the corner of my eye, I saw something in the water. I looked down and froze like a deer caught in headlights. Through the film of soap on the sloshing water, I could see the head and shoulders of a woman facedown at the bottom of the tub.

"Oh, God." I grabbed my daughter and ran into the hall.

"What's the matter, Mommy?" she asked, standing naked and wet beside me.

My pulse was racing, not in fear of what was in the tub, but of what was in my head.

"I'll get you a towel, honey," I said.

I went back into the bathroom, knowing there was nothing there, nothing but bathwater and the soap crayons Ashley had dropped when I scooped her up. Not for a second did I expect to see a body in the bathtub. Why, I wondered, had that particular illusion presented itself? Of all the possible hallucinatory concoctions, why a woman facedown in the water? Does the subconscious communicate in code?

It wasn't the first time I had wrestled with such questions, and I decided to say nothing to my husband. What would I tell him? We had a dead woman in our bathtub? I had a psychotic delusion? My complaining about noises in the attic and phantom burglars rattling the door had halfway convinced him I was a candidate for the psycho ward. Better not to build the case against myself.

I think I had always expected to go crazy, and now I found myself wondering if this was what it felt like.

When I was six weeks old, my mother gave me away. She gave birth to me in Gary, Indiana, and, just as she had done with my older sister and three older brothers, she waited until she was able to travel and then carted me off to Cocoa Beach, Florida, and turned me over to my grandparents. She went back north to work in the bars around Chicago.

Grandpa was a housepainter and must not have made much money, but he and Grandma always took in my mother's offspring as though they had a solemn duty to do so. Why Grandma was so charitable to my mother is a mystery. Grandma was a stern fundamentalist Pentecostal with narrow views toward sex (it was taboo), alcohol (it was taboo), and drugs (worse than sex and alcohol). She had to have known something about my mother's lifestyle, her work in bars, the succession of men in her life, and yet she loved my mother and shouldered her burdens with amazing forbearance.

At the time, my mother was married to Patrick Carrow, the father of her first three children. I was given his name but was told later that he adamantly renounced his parentage and claimed I was the product of a union between my mother and a Gary physician. It was just as well with me. Pat Carrow had been a boxer and was as mean and ruthless as any of the men my mother took up with. Marilee, Patrick, and Larry lived with Pat Carrow off and on as they were growing up and Patrick told me that Pat Carrow beat them and sometimes made them eat from dog bowls.

Giving me to Grandma may have been the kindest thing my mother ever did for me. By Grandma's account, I arrived in Florida with a full head of cradle cap and skin that cracked and bled. I was sick half the time and slept the other half. "You weren't much bigger than a biscuit," she said. Mother told her she was going back to Gary to finalize her divorce from Pat Carrow and would return in a few weeks to be with her children.

She went back to Gary and hooked up with a guy named Jimmy Mikos, a professional thief and all-around loser. The next time I saw her, as far as I can remember, was nearly three years later. I might not have seen her then if my health had not steadily deteriorated. I caught colds and pneumonia easily. Crawling was an effort and I was more than a year and a half old before I took my first steps. My aunt Reda, who lived near us and sometimes looked after me, suspected I had a heart problem and encouraged Grandma to take me to a specialist. She was correct. The diagnosis was a deformed heart—patent ductus arteriosis—and without surgery, the doctors said, I would die. They recommended a team of heart specialists at the University of Indiana in Evansville.

Grandma never told me many details, except that she and Grandpa had no money for the operation, so she called my mother at the only telephone number she had, the number of the bar where she worked in Chicago.

"They said she couldn't come to the phone because she was busy with a customer," Grandma said. "I told them, 'You've got five minutes to get her on the phone or I'll have the vice squad there in ten.' Your mother got on the phone and said, 'Are you crazy? These people wouldn't think twice about blowing up your house with you and the kids in it.' She worked for a bunch of gangsters but they didn't scare me."

Mother and her new husband, Jimmy Mikos, rented an apartment in Evansville and then came to Florida to get me. Apparently, I was too weak to undergo heart surgery. The Indiana doctors decided to wait a few months until I had acquired enough strength for the operation.

Grandma and Grandpa also moved to Evansville to be near the family. I lived with my mother and stepfather for several months before the operation, but my memories of Jimmy Mikos were always vague. Grandma never told me much about him, except that he loved me and treated me well. At any rate, he wasn't around very long. The day after my surgery, the FBI kicked in the door of our apartment and arrested him. I never saw him again.

Not long after I left the hospital, my mother gave me back to Grandma and returned to her career as a B-girl in bars around Gary and Chicago. That's where she met Danny Daines, my next stepfather.

To my recollection, I never thought much about the surgery until years later, when I was about twenty years old. I began to have flashbacks, dim memories that moved in and out of my head like changing wind. I would see metal bars, like the bars of a jail door, or the bars that surround a child's hospital bed. Sometimes it was clearer . . . it was a hospital bed. I saw a man's featureless face superimposed over the bars and a distraught little girl—angry or scared, I couldn't tell which.

Over a period of weeks, the flashbacks became more vivid but the images fit no comprehensible scenario. A little boy, a teddy bear, a man wearing a turban, the smell of disinfectant. Gradually, they began to merge and sort themselves into sequence. The man in the turban was a doctor and the little boy shared my room. His parents were always there and he was surrounded by toys. I was almost always alone. Mother rarely came to the hospital. Grandma had no transportation and could not come as often as she wanted. I remembered lying in my bed and crying and the little boy's father walking over and handing me a teddy bear. I fell asleep cuddled next to it. When I awoke, my mother was reaching into the bed and picking up the stuffed animal. "It's not yours," she said. "You have to give it back." I remembered a burning rage. I screamed and shook my bed rails and reached out for the teddy bear. The next thing I remembered was the bear lying on the floor, a hole in its body and stuffing scattered everywhere. The little boy was crying and his parents were upset. Everyone seemed to be angry with me. My mother pulled me from the bed and shook me violently. Grandma grabbed me away from her and held me and soothed me. I never knew what happened to the teddy bear. When the memories of that hospital room began coming back, I asked Grandma about it but she never gave me details or an explanation.

For years I was troubled by the stuffed bear and my inability to recall how it became torn and disemboweled. I was also confounded by the shaded face of a man who appeared in the flashbacks. Maybe there were some things my mind refused to resurrect.

Except for a few years when Mother was married to Danny Daines, my time with her was intermittent and usually ended with her dumping me at a relative's house and disappearing into the night. Grandma and Grandpa had me most of the time, but even they presided over a family that was morbidly dysfunctional.

My grandmother's parents had married her off to a drunken and abusive older man—in settlement of a debt—when she was thirteen, and she had five children before she was old enough to vote. She left her husband and sought welfare assistance for her children. The welfare agency did help—by putting her kids in foster homes. Until she was able to get a job in a plant that made pies and cakes, Grandma lived on the streets, sleeping in doorways and empty buildings and scrounging for food wherever she could find it.

With her first paycheck, she rented a small apartment and collected her children. They lived on the edge of hunger and destitution until she married the man I call Grandpa, although he was not my mother's father.

For the rest of her life, Grandma carried those years of deprivation like a backpack full of sand. Christmas was the worst time for her, and it was miserable for everyone around her. She always went into a deep depression and relived the pain of all the holidays past, the Christmas mornings when her children woke up to a barren apartment and cried because they thought Santa Claus had overlooked them. She never wanted to put up a tree or buy gifts. The depression would stay with her until the new year and then vanish like the haze before a rising sun.

Still, she had a very strong faith in God, which often assumed a curious configuration. She believed in corporal punishment and backed it up with a violent streak that terrorized her grandchildren. She didn't just spank us, she whipped us, regardless of the seriousness of our transgressions. The ferocity of her whippings was usually amplified by the Holy Spirit.

"Bless me, sweet Jesus," she would say with the first swing of a belt or stick, drawing fervor and energy from the rejoicing. "In . . . WHACK . . . the . . . WHACK . . . name . . . WHACK . . . of God . . . WHACK . . ."

Yes, I had always expected to snap someday, and the longer we lived in the house on Clifty Drive, the more reasons I had to suspect that my mental state was growing brittle with age.

For her second birthday, in May of 1988, Ashley received a battery-powered, voice-activated, talking doll. It responded to a human voice by saying, "Mama, Mama, Mama." Ashley loved dolls and carried one with her all the time.

For some reason, that particular doll annoyed me. In fact, I disliked it intensely. A few weeks after her birthday, I was lying in bed and heard a soft voice coming from Ashley's room. My first thought was that she was up playing. As I approached her door, I recognized the doll's voice saying "Mama, Mama" over and over.

I pushed the door open and looked into the bedroom. Ashley was sound asleep but I could hear the doll's voice droning on. I looked around the darkened room, trying to figure out where it was coming from. Suddenly, the doll fell to the floor in front of me, its rubbery mouth still moving and calling, "Mama, Mama."

What could have activated it? Steven had moved into his own room by then and Ashley was alone and asleep. The doll kept crying "Mama" as I picked it up and turned off the power switch. It continued to speak. I flipped the switch on and off to no avail. I opened the back compartment and tore out the batteries. It fell mute and stared back at me with vacant glass eyes.

The next time I heard the doll's voice coming from Ashley's room, I was halfway out of bed, intending to turn it off again, when I remembered that I had removed the batteries. I lay back down and listened. *Am I actually hearing it or is the voice in my mind?* It soon stopped talking, but the next day I sneaked the accursed device out of Ashley's room and threw it away.

Most of the things that caused me to wonder about my own sanity seemed to be centered on my daughter. Whenever something happened that I couldn't quite figure out, Ashley was somehow involved.

We bought her a little antique rocking chair that had round, wooden braces, three or four inches apart, just above the rockers. We kept it in the living room and she sat in it while watching television. One morning I was doing the dishes while she was watching "Sesame Street." I had just walked to the sink when I heard her scream. She was caught in the rocking chair, wedged between the dowel braces under the seat, howling in pain and barely able to breathe. I tried to free her, but the chair had a deathly grip. I ran into the laundry room, got a hacksaw, cut through the dowels, and tore them from the chair to release her. Ashley had long bruises across her back and abdomen.

When Ron got home, I showed him the chair and told him what happened.

"How could she have gotten between those braces?" I asked him. "There's barely room to put your fist between them."

Ashley couldn't tell us what happened, but Ron came up with a theory that we both accepted, more or less; it was thin, but better than no theory at all. Ashley must have jumped off the sofa and hit the chair, and her momentum carried her through the narrow space between the rocking chair's slats. Improbable but not impossible.

We didn't bother to fix the rocking chair. As with the talking doll, I threw it away.

During the time I was working until midnight, I usually slept later than the rest of the family. It wasn't uncommon for Ron and Steven to be gone when Ashley and I got up. They always locked the door behind them. One morning, I went into the kitchen and found that the door was open and Ashley was outside, playing on the porch. *Ron's been careless again,* I thought. Then I saw the yellow sticker on the inside of the kitchen door. It was from a UPS deliveryman and it said he would return later with the package.

When he came back, I asked how he got into the house.

"I knocked on the door and it opened and a little girl was standing there," he said. "I asked if her mommy was at home and she didn't say anything. I called out several times and no one answered, so I left that note and went on my way."

I was astonished that Ashley could have unlocked and opened the door. I pushed it shut, engaged the lock, and asked her to open it. She could barely reach the knob and couldn't turn the lock at all.

Chapter 5

During our second year in the house, Ashley began to get up at night, go into the living room, turn on the television, and raid the refrigerator for cookies or snacks or peanut butter sandwiches. We found it more amusing than upsetting. To us, she was just a child who enjoyed being alone and was not afraid to prowl around a dark house by herself. Apparently, she did not consider herself to be alone. After her nighttime forays, we usually found that she had fixed two of everything—two glasses of milk, two plates of cookies, two of whatever she had.

Then she began to talk about the little girl.

The first time it happened, I had been wrestling with health problems—the female variety—and fatigue, occasionally falling into such a deep slumber that I awoke feeling as if I had been drugged.

One such morning I was roused by Ashley crying and tugging at me. She was extremely upset, and I fought to shake off the grogginess that was like cement in my head.

"What's wrong, baby?" I asked.

"My neck was hurting and I yelled for you," she said. "I yelled and yelled and you didn't come. The little girl said you couldn't hear me."

My eyes were still unfocused and my head was begging for the pillow.

"What little girl?" I said.

"The little girl who comes to my room," she said.

Obviously, she's had a bad dream. I pulled her into bed with me and rubbed her neck.

Nothing more was said about the little girl until two weeks or so later, at the dinner table. As was customary at our house, we each talked about our day and anything interesting that had happened to us.

"I have a friend," Ashley informed us.

Ron and I smiled at each other.

"A little girl," Ashley said. "She comes to my room at night and plays with me."

Later, Ron and I discussed Ashley's *imaginary* friend. Children who are alone a lot often dream up playmates, so we figured it was time to enroll our daughter in a preschool so she could be with children her own age. She loved preschool but she continued to talk about her *imaginary* friend and I realized that Ashley had formed a special bond with her, was defensive about her, and protective of her.

We were sprawled on the floor with her coloring books and crayons one day and Ashley said, "The little girl doesn't get to color."

"The little girl who comes to your room?"

"Uh-huh."

"What does she look like?" I asked.

"I didn't see her, Mommy," she said.

"Where does she live?"

"She lives in the attic most of the time. She's very sad. She doesn't have a mommy and she doesn't have a home of her own."

"That would be very sad, wouldn't it?" I said. I didn't want to encourage her fantasy, but it seemed important to discuss it with her and let her know it was all right to have the feelings she was experiencing. I had never heard of a child suffering serious damage from conjuring up a playmate.

She said, "Yeah, they stay up in the attic."

They? The cast was growing. Before, she had always spoken of one friend.

"Who are they?" I asked.

She wouldn't answer and I repeated the question. Her mood visibly changed. She became angry and rubbed her crayons hard across the paper.

Trying to lighten the conversation, I said, "Let me guess. Every night after I go to bed they come out and get peanut-butter-and-jelly sandwiches."

That seemed to upset her even more, as if she felt I was mocking her. She stood, glared at me, and said, "How would you like to have to live in somebody's attic and not have a mommy?"

She gathered up her crayons and went to her room.

*   *   *

Weeks would pass during which things seemed perfectly normal in this house and in my head, but every time I thought we had reached level ground, the mountain rose up before us.

Through dogged persistence, we had made the house livable— actually very comfortable and attractive, I thought—but every day was a hassle to keep it that way. Appliances shorted out and when we replaced them, the new ones did the same. Lightbulbs flickered and exploded in the sockets. By the spring of 1989, the engines in two of our cars had blown up. Cats, dogs, goldfish, every pet we acquired for the children, died within a few months.

We had not yet tackled the five former motel rooms and we rarely talked of our plans to convert them to a day-care center. My husband's moodiness deepened and he was spending less and less time working on the house.

Other strange things befell us.

The word HELLP was scratched into the wall paneling. Ashley was too small to have done it. Steven denied that it was his handiwork. "Mom," he said, pleading his case, "I know how to spell 'help.' "

Charges for long-distance calls we had not made—some to the Virgin Islands—appeared on our phone bills. We were not held responsible for them by the phone company, but it was another in a growing catalog of irritations.

We did not dismiss the possibility that someone somehow was getting into the house while we were away. That suspicion had been aroused by the broken washing-machine hose that appeared to have been cut, the wallpaper taken from the walls and laid out on the floor, the birds—all suggested that the house was being opened in our absence. There was never any sign of forcible entry, and we had no idea who would be harassing us or why, but we could arrive at no other conclusion.

The Cyruses, who occupied the small house behind ours, were our closest neighbors, and shortly after we moved in I had a mild run-in with them. Their children had a habit of riding their bikes through our yard and entering the house without knocking. I was still new enough to Madison not to be familiar with local customs: People thought nothing of walking into a neighbor's house unannounced. I held my tongue and remained courteous until one day I was looking for our wheelbarrow and saw it leaning against the Cyruses' house. I walked over and firmly told them to refrain from taking things from our property without permission.

But we were not enemies and I had no reason to suspect them.
But who?

We had not seen each other in seven years, and therefore my sister
Marilee's call caught me completely by surprise. She was living in
Clarksville, Indiana, sixty miles from Madison, and wanted to come
visit me.

My first memory of Marilee was when our mother married Danny
Daines and settled down long enough to reunite her brood for a few
years. She was ten years older than I and teased me mercilessly, but
we got along fine. In later years, though, we did not stay in close
touch. That's the way it was with all my brothers and sisters. We
faded into and out of each other's lives almost randomly.

We had the house in pretty good shape and I was anxious to show
it off. As soon as Marilee arrived, I led her from room to room, telling
her about the hard work we had put into the place. I was proud of
my home and pleased that after all this time, it had come together
nicely.

"We've still got a lot to do," I said. "We're going to knock out
some walls in that motel wing and fix it up. Ron thinks we can turn
it into a day-care center."

She was hardly enthusiastic about the place. In fact, she was visibly
ill at ease.

"You don't like it?" I asked.

"Well . . . there are so many hallways, or something," she said.
"It gives me a funny feeling."

Kellie had said almost the same thing. First my best friend and
now my sister. The hurt must have been written on my face.

"But it's nice," she said. "It really is. I'm happy for you."

That night we made herbal tea and talked into the wee hours. I
began to confide in her about some of the strange things that had
happened since we had lived in the house—problems with the paint
and wallpaper, the birds, animal noises in the attic, the unexplainable
flooding, car engines blowing up, Ashley and the rocking chair.

I told her about the vision I had of the woman in the bathtub and
Ashley's imaginary friend who lived in the attic and only came out
at night. "This house has caused us a lot of stress," I deadpanned.
"I think it's affecting our minds."

"It may not be in your mind," she said, more serious than I
expected.

Marilee told me she had become good friends with a woman she met at a psychic fair she had visited with a girlfriend the previous year. They signed in and a woman asked her if she wanted to see a palm reader, a fortune-teller, or a numerologist.

"I told her I wanted to see a psychic," Marilee said, "a gifted one. I told her I would recognize a phony. So, she took me to this psychic named Susie. I felt kind of silly, but we were just there for a good time. Well, she told me things that nobody could have known unless they knew me real well. She told me about my relationship with my son, his age, and all that. She told me my father lived with me and I was going into business—this was just before I opened my beauty salon. She told me about a relationship I was in. I mean, it just blew me away."

I kidded her about falling for some sideshow hocus-pocus but she was a firm believer. In fact, she and Susie had become good friends, and through that friendship Marilee had become enthralled with the supernatural.

"Sis, have you ever played with a Ouija board?" she asked.

"Well, sort of," I said. "Steven got one for Christmas a couple of years ago. We messed with it a couple of times, but nothing happened."

A Ouija board has the letters of the alphabet and a few simple words, such as YES and NO, in a circle along the outside edge. An arrow mounted in the center points to the letters or words to answer questions posed by the participants. Supposedly, the board acts as a medium through which the dead communicate with the living.

"They're weird," she said, describing a night at the beauty shop when she and her partner, Cindy, set one up after closing time, lit candles, and proceeded to communicate with the board. Several times, she said, the pointer spun wildly and the candle flames shot up like propane torches. "That made us a little squeamish. We put it away."

"Aw, those don't work. Steven's never moved," I said. "I think it's still in his closet."

"Go get it. Let's try something," she said.

"Marilee, you're turning into an old fortune-teller," I laughed.

"You listen to me and take this seriously," she said. "There's something wrong with this house. Let's see if we can find out what it is."

Ron and the kids had been in bed a long time. I crept into Steven's room, got the board, and placed it on the kitchen table. We turned down the lights and lit candles, and Marilee gave me instructions. We sat facing each other with our fingertips barely touching the board. She began by asking it simple questions and the needle moved slightly from side to side.

This is a trick, I thought, *Marilee's still teasing me.* But try as I might, I couldn't figure out how she was doing it.

"Is someone there?" she asked.

Without hesitation, the arrow rotated to the word YES.

"Who are you?"

Slowly and deliberately, the arrow spun to one letter after another, spelling out S-P-I-R-I-T. I studied Marilee's hands, trying to detect her method of manipulating the arrow. Feigning fear, I exhaled a low "Ooooooooh."

Marilee was not amused. "You can't make fun of the Ouija board," she snapped. "You'll make the spirits mad."

She lowered her head again and asked, "Do you know my mother?"

The arrow pointed to YES and then, as if struck with a hammer, the pointer flew off the board and landed on the floor. Marilee's hands had not moved and she appeared no less startled than I. *Maybe she isn't teasing me.*

She retrieved the pointer from the floor and placed it back on the board. "Maybe we'd better change the subject," she said.

"Are you male or female?"

F-E-M-A-L-E.

"What is your name?"

C-K.

Marilee repeated the question and the answer came back the same: C-K. The letters meant nothing to either of us, but they were all the board would reveal.

"Are you dead?"

YES.

"How did you die?"

M-U-R-D-E-R.

"Do you like Doretta?"

NO.

"Do you like Ron?"

The arrow didn't move.

"Do you like Ashley?"

Nothing.

"Do you like Steven?"

Nothing.

Marilee went back to her initial question. "Do you like Doretta?"

For an instant, the arrow twitched and then swung toward the word NO.

Marilee looked grim, but I still believed this was another one of her jokes. When she came to live with us in Danny Daines's house, she told me she was not my sister, but an alien from another planet. I was only five years old and could be convinced of anything. Now, I was a complete disbeliever in such things as aliens, spirit worlds, and Ouija boards, but something about this experiment tantalized me. The truth is, I was having fun.

With my finger resting lightly on the board, I asked, "Is this house haunted?"

YES.

"Is it haunted by a man or a woman?"

Before the arrow could move, Marilee yelled "You pervert!" and the arrow again flew off the board.

"Did you call me a pervert?" I laughed.

But Marilee's eyes burned with rage, a fire from a boiler that smoldered somewhere out on the edge. "No," she said, surprised that I had asked. "I don't know why I said that. It just burst out of me."

What had begun as a playful evening had turned glum, nearly spooky.

"All right, that's enough," I said. "Do you realize it is nearly five o'clock?"

We put the board away and went to bed.

We were up by nine or ten and were planning to go shopping. In a state of mild panic, Marilee strode into the kitchen. Her face was the color of skim milk. "Doretta, you're not going to believe this," she said. "I walked into the bathroom and your blow-dryer came on. I didn't even touch it, it just started running."

It wasn't unusual for me to leave the dryer plugged in and resting in the towel rack. That's where it was when she walked in.

"I didn't touch a light switch or anything. It just came on," she said. Her uneasiness with my house was intensifying.

"Casper the Friendly Ghost," I chided her.

"He may not be so friendly," she said.

"Come on, sis. I told you we've had a lot of trouble with the wiring. Screwy things just keep happening," I assured her.

"I picked it up and turned it off, Doretta," she said. "The switch had been turned on."

"I wouldn't be surprised," I said.

We drank a cup of coffee and I went into the bathroom to get ready for our shopping trip. I took a shower and washed my hair, and before reaching for the dryer, I slipped on a pair of headphones connected to a small radio. My hair is fairly thick and doesn't dry quickly. I prefer listening to music rather than the hum of a blow-dryer.

I was bent over, letting my hair fall past my face, when I heard static. Thinking the broadcast signal was fading, I raised up to adjust the radio. Still holding the dryer pointed toward my head, I looked in the mirror and saw flames and smoke pouring out of the dryer. I let go of it and it flew threw the air and landed in front of the bathtub. As soon as it hit the floor, the dryer split in half and the flames went out.

Marilee heard the commotion and ran into the bathroom.

"Oh, my God," she said. "I told you, Doretta, I told you."

"It just shorted out," I said. "It's not the first time."

"You've got to get out of here," she said. "You can move to my house."

"Marilee, that's ridiculous," I said. "It was just an electrical short, that's all."

A light rain was falling when we left the house, dropped Ashley off at preschool, and headed downtown. Marilee continued to nag me about leaving the house, and nothing I could say would put her mind at ease. What happened when we returned home certainly didn't help matters.

In the kitchen, we had installed a ceiling fan and light fixture with five decorative globes arranged in a circle pointing out from the center of the fan. When we walked in, I flipped on the switch and the five bulbs exploded in a rhythmic sequence. POP, pause, POP, pause, POP, pause, POP, pause, POP.

Marilee was going to pieces. I ushered her into the living room and tried to calm her down.

"I'm getting out of here," she said. "I can't stay here any longer."

"Marilee, don't be silly," I said. "This is an old house. It's no big deal. We've lost toasters, coffeepots, irons, a lot of things the same way."

"Sis, please," she urged, "you've got to get out of here. This house is mad at you."

I persuaded her not to leave until morning, and when Ron came home that evening, Marilee tried to convince him that I was in some sort of danger here.

"Look," Ron said, "there's a good explanation for what happened."

"What?" Marilee demanded.

Ron didn't know precisely, but he came up with a theory.

"When the blow-dryer shorted out, Doretta took an electrical charge that stayed in her body. She was wearing tennis shoes, so she wasn't grounded, okay? The electricity couldn't leave her body. Maybe when she touched the light switch, it left and caused the bulbs to blow out."

Marilee wasn't buying it and, frankly, I had a little trouble with it myself. My opinion was that the electrician had done a faulty job of rewiring the house.

The next morning, Marilee packed up to leave and informed me she had no intentions of coming back. We walked out to her car. The morning was cool and golden, and scattered clouds from yesterday's rain stuck to the powder blue sky like wads of lint. Such mornings always brightened my mood.

"That Ouija board was right about this house, Doretta," Marilee warned. "You'll regret it if you stay here."

Teasingly, I said, "Ooooooooh."

"It's not funny, sis," she said.

"I really enjoyed your visit, Marilee. Promise me you'll came back soon."

"Hah."

She started up her car and I waved good-bye. She looked at me one last time, shook her head, and drove away. *Poor Marilee,* I thought. Like all my mother's children, she had her problems. I shouldn't be surprised that she would end up talking to Ouija boards, hanging around with fortune-tellers, and rambling about a vengeful house.

A few days after her visit, Marilee called and told me her father, Pat Carrow, a man I barely knew but whose name I carried for the first fifteen years of my life, had died. I drove to Clarksville to be with her. My brother Larry was there also, and the three of us went to the funeral home to make the final arrangements. Pat Carrow meant nothing to me. He disavowed fathering me and treated me like a leper my entire life. While we three siblings sat like toy soldiers on a store shelf and waited for the mortician, I studied Marilee's face, her high cheekbones, her deep-set brown eyes and wavy, auburn hair. I turned toward Larry and saw a mirror image of Marilee. Both were a mirror image of me. How could Pat Carrow deny me and claim them?

The funeral director asked the perfunctory questions, and Marilee made it clear that her father had no insurance and we had little money for his burial. She and Larry looked to me for an opinion and I said, "Just cremate him." I suppose a part of me wanted to make certain that he burned for the terrible way he had treated me.

Marilee and Larry agreed that there was no reason to hold a visitation or service of any kind. Pat Carrow had been a vicious man, liked by very few. Among the three of us, we could not think of a single person who might attend his funeral.

"What do you want to do with the ashes?" the funeral director asked.

Marilee, Larry, and I exchanged quick glances and answered in unison, "Just throw them away."

Chapter 6

Sparks leaped from my fingers and an electrical arc buzzed between my hand and the door of the microwave.

Kellie looked over and raised her eyebrows. "I swear, D. J., I think you're a witch."

Witch. I'd get used to that. Most of my friends and coworkers at the Coach House had seen the sparks that flew when I reached for metal and they kidded me about it. The fact that more often than not I wore black, a common color for restaurant workers, contributed to the illusion. With dark hair, dark eyes, dark clothing, and electricity shooting out of my fingertips, I probably fit a lot of people's mental picture of a witch.

"I may be," I joked with Kellie. "My grandmother was a witch, you know."

Grandma and Grandpa always lived in impoverished neighborhoods, the kinds of places where people could not afford to take the children to the doctor unless they were seriously ill. Many women brought their kids to our house to be cured. At certain times of the year, Grandma didn't just run a household, she presided over what amounted to a local clinic for minor childhood maladies.

The mothers who sought her treatment affectionately called her "the old witch" because of the curative prowess she demonstrated. Although it was a term of endearment, I disliked the connotation. Witches were evil and there was no witchcraft in Grandma's methods. She was a great believer in home remedies, brewing up concoctions of broths and herbs to treat colds and sore throats and the like. She was also quick with a poultice to treat sores, cuts, insect stings, rashes, and boils.

But she had another talent, something that as a child growing up in her house I heard people refer to as a "sixth sense." She just knew things.

My little sister, Nancy, ran away from home once. Grandma ordered Grandpa into the car and made him drive around, following her directions, which, to anyone but Grandma, would have seemed random and aimless. But her instructions eventually took them far from our neighborhood to a housing project my grandparents had never seen. She got out of the car and walked straight to an apartment, knocked on the door, and confronted the tenants and an astonished Nancy.

Grandma never explained how she divined Nancy's whereabouts, if she even knew. Hunches and intuition were not subjected to critical analysis in her house.

Although Kellie's remarks about me being a witch were made in jest, I sometimes felt that there was a serious core to them, that she watched me with the same anticipation with which a child might watch a magician, always expecting the unexpected.

"Have you talked to your doctor about this stuff?" she said, referring to the electrical charge that drained out of my fingertips.

"No. What would I do, ask him to check my battery?"

My husband's hypothesis may have been partially correct. When I flipped on the kitchen light switch and five bulbs exploded sequentially, I probably was carrying a charge in my body, but there had to be more to it than picking up a stray volt or two from a defective blow-dryer. I was convinced that rather than being the victim of the dryer's malfunction, I was the cause of it.

Whatever I was carrying around wasn't mere static electricity. That will make your clothes cling and your hair stand up—it will even knock out a computer—but it won't cause a stove to overheat.

Many times, I put food in the oven to bake at 350 or 400 degrees and it would be broiled within a few minutes. At other times, the heating element would burn out and have to be replaced. I was tearing up so many appliances that Ron must have suspected me of trying to sabotage our home. Most of the time he wasn't around when those things happened and he had a hard time accepting my explanations of *how* they happened.

It wasn't until he witnessed one incident that he took me seriously. I was getting ready to take some clothes out of the washing machine. I reached over to open the dryer door and received a jolt powerful enough to knock me off my feet. I literally fell to the floor.

"Are you all right?" Ron said, rushing over to help me up.

"Now do you believe me?" I snarled, furious that it took a near electrocution to dispel his skepticism.

"I'd better check this dryer," he said. "There must be a power leak in it somewhere."

Ron is an electrical technician at the Kentucky Utilities power plant and he has meters and other instruments for checking current flows and things like that. He tested the dryer carefully and found nothing wrong with it. On the chance that the errant current could be showing up intermittently, he rigged a lightbulb that would flash on if electricity got into the metal body of the dryer. The bulb never registered an impulse. In fact, the dryer worked fine when anyone else used it. Obviously, the electricity was coming from me. How did it get inside me? Where did it come from? Who knew?

At the plant where Ron works, they have an area they call the brushyard because when you walk through it you feel like you have been brushed with electricity. The workers, who pick up a lot of electricity on the job, test themselves periodically by gripping a wire connected to a meter that measures the amount of electricity stored in their bodies.

Ron came home one day and told me he had registered thirty-eight amps on the meter. No one else went above eighteen or nineteen.

"Maybe I'm bringing the electricity home," he said. In the absence of another sound presumption, we let it go at that. But if Ron carried a high charge, I wondered, why did the appliances not short out when he used them? How was the electricity transferred to me? It didn't make sense, but at the time very little did.

Steven walked out of the bathroom and into his bedroom to get dressed for school. He was shirtless and what I saw shocked me. I followed him into his room and asked, "What happened to you?"

Bruises covered his back, chest, and arms. He had been quiet in a cranky sort of way for a few days. This probably explained why.

"I don't know," he said. "My back felt sore when I woke up and these bruises were there."

I looked closely at his skin. There were large splotches, the kind that would come from heavy blows with a broomstick.

"Steven, I want to know how you got these marks." My first thought was that he had been in a fight or a car wreck. He was fourteen years old, an age when kids start riding around with older friends.

"Mom, I don't know," he said.

"Did someone beat you up?"

"No." He was emphatic but not defensive.

Within a day or so the bruises were gone. Then he woke up one morning and they were back.

"I'm taking you to the doctor," I told him.

Our family physician looked him over and asked the same questions I had asked. Steven denied knowing how the bruises got on his body.

"I'd like to talk to Steven alone," Dr. Stack said. Under those circumstances, it is reasonable for a doctor to suspect child abuse by one or both of the parents. I knew I hadn't beaten the child and it would have been next to impossible for Ron to have done it without my knowledge.

They were alone for fifteen or twenty minutes. When they came out of the examining room, Steven proceeded into the waiting room and I stayed behind. The doctor shook his head and said, "He insists he doesn't know what happened. I don't think he's lying . . . or trying to protect anyone."

"Could it be caused by something internal?"

"Maybe. We'll run some tests and see what we find."

He found nothing. All the tests came back normal, and the doctor was stumped.

"Just watch him pretty close and bring him back in if this continues," he said.

No prodding was necessary for me to watch my son closely. He and I had been through some times together, and twice in his infancy I had come close to losing him. If anything I probably was too watchful and too protective of him.

Steven was the only good to come of my first marriage, which occurred at a time in my life when I was struggling to find my own way. I was fifteen years old, had recently buried my mother, dropped out of school to work in a film-processing plant, and was still living with my grandparents. Ray Holmes was sixteen years old, a temp worker who had hair longer than mine, a fondness for marijuana, and a family history about as miserable as mine. I met him at a high-school football game and considered him generally obnoxious. He kept pestering me to go out with him, and eventually I caved in. He was one of the few boys I had dated whom I could invite to my house and not feel humiliation for my dysfunctional family and the poverty in which we lived.

In the two years before I met him, I had been despondent and suicidal. Mother got sick and came to live with us at Grandma's house. The place was in constant turmoil. Patrick was rebelling at being sent to a school for blind children and caused so much trouble that he was expelled. Mother got better and went back to her old life, deserting her children once again. I was thirteen and in a lot of emotional pain. I started smoking cigarettes, hanging around with a rough crowd, and defying my grandmother's orders. One infraction led to a beating with her belt. She laid me across her bed and hit me with the belt until I couldn't take it anymore. I pulled one leg back and thrust my foot into her stomach and screamed, "No more! You're not going to hit me anymore!"

Crying and yelling, Grandma ordered me upstairs to my room. "I'm calling your mother to come and get you," she threatened. "Nobody hits me and gets away with it. You can just go live with your mother."

Nothing terrified me more than the thought of living with my mother. I lay across my bed and cried. I wanted to die. If I died, the pain would end. I wasn't afraid to die, but I was afraid to go to hell. Grandma had told me that people who killed themselves could not get into heaven. What was the point of leaving this hell if I was only bound for another.

Dying by natural causes made more sense. The window of my bedroom led to the rooftop. When everyone was in bed, I crawled out the window and sat in the wet snow in my nightgown. I sat and shivered until I couldn't take the cold anymore. I went back inside and went to bed in the wet nightgown. By morning, I hoped, I would have pneumonia and in a week I would be dead.

All I got from three nights on the roof was a bad cold. The aches and fever and chills diminished my death wish, but not my emotional distress. I became self-destructive, biting myself on the arms when I was upset, rarely eating, swearing and acting rowdy. I even got in a fistfight with a boy and whipped him.

One day I came home from school and Grandma was crying. Mother was sick again, she said, and was coming back to stay with us. Later I would figure out that she was coming home to die.

It was during that time that I met Ray Holmes. I had had enough of my family's agony and wanted out. He was in the same boat. Breaking away was something we both longed for. Grandma had essentially raised me, but after Mother's death her health began to fail and I felt like a permanent burden to her. Besides, she and my mother both had married at thirteen. I was two years off the pace. Time to move on. It made sense for Ray Holmes and me to team up, get away from the past, and start our own lives.

We married and moved to Gary, Indiana, and for a while Ray had a pretty good job. He made about thirteen dollars an hour but he didn't know what to do with the money, except buy marijuana. Our son was born a year later but that did nothing to bolster my husband's sense of responsibility.

When Steven was about three months old, Ray was out of work and we had drifted to Salem, Indiana, to stay with his sister. We were broke, living off relatives, and had few prospects for the future. One morning, I looked out the window and saw my seventeen-year-old husband riding a skateboard with a couple of twelve-year-old neighborhood kids. *He's still a child, Mrs. Holmes. You're going to have to leave and let him grow up.*

I called my grandparents in Louisville and they came to Salem to get me. I got two jobs—one at Schuler's Food Mart and another at a Quick Stop Food Mart, where I put a playpen behind the counter and watched over Steven while I worked. I had an apartment and was doing fine until Ray Holmes blew into town.

He hadn't grown up much, but I let him see his son as often as possible. He was, after all, Steven's father, and since we had not officially divorced, he was still my husband. Therefore, the custody issue had never been addressed, much less resolved. He picked Steven up one day to take him for a drive and I didn't see my son again for nearly five months.

With no experience at tracking down missing persons and no one to rely on, I was lost. I called the police, friends, relatives, anyone I could think of but could not get a line on my son's whereabouts. I looked everywhere but soon realized that Ray had left town.

My initial panic and anger turned to a dull and constant numbness—loneliness, depression, and futility rolled into one bleak wad. I began hanging around with a group of people from my apartment building, staying out late and, eventually, dabbling in drugs, first smoking marijuana and then shooting speed, something the others called "beans."

Grandma had not shown much concern for my son's absence, and a few months would pass before I understood why. On New Year's

Eve, I went to her house. I had lost a lot of weight and that was the first thing she noticed. The second was the needle tracks on my arm.

"My God, you're shooting drugs," she said.

"Yeah," I said. There was no point in denying it. She couldn't beat me anymore and her lectures bounced off me like Nerf balls. I loved her and wanted her acceptance but, if it became necessary, I could live with her rejection. For once, she was more concerned than reproachful.

"You're going to kill yourself . . . with that heart . . ."

"I don't care anymore. I don't have anything to live for. I hope I do die."

She took me into another room, away from the rest of the family, and said, "What would it take for you to want to live . . . to stop messing with that stuff?"

"I just want Steven back."

"You're going to have to prove you're off drugs first," she said. That was when I realized she knew something about my son.

She wanted me to go into a detox program, but I refused. "I'll quit on my own," I promised her.

Nearly two weeks passed before she was convinced. Feeling better and starting to regain weight, I went by her house. She looked me over like a produce buyer inspecting a box of squash. "Let's go get him," she said. She had known all along where my son was. Why hadn't she told me sooner? She may have thought that I was better off without a child, or she may have believed that sooner or later I would be forced to move back into her house and she would be saddled with the burden of a great-grandson. I couldn't blame her for being weary of raising other people's children.

We drove to Gary and found my son. He was staying with the parents of Ray's girlfriend, a block from my aunt Mary's house. Ray was at work.

"I want to see my baby," I said when the door opened.

"You're not ever going to see him again," the woman said.

I went back to my aunt's home and called the police, who sent two officers to the house where Steven was staying. Because neither Ray's girlfriend nor her parents had legal custody of my son, they were forced to let me see him. They also were unable to stop me from walking out with him and taking him back to Louisville.

A year later, Ray stole our son again, taking him from my grandparents' house while I was working. It was no problem finding them that time. I knew they were back in Gary.

I scraped together some money, reserved a seat on a Greyhound bus, and packed a set of clothes for Steven, including a heavy coat.

In Gary, I went straight to Aunt Mary's house. Ray had been dating one of her daughters, so she knew how to reach him. From the demeanor of my aunt and cousins, I suspected they were actually in cahoots with my ex-husband and might, therefore, try to thwart my plan to take back my son. This time it might not be so easy to just walk away with him, I thought. I was correct.

"I'm going to sign some papers for you to have the kid," I told Ray on the phone. "I don't want him. He costs me money, he cries all the time, a real pain.

Remembering how I had taken Steven back a year earlier, he was testy at first.

"I mean it," I said. "He's all yours. I'd just like to come by and see him for a few minutes, then I'm gone."

To my surprise, he consented. I borrowed a car and drove over to the trailer house Ray was renting. The place was a sty and the first thing I saw was a bag of marijuana on an end table. I picked Steven up, said a few words to him, and tried to appear as disinterested as possible.

"Look, let me take him and spend one more night with me at Aunt Mary's," I said.

"No way you're leaving here with him," he said.

"Okay, you can take him over there. Aunt Mary and Uncle John will be there. They won't let me leave with him. I just want to spend one more night with him. We'll go to a lawyer in the morning and sign whatever papers we have to sign."

Apparently, he was convinced. He bundled Steven up and we drove to Aunt Mary's house. When Ray left, he took Steven's coat with him, thinking that was sufficient to keep the child homebound until he returned for him.

The next morning, I was dressing Steven with the clothes I had brought when Aunt Mary walked in. "What are you going to do?" she asked.

"I'm taking my baby and I'm going home," I said.

My plan was to take a cab to the bus station, but when I went through my purse, I discovered that someone had taken my money. To hell with them, I was leaving anyway.

It was biting cold and snow and ice covered the ground, but I set out walking with my two-year-old son in my arms. Three blocks away, I flagged down a police car and told the officer my story. What happened next still amazes me. The officer drove me to a truck stop and checked with the drivers until he found someone going in the direction of Louisville.

The first driver took us part of the way and, using his CB radio, located another trucker who could take us a little farther. We changed trucks two or three times and the last driver dropped us off right in front of Grandma's house.

It took me a year and a half of cleaning toilets and bedpans in a hospital to save enough money to divorce Ray Holmes. I asked him to sign papers giving me complete custody of our child and he said, "For a hundred bucks I'll sign them."

It was the best money I ever spent.

Steven's mysterious bruises vanished and did not return, but the rest of the family was visited by physical ailments that were just as mystifying.

Dressing Ashley one morning, I smelled a rancid odor on her. I checked her undergarments and found an orange stain unlike any I had ever seen. She suddenly complained of a pain in her abdomen and a fetid orange substance ran from her bowels and down her leg. Back we went to the hospital. Several doctors were called to try to identify the substance and its cause, but all were baffled. The condition vanished in a few hours and Ashley was released.

My health went from bad to worse, and there were times when I truly believed I was dying. I had colds, flu, fever, headaches, and one bout with pneumonia.

In one two-week period, I awoke nearly every night with swollen legs and a blistering rash all over my body. The first time it happened, I stared in the mirror in horror at the bloated, scaly monster looking back at me. It wasn't like poison ivy or any allergic reaction I had ever seen. Curiously, I felt no pain and by morning the swelling and rash were always gone.

After several episodes, those symptoms stopped but others appeared. My eyes became so sensitive to sunlight that I had to wear dark glasses indoors. My doctor told me my eyes had become allergic to themselves. After being treated with steroid drops for a while, my eyes returned to normal.

It seemed we were constantly en route to or from the hospital or doctor's office. I came down with severe bronchitis. The coughing and choking spells were so violent that Ron had to drive me to the emergency room, where I was put on a breathing machine. For two or three weeks, I slept sitting up in a chair in the living room holding an inhaler in my hand.

Most of the time I felt suffocated by a world closing around me. The family illnesses, the chronic problems with the house, the long hours I was working at the Coach House, where I had become a manager—it was too much. Ron and I had sort of disconnected from each other. I was with the kids all day and when he came home, I left for work. We hardly ever talked and he had almost completely stopped working on the house. Our dream of running a business out of the motel wing was fading, and I felt like a waterlogged stump being pulled along by a muddy current.

Many of my health problems, the doctors thought, were brought on by fatigue and lack of sleep. I agreed and began to think about quitting my job at the Coach House. That caused serious problems between my husband and me.

Ron knew that the owner of the restaurant was planning to sell out and retire, and he became obsessed with buying the place. It was the last thing I wanted. For starters, owning and running a restaurant would require more time than I was willing to give; I would never see my children. Also, I was uncomfortable with the level of debt we would have to take on—assuming we could find someone who would lend us the money.

"That place is a gold mine," Ron argued. "If you won't do it for me, how about the kids? You could send them to college. It could change our lives."

Owning a business was his obsession, not mine. Money was always more important to Ron than it was to me. Having time for my children and my husband and my home was far more valuable to me than amassing wealth. Our relationship went from argumentative to acrimonious. I resented the guilt he was foisting on me and the lack of concern he was showing for my welfare. No doubt he resented my stubbornness, my unwillingness to consider what he felt was a glorious business opportunity. We fought bitterly and the tension wore on me. I began to have horrible nightmares. They were not always the same, but the theme consistently involved the death of my son.

Chapter 7

Everyone probably has experienced the sensation at one time or another: You're alone, absorbed in some activity, and you feel eyes boring into you. You look up, look around, and no one is there.

In the fall of 1989, that sense of being watched became a constant distraction.

It began after I quit my job at the Coach House, thereby settling the argument over whether or not we would buy it. I wanted to get as far away from the restaurant as possible. I enrolled in accounting classes at Ivy Tech, and for a brief time things improved at home. Although my classes required long hours of homework, a huge burden had been lifted from my shoulders and a point of contention between Ron and me had been removed. With those pressures gone, and my marriage showing modest improvement, I had no doubt that I had made the right decision.

That September, the kitchen became my study. Ron and the children usually went to bed early and I could be alone with my books and my herbal tea. It was not unusual for me to sit at the dining table working on assignments until after midnight.

It is difficult to remember exactly when it started, but on those long, quiet evenings I began to feel that I was being watched. I would look up from my books expecting to see someone in the room with me.

It was a nightly occurrence and a decided hindrance to concentration, but it was not worth mentioning to my husband until one evening when the feeling was unusually powerful. My skin tingled like an antenna receiving a signal. My head jerked up in time to see movement in the doorway, a kind of residual blur, like someone jumping quickly out of sight.

I hurried over to the door, thinking I would catch one of the kids scurrying back to bed. The hallway was empty. I checked the bedrooms and found everyone asleep.

The next morning I told Ron what had happened and about my nagging sense of not being alone late at night.

"You're just tired, Doe," he said. "You're studying too hard. You need to start getting more sleep."

As the weeks passed, the feeling of being watched became more powerful and, though they never told me, I suspected Ron and Steven were beginning to sense it also. Several times I saw them suddenly look over their shoulders as if someone had walked up behind them.

Or was I imagining that? Ron was convinced that fatigue was playing tricks with my mind. Maybe he was right. What else could it be? When those eerie feelings came over me, when I *thought* I heard or saw something, no one else was around to verify or refute it. Still, it seemed that too much of what was happening was being blamed on my fatigue when, in truth, I was more rested than I had been in months.

After seeing the vision of the woman facedown in the bathtub, I had been quick to assess my own mental state. This was different. I was not exactly seeing things, just sensing a presence, and I was not the only one.

Hadn't my sister sensed the same thing from the Ouija board? Several times I had called Marilee and invited her back to my home, but each time she refused and made no secret of her reasons.

Hadn't my best friend sensed something here that gave her the creeps? Unlike Marilee, Kellie was not immersed in Ouija boards and otherworldly mumbo jumbo, but more and more she balked at coming here. The time came when she would not come at all.

I invited her and her girls over one night when Ron was working late. She declined and told me she preferred not to visit me after dark.

"No hard feelings, D. J.," Kellie said, "but there's something wrong with that house. You've got ghosts or something in there."

"Give me a break," I laughed. "You're acting as bad as Marilee. You don't really believe in ghosts."

"Why don't you come to my house tonight," she said with a touch of nervous levity. "Just in case."

Since Ashley's birth, Ron and I had spent very little time together without the children. We picked a nice spring weekend to let them stay at his mother's house in Louisville so we could be alone. We planned a quiet two days of good food, wine, and the intimacy that had been missing from our lives.

We spent Saturday just hanging out together, talking a lot and getting reacquainted. It may sound odd that after more than a decade of marriage we would have to get to know each other all over again, but the past three years had been tough on us. A lot of anger and frustration and resentment—sometimes over minor issues—had grown like dense brush between us and we needed some breathing room to chop through it.

About ten o'clock that evening we went into the bedroom and, uncharacteristically, I left the door partially open. Normally when Ron and I were going to make love, I closed and locked the door to prevent one of the kids from walking in on us. That night we were alone, so I didn't bother.

Ron was lying on his side with his back to the door and I was sitting cross-legged on the bed, facing him. I was looking down, but movement from the hallway caught my eye. I raised my head and saw a little girl holding the knob and pushing the door open.

"Ashley," I gasped.

Ron bolted upright and the little girl evaporated before he could turn his head toward the door. He saw only an empty doorway.

"Doe," he said, "The kids are sixty miles away. Can't you let go of them for one weekend?"

My heart was pounding against my chest and I trembled all over.

"I saw a little girl," I said. "She looked like Ashley."

"Ashley isn't here, Doe." He was becoming irritated.

"I didn't say it was Ashley. I said she looked like Ashley . . . the way Ashley looked a couple of years ago . . . her hair cut in bangs. She was carrying a doll, just like Ashley always does."

Ron laid back down and I could feel the romantic air seeping out of this evening. "You know what I think?" he said. "I think you were just edgy because you didn't lock the door. That old fear of Ashley walking in made you imagine that she did."

"I didn't see Ashley," I said. "I saw another little girl. Ron, I saw her."

Obviously wanting the discussion to end, he closed his eyes and didn't answer.

"Look at the door," I said, nudging him. "I didn't leave it that far open."

He ignored me and I couldn't blame him. The room was dark except for a faint light that found its way down the hallway from the living room. I sat for a long time staring at the door and listening to my husband's breathing, the slow, rhythmic respiration that precedes sleep. It was the first time I had been away from my daughter overnight, so maybe some stray thread of anxiety had gotten tangled up in my imagination. *Maybe I just thought I saw her . . . a mental picture of her at a younger age . . . or something. But why a vision of an earlier time? If something was bouncing around in my subconscious, why the distortion?* I lay back on the bed and tried to relax, but my brain wouldn't gear down. The little girl at the door had been as real as . . . as what? The woman in the bathtub?

Each time I convinced myself that my mind was playing tricks on me, something happened to challenge that rationalization. A few nights after we brought the children back home, Ashley woke up screaming. I was out of bed and halfway to her room when, over her shrieks, I heard noises in the attic, not the animal scratching we had previously noticed, but loud pounding and banging, like objects being tossed about. Birds hitting the rafters, I wondered, or beams settling under years of strain?

"He's hurting her," Ashley yelled. "I can hear him hitting her."

"Sweetheart," I said, lifting her out of bed, "you've had a bad dream."

"No, Mommy, he's hitting her. Make him stop." She stopped squirming in my arms and I realized the attic was quiet. I put her back in bed, pulled the blanket up, and kissed her forehead.

"Go back to sleep," I said.

As I moved away from her bed and reached for the light switch, Ashley raised her head. "It wasn't a dream, Mommy," she said. "I was awake all the time."

For a long time, the things that happened in this house had seemed odd or peculiar, but now they were becoming absolutely weird, not the kinds of things I could accept as coincidental or purely figments of my imagination. Even if I were loony enough to see dead women in the bathtub and little girls walking our halls, that didn't explain Ashley's insistence that a little girl lived in our attic. Had she planted the notion in me? Sure, the power of suggestion is strong, but it was absurd to think I was seeing ghosts because of my daughter's imaginary playmate.

As hard as I tried to resist it, the preposterous notion that some kind of force dwelled in this house began to take root. Not ghosts or spirits or demons, but an elemental presence, like the tide in the ocean or the wind on a mountaintop, some kind of energy inexplicably bound to this house or this land.

Except for the illnesses we all had suffered, most of the oddities tilted toward Ashley and me. They could have been the work of brain warps or inventive subconsciousness, but something happened with Steven one evening that suggested that none in the family was immune to the whims of this house.

He went into the kitchen, poured a glass of water, and started back to his room. The glass flew out of his hand and landed several feet away. I was sitting on the sofa watching him. He didn't drop it. It didn't bounce or roll away from him. It left his hand as if it had been thrown.

"What was that?" he sputtered. "It felt like something jerked it out of my hand."

Then things began to turn up missing. Or things I didn't know were missing turned up in the most unlikely places. The first incident I can remember involved my wedding ring. I was washing dishes and Steven was standing beside me talking about nothing in particular. He said something about my wedding ring and asked if he could look at it. I slipped it off my finger and handed it to him.

He examined it for a second, tried to fit it on one of his fingers, and then handed it back to me.

"Just put it on the counter," I said. My hands were slick with soap and cleanser.

He placed the ring beside the sink and walked away. After finishing with the dishes, I dried my hands and reached for my ring, but it wasn't where I had seen Steven put it.

"STEVEN!" I yelled. He came back into the kitchen. "Where's my ring?"

"Mom, you saw me lay it down right there."

"Well, it's not there now. You're going to help me find it."

We combed every inch of the kitchen before giving up the search. Steven left to spend the night with a friend, and later in the evening, before going to bed, I wiped off the counter once more and made another quick look for the ring. If it had fallen into the sink, I figured, it might still be in the drain trap. I would ask Ron to check that tomorrow.

The next morning, I went into the kitchen to make coffee and found my ring on the counter beside the sink. Since Steven had been gone, he could not have placed it there. When Ron got up, he insisted he didn't even know the ring had been missing. No one had been in the kitchen since I wiped off the counter the night before.

Oh, well, stranger things had happened in this house. Delighted to have the ring back, I slipped it on my finger and pushed the matter out of my mind—until the incident with my marriage license.

Marriage licenses are not something most of us carry around. Anyone who has been married more than a few years would probably have a hard time locating theirs. Although I've always been inclined to keep things—receipts, old photographs, tax returns, medical records, and the like—my filing system leaves something to be desired. I probably could have produced my marriage license, but not on short notice. It was tucked away in a box with other personal papers and I had not looked at it in years.

One night I sat down to study and reached for a new accounting textbook I had purchased a day or two earlier but had never opened. I flipped through it to get some idea of the material that it covered. Near the middle of the book, I turned a page and there was my marriage license.

My relationship with my husband had been touch and go for several months and at times divorce had crossed my mind. *Maybe it's been on his mind, too, and he planted our marriage license here as some sort of suggestion that we reexamine the contract.*

He had the look of exasperation that was becoming familiar. "Doretta," he sighed when I confronted him, "I don't think I've seen that license since the day it was issued. I don't even know where you keep it."

It was impossible for me to rule out lapses in my own lucidity as being responsible for some of what I was experiencing. Could I be having blackouts and doing things—misplacing my wedding ring and my marriage license—without being aware of them?

It was possible, I suppose. About the same time, I began seeing doubles of myself. Doppelgängers, I learned later, is what they are called. It's a German word that means a ghostly double of a living person. The first time it happened was at a convenience store near our house. A woman in a blue car pulled up beside me, facing the opposite direction. She looked directly at me and smiled. I stared back in shock. She didn't just resemble me, she was a mirror image of me. She smiled, lowered her head, and drove away. I looked in the rearview mirror but could not see her car.

For the first time, these mental contortions were getting scary. After I regained my composure, I put the car in gear and drove home. In the bathroom, I stood in front of the mirror and looked at my eyes and mouth, looked for some outward sign of dementia. Does madness have facial characteristics? I didn't know.

After seeing the doppelgängers two or three more times, I told my husband—at the risk of widening the gulf between us.

"It was just someone who looks like you," he said. "You know we've been told there is a woman here in town who resembles you a lot."

"I've seen that woman and this wasn't her," I said. "It was me."

A faraway look slid across his eyes. "Well, you thought it was you," he said with obvious indifference.

"If I'm seeing things, things that aren't there, there must be a reason," I said. "I don't understand what's going on. I don't understand any of it."

Chapter 8

"It could be a tumor or blood clot putting pressure on a nerve in the brain," the doctor said, after a battery of tests revealed no other possible cause for the temporary blindness. The search for a tumor would require injecting dye into my brain and then scanning it for irregularities.

If not for the numbness inflicted by recent events, the prospect of a brain tumor would have unnerved me. But I was weary of the things that had been happening to me and would have been relieved to uncover any plausible foundation for them, no matter how unpleasant it might be.

We were at the emergency room of Norton Hospital in Louisville because a few hours earlier I had been hanging clothes on the line and saw what I thought was a bright flash just as I returned to the house. I stood for a moment, trying without success to focus my eyes and adjust to the dim interior. My head throbbed and I could see only the shadows of my children in the living room. Then everything went completely black.

"Steven!" I yelled. He came into the kitchen and helped me to a chair. "Call your father." I sat wrapped in blackness until Ron came home. He called Dr. Green, who had treated my earlier allergy of the eyes, and explained what had happened.

"Don't bring her here," Dr. Green said. "Take her to Louisville. They have better facilities."

We had driven twenty or thirty miles when my vision returned. The curtain lifted as quickly as it had fallen. I could see perfectly and my headache was gone.

"Let's go back home," I told Ron. "It's over."

"We're going on to the hospital," he insisted. "We're going to find out what caused it."

The doctor's suggestion of a possible brain tumor made a lot of sense. It could explain the visions, or hallucinations if you prefer. It might even explain a lot of other things I was experiencing in the spring of 1991.

Before the blindness, I had begun to have periods of time lapse, hours that unaccountably vanished.

It first happened on a warm sunny day as spring was beginning to break winter's rigid grip on Madison. In high spirits and filled with the season's renewal, I left home about eleven o'clock in the morning to drive to Kellie's apartment. I turned on the car radio, rolled down all the windows, and enjoyed the feeling of freedom that comes with a bright sky and wind in your hair. On impulse, I decided to take a different route to Kellie's. I left the main road and turned down a country lane that ran past fields of swaying grass.

The car radio began to sound strange, as if the music was playing at a slower speed. Then everything shifted to slow motion—the car, the tall grass bowing to the wind, my own movements. The next thing I knew, I was at the same spot in the road but everything was normal. Something peculiar had occurred but I had no idea what it was.

When I got to Kellie's house, she said, "Where have you been?"

I looked at the clock on her wall. It was four in the afternoon. Somehow on that rural byway I had lost five hours.

My body chemistry also was changing. Rings, necklaces, and other jewelry I had worn for years turned dingy and left stains on my skin. I was losing weight. Foods I had always liked repulsed me and I developed a taste for others I had never liked before.

My hair, which had been dark since I was five years old, began to change color. At first, I noticed light streaks but because I spent a lot of time outdoors I attributed them to sun bleaching.

One day Kellie looked at me closely and said, "My God, you're turning blond."

I went into the bathroom and examined my hair in the mirror. The color was changing not at the ends, where the sun would affect it, but at the roots. The new growth was the flaxen hue it had been in my early childhood.

A couple of weeks later, I went to the Fiesta Hair Salon. Patty, the manager, tried to figure out what could have caused it. "They didn't cover this in cosmetology school," she laughed. "All I know to do is color it."

She used a dark, permanent dye. But when I shampooed my hair the next day, the dye washed down the sink and my hair roots were blond again.

"That shouldn't have happened," Patty said when I returned to the salon. "Maybe the bottles got mixed up and I used the wrong stuff." She doubled-checked her chemicals and dyed it again. As before, the dye washed out. I stopped trying to permanently change my hair color and used rinses to keep it temporarily dark. Eventually, it began to grow in dark again.

Could a tumor have caused my hair to change color? It had not occurred to me before. Could that also explain the change in my taste buds, the weight loss, and the recurring bouts with depression and lethargy? Certainly, it could explain the time lapses and doppelgängers and other ghastly illusions. It almost would have been a relief to find a physiological cause. At least I could stop worrying about lunacy.

"We can't find a thing," the doctor said after the dye had coursed through my brain. "No blood clots, no tumors, nothing. It may have just been a migraine headache."

After all the time and money we had put into it, the house still seemed to rebel against us, and as summer approached, that mutiny turned ferocious.

Odors we could not identify appeared in different parts of the house. Sometime it was the smell of a sewer and sometimes it was like foul body odor. Less often, it was the sweet aroma of perfume.

Once, when the fetid odor was especially strong, Ron opened a trapdoor into the crawl space to check for a broken sewer line. Thousands of bizarre-looking insects swarmed into the house. They appeared to be a cross between a mosquito and a daddy longlegs spider—unlike any insect we had ever seen. If they were mosquitoes, they blessedly were of a variety that didn't bite.

Not long after that, wasps began a long siege of the house. They entered through the vents, half a dozen or more at a time, and everyone in the family suffered stings on the face, neck, and arms. Each time we killed off one group of invaders, another batch arrived. It was like orchestrated aggression calculated to drive us out.

No sooner had we repelled the wasp invasion than we were assaulted by ants, red and black, that were unaffected by insect sprays. They infested the house and blanketed the yard, announcing their presence by attacking Ashley as she rode her bicycle. She crashed her bike and was screaming on the lawn when I got to her. She was covered with ants and more were pouring out from the hollow handlebars.

The whole family was tired and irritable from losing sleep to the insect war. Each of us suffered severe mood swings and personality changes that caused violent outbursts and other behavior that was completely out of character.

Ron had often been sullen and moody and withdrawn over the past few years, but now he was cold and, at times, menacing.

Our fighting had resumed with a vengeance, and I told him I wanted a divorce.

"If you divorce me, I'll take your kids," he said during one argument. Another night, lying in bed, he told me he would kill me if he ever caught me with another man. "I don't have a conscience," he said. "I could kill somebody and it wouldn't bother me."

This was not the man I married. Ron was never a violent person, never even physically aggressive. Now, the icy malevolence in his voice sent a chill through me. For the first time, I was afraid of him. Was it some kind of game he was playing? I thought not. There had been other changes in him. His health had deteriorated and he was almost always in pain.

He began working longer hours, volunteering for overtime and filling in for coworkers who wanted time off. It was as though work was his refuge from this house. Or from me. The thought that he was seeing another woman occurred to me more than once.

I answered the telephone and a tentative female voice said, "Doretta?" I recognized my cousin who lives in Rineyville, Kentucky.

"Hi, Jenny," I said.

"Where have you been."

"I've been home all day."

"I've been trying to call you for three weeks," she said. "Have you been away?"

"Not for three weeks," I said. "Nobody answered the phone?"

"Ah . . . yeah." She was even more halting now.

"Who'd you talk to?"

"Ashley."

"Why didn't you have her call me or Ron to the phone?"

"Every time I called, she said you weren't there."

"Jenny, you know I never leave that child here alone."

"I thought it was pretty strange, too. Every time I called a little girl answered and I said 'Ashley?' and she said 'Yes.' I said, 'Is your mama there?' 'No.' 'Is your dad there?' 'No. I'm all alone.' Then she'd hang up. I was about to give up on getting in touch with you."

If she had been dialing my number, I would have heard the phone ring. Also, Ashley was not inclined to answer the phone. She was more likely to let it ring until someone else picked it up. Was Jenny reaching a wrong number? Maybe. But for three weeks? What were the odds that she would have reached a household with a little girl named Ashley?

After we hung up, I turned to my daughter. "Why didn't you tell me Aunt Jenny was calling here?"

She said, "I never talked to Aunt Jenny."

"Are you sure you didn't answer the phone and forget to tell me?"

"I'm sure."

Ashley still talked about the little girl who came to her room to play. How long had this been going on? Two years, maybe more? It was a long time for an imaginary friendship, but Ashley talked about her as casually as she spoke of any of her other friends.

Once in a while, I would walk into a room where she was playing and ask, "Is your friend here?"

She would give me a look of utter impatience, as if I could see for myself, and say, "No, Mommy, she isn't here."

Is it healthy, I often wondered, *for this imaginary relationship to have such an enduring tenure?* I considered discussing it with Ashley's teacher or a counselor but by the time school was out, I had other things on my mind.

Not only were the house disasters accelerating, but summer brought renewed personal stress for the whole family.

I discovered that Nancy, who now had two children, was living in a shelter in Louisville and, though Ron was not excited about the idea, I brought her and the kids to Madison to stay with us.

I had not been in close touch with Nancy since she was released from Madison State Hospital nearly four years before. The therapy sessions with her had been painful and dredged up buried memories I preferred to leave alone. This was not the happiest time for our lives to converge again, but her blood was my blood and it grieved me to see her children homeless.

As it turned out, they might have been better off in the shelter. Within days of arriving at our home, Nancy's children began waking up at night, crying from nightmares. Jessica came howling to my bed one night. "Aunt Doretta," she said, "an old woman was in Ashley's room. She was so horrible. She was standing at the foot of the bed." I assured her it was just a bad dream, but she never again would sleep in Ashley's room without her mother.

The insects also returned that summer. Nancy and I were in the backyard one afternoon and heard a loud humming coming from a tree near the house. I stepped over for a closer look, and huge green flies swarmed out at me. The tree was covered with them. Ron tried insect sprays, but nothing drove them away. As a last resort, he tried to cut down the tree, but each time he approached it, the flies swarmed over him like a dense fog.

I had told Nancy little of the things we had experienced since moving into this house, but, like Kellie and Marilee, she became edgy and made offhand comments about the "weird" feeling she got here.

More and more I was sharing that feeling. Acrimony, thick and palpable as warm caramel, oozed over the house that spring and summer. We were at each other's throats like wounded wolves, usually for reasons so minor that we could not recall later what aroused us.

For the first time in our marriage, Ron and Steven tangled and Steven got the worst of it. The fight just came out of nowhere.

There is a small opening in the hall wall that leads to the bathroom water pipes. At that time, we were still working on the plumbing and in order to shower, we had to open a valve behind the small door of the opening. Steven had opened the door and was leaning across it, reaching for the valve. Ron saw him and shouted something about him breaking the door. He hit Steven with his fists and Steven, who was fifteen years old, hit back. I ran into the hall and tried to get between them, but Ron threw me back into the living room. When they finally stopped fighting, Steven was black and blue. Nancy took him to Louisville to spend a couple of days with my grandfather.

I was astonished and enraged. There had never been violence in my house and I had always sworn not to tolerate it. Ron seemed to forget the incident as soon as it happened. That's the way he was these days—detached from everything that was going on. I screamed at him for beating our son and the words rolled right off of him. To him, it never happened.

I was still shook-up when I went to pick Steven up at Grandpa's a couple of days later. Grandpa was as livid as I had ever seen him. "If I ever see my grandson like this again, you'll lose him," he promised.

Steven's disposition became much like Ron's. He was irritable and noncommunicative much of the time. He had always been loving and protective toward me. Like most teenagers, he grumbled about household rules now and then, but he never talked back to me.

He came in one day and asked my permission to do something and I told him no. He stomped off to his room and I went in a few minutes later to explain why I didn't want him to do whatever it was he had asked permission to do. Normally, he might pout a little but he rarely challenged my authority.

That day he was different. He quarreled with me, accused me of treating him like a baby, of never letting him do anything. His voice got louder and I turned to leave the room. I was pulling the door behind me when it was jerked out of my hand. Steven picked me up and threw me against the hall wall. I let out a shriek and Ashley came running from the living room. Steven grabbed me again, lifted me off the floor, and flung me into the living room.

I hit the back of the couch and thought my neck was broken. He pounced on top of me and sat on my chest. Dazed and barely able to breathe, I begged him to let me up. I twisted and squirmed, but couldn't break the grip that was pinning me to the floor.

I looked up at his face and was horrified. His cheeks and jaw were as hard as stone; his eyes were on fire; his mouth was twisted and white foam drooled from his lips. I was vaguely aware of Ashley pleading with her brother to stop.

"Steven!" I yelled. The foam from his mouth dripped onto my face. He didn't respond to my cries, showed no recognition of me at all. "I love you, Steven, I love you." Gagging and gasping, I said those words over and over.

Suddenly, he went limp. His eyes closed and he rolled over onto the floor. I got up and went into the kitchen to call Ron. I thought Steven had suffered a psychotic episode of some kind. Ron suggested that I leave him alone and let him calm down. I hung up the phone and went toward the bathroom to clean up. When I passed his room I could see Steven lying across his bed, apparently asleep.

The next day he saw the bruises on my arms and back and asked me what happened.

"Those are from our wrestling match yesterday," I said.

"What are you talking about?"

He looked dumbfounded while I recounted the altercation to him.

He said, "Mom, I would never hurt you. If I did that there's something wrong. You should put me away someplace."

"You don't remember anything?" I asked.

"The only thing I remember was you coming into my room and us arguing. Then I woke up on the floor."

Judy Nestus, Steven's school psychologist, was a good friend, so I stopped by her office.

"That certainly doesn't sound like Steven," she said after hearing my story.

"It was not Steven doing those things to me," I said. "The eyes and face I saw were not Steven's. He swears he doesn't remember any of it. Judy, I'm at the end of my rope. What could cause him to do something like that and not remember it?"

She had no professional opinion, but offered to talk with Steven. But the school term would be ending in a few days and she would not have time to learn much before the summer break.

Chapter 9

Reconstructing the summer of 1991 is not easy. Those weeks lie in my mind like a pool of inky backwater. Rancor was all around me and I was powerless to control it.

Tensions between Nancy and me grew steadily as her stay lengthened. At first, she had been well behaved and conformed to the rules I imposed, which were not severe but were, nonetheless, a rein on the lifestyle she preferred. She found a boyfriend in Madison and began staying out later and later, hanging out in bars and living a life that reminded me too much of my mother's. When my rules cramped her style, Nancy sometimes stayed with Kellie, who was single and more tolerant of her hours and activities.

One night after a full week of turmoil, I fell asleep on the loveseat and had a dream about Jessica, Nancy's daughter. In the dream, Jessica was more like me, like me as I was as a child, a child tormented by a mother who drank hard and brought home strange men.

I woke up at three o'clock in the morning, agitated and mildly confused, not certain if I had dreamed of Jessica or myself. Ancient memories crowded into the jumble.

We're riding in a car with Mom and Joe Milovitch, her boyfriend. They're both drinking. Nancy is in the front seat between Mom and Joe and I'm in the back. Nancy begins to cry. Joe yells at Mom to shut her up. Mom slaps Nancy hard and she cries louder. My mother throws her over the seat into my lap. Blood runs from her mouth onto my blouse.

Of all people, Nancy should know what she is doing to her daughter. I thought of what she had told the psychiatrists during the therapy at Madison State Hospital and my denial when I was confronted with it. Nancy was right, at least partially. There were men in the

bed she and I shared with our mother in a small apartment in Gary.
Was there more?

*I'm not sure what awakened me; the movement, the noise, the smells.
I turn my head to the side. Joe is on top of my mother and they are both
naked. It isn't Joe, it is a man I have never seen before. Now it is Joe
again. Mom is moaning. Is he hurting her? I'm frightened that they will
know I'm awake. I close my eyes and try to slide toward Nancy, so their
bodies won't touch mine. My eyes are closed tight and I'm pretending I'm
not there. . . .*

A bell sounded somewhere in my head and the memory scampered
back into its box.

It must have been three-thirty when I woke Kellie up by kicking
on her door. She had been sleeping on the sofa and was flabbergasted
when she saw me through the screen door, wild-eyed and spoiling
for a fight.

"I want to talk to Nancy," I said, pushing my way in without
waiting for an invitation.

"She's upstairs," Kellie said. "Her friend is with her."

I walked to the foot of the stairs and yelled for Nancy. Kellie tried
to calm me down, but I pounded on the wall and shouted until my
sister appeared at the top of the stairs. I insisted she come down.
Kellie, who had never seen me in such a state, looked frightened
and tried to get between us.

"I've had it with you," I told Nancy. "I've done everything I can
do. I'm going to help Timmy keep Jessica away from you. I'm not
going to let you do to her what was done to us."

Taken aback by my tirade, she didn't respond at first, but as I
ranted on, she became contentious.

"You're crazy, Doretta," she spat. "You're possessed. You've got
a demon in you."

That sent me further over the edge. I grabbed her by the throat
and lifted her off the floor and in that instant I was looking into the
terrified eyes of a fragile little girl cowering in a corner while her
mother, soaked with vodka, cursed and threw dishes and threatened
to kill her. My heart broke first, then my grip.

"Oh, God," I said. Nancy held her neck and stared at me. I turned
and ran out of the house. I was too full of shame and guilt and
sadness to even attempt sleep that night. I sat like a zombie waiting

for sunrise and brooded over the realization that there was some of
my mother in me after all.

*Mother is on a rampage. Grandma and Grandpa have moved out of
the house and left her to care for her own children. She is cursing them
and cursing us. I crawl under the dining table to hide from her. "Get
your pathetic ass out from there," she screams. I burrow deeper into my
hole. She reaches under the table, grabs me by the hair, and drags me out
of hiding. I can smell the liquor as she pulls me upright by the hair and
slams her hand across my mouth. My nose and eyes burn and I can taste
blood on my lips.*

*Pea soup again. Three times a week we eat split pea soup over rice.
"I'm sick of pea soup," I say. Patrick and Nancy look at me in disbelief.
Mother goes nuts. She throws her plate against the wall and scoops food
off my plate and smears it on my face. She swings at me and I duck. She
swings again and I run. She chases me around the room. Patrick tries to
distract her by grabbing dishes from the sink and throwing them to the
floor. It works. She turns away from me and begins beating him. Patrick
is legally blind and wears glasses as thick as Coke bottles, but he is tough
as rope and as brave as a soldier. Thank God for Patrick.*

*"Fix your sister's bottle," my mother says. Nancy is four. "She's too
old to be taking a bottle," I say. She grabs my hair with both hands and
beats my head against the floor. Patrick struggles with her, but she drags
me across the floor and kicks me in the stomach. She shoves me into a
closet, closes the door, and locks it. Curled up on the floor, my head spinning
and throbbing, I can hear her ranting, "I'll kill all you fuckin' kids."
Hours pass. She collapses into a drunken slumber and Patrick sits outside
the closet door talking to me. "We could run away from here," he says.
We both know we can't.*

*For a change, Mother isn't drunk. She is smiling and happy and tells
me what a wonderful time we will have. She combs and braids my hair,
dresses me in my best clothes, and takes me to a beautiful restaurant. I
can have anything I want. She orders lobster and dips it in lemon sauce
and shares it with me. I feel like a princess. Mom really does love me.
Later that night, she gets drunk and hits me over and over. No matter
how much pain I feel I won't cry. She'll stop beating me if I cry but I
want to hurt her the only way I can . . . by showing her I am as cold and
unfeeling as she. I win. I don't cry. I stare at her with the pain held inside
me. "Take those damned evil eyes off of me," she yells. There is loathing*

in her voice and maybe a trace of fear. Never make the mistake of thinking your mother loves you, *I say to myself.*

When Ron got up at five-thirty, I was sitting on the sofa.

"What are you doing up?" he asked.

"I'm waiting for the police to come and get me," I said.

Nancy didn't call the police. Not long after our confrontation, she moved back to Louisville, found another boyfriend, and gave Jessica to her ex-husband.

My grounding in Catholicism was shallow at best, but that summer, probably because of the turmoil in my life, I felt myself being tugged back toward the Church from which I was long estranged. My attitudes toward religion are ambiguous and imprecise—I believe in God, but I have many reservations about the rituals and trappings and demands of most churches—and my days in parochial school under the stringent eyes and punitive command of the nuns had left a bitter aftertaste. Still, this sudden longing for a spiritual connection seemed perfectly natural. If the Church held no hope for troubled souls, what was its purpose?

Though I still didn't attend Mass and had no contact with the local parish, I found myself, a few weeks before classes were to begin late in August, in the office of Judy Gavin, principal of the Pope John Catholic School, discussing Ashley's enrollment for the fall term.

"I don't think I learned anything in parochial school," I told her, "except to pray a lot and keep my mouth shut. The nuns were very stern."

A nod of the head suggested she understood.

"Will Ashley be taught by nuns?" I asked.

"No, we have regular lay teachers," she said. "We don't teach Catholicism. We have a prayer time, but the rest of the day is devoted to regular educational classes."

Putting my daughter in parochial school would be an unceremonious and halting first step toward reentering the Church's dominion, but something held me back. In my childhood, the Church was an autocratic and judgmental place. That summer, I had all the discord I could deal with.

Besides the antagonism of my little sister, things also could not have been much worse between Ron and me. I felt betrayed and abandoned by him. It was as though he had cut himself off from the ordeal we were living, refusing to acknowledge it or help me find a way to cope. He had his own world apart from the house and the relentless misery it inflicted. He had places where he was free from the hell I could never seem to escape.

As he spent more and more time away from the house, my suspicions that he was having an affair deepened and eventually I accused him of it. His denials, to my ears, were hollow and unconvincing. *Ron,* I began to tell myself, *is not honest. He has no compassion for me, perhaps no conscience at all. Even if he has not slept with another woman, he has cheated on me in other ways—breaking promises, putting other things before me, ignoring me when I needed his attention and support the most.*

As the summer wore on, separating from him in spite of his threats appeared inevitable. Neither of us really wanted a divorce, but for different reasons. He wanted me, I believed, the way a man wants a power tool or a bass boat; a possession, something to be owned and played with when the mood struck.

I still loved him, although I was unsure how much. I loved my children, loved having a family and a home, the kind of normal life I never knew as a child. Growing up, I would see kids with real families—a mother and a father, brothers, sisters, a house of their own—and think how lucky they were.

With Ron, I had those things; my children had those things and I didn't want to take that away from them. But I wanted a husband who loved me, who was open and honest with me, who had the courage and strength to fight whatever battles I had to fight.

We stayed together out of hope, I suppose, the hope that one day we could defeat the hardships this house had brought us and defeat the bitterness we held for each other. I did not want to believe that the damage to our marriage was irreparable. Our arguments had never become physical, and around the children we always tried to keep the facade of civility intact. Maybe we had not passed the point of no return.

On Saturday morning we went to the Kentucky Utilities company picnic and took a brief tour of the plant. It was hard to imagine a more innocuous outing, and so the last thing I expected was that it would provoke the worst fight we had ever had and make me wonder if perhaps Nancy had not been right, maybe there was a demon inside me.

It wasn't the *Playboy* magazines. Ron had bought girlie magazines before and brought them home and I never objected, as long as Steven and Ashley could not find them. It was the deception. He had often talked about other guys at the plant who kept *Playboy* magazines in their lockers.

"And you don't?" I had asked him.

"Of course not," he said.

When I saw the magazines in his locker that Saturday, I felt a rush of anger. Why would he lie to me about something so silly? Why would he lie when the truth wouldn't hurt? It was a small thing but enough to arouse, once again, the feelings of betrayal. If he would deceive me about things so unimportant, could I trust him in things that really mattered?

I kept my anger inside me all day, thinking it would go away. Instead, it festered and grew like a fungus until I couldn't hold it any longer.

"Why did you lie to me about your *Playboy* magazines?" I asked him when we were back at home.

"Aw, Doe, what's the big deal about a few magazines?"

"It's not the magazines. It's the lie. You lie about everything. You lie so much you don't know the truth anymore."

Our voices were rising, and I was aware that Ashley was watching us. I didn't like arguing in front of her, but I had pulled the cork and everything came spilling out of me.

"No more!" I screamed. "I've had it with your lies! No more!"

Ron moved across the room and towered over me. His face was flushed and his eyes burned with rage. Suddenly, I felt the inside of my cheek crush against my teeth, tasted the blood that spurted from my lips as my head snapped back and hit the wall with a force that nearly buckled my knees.

Reeling and trying to stay on my feet, I watched Ron turn and storm out of the house. I went into the bathroom to wash my face. The corner of my lip was cut and blood had dripped onto my blouse. Ashley watched me but said nothing.

What in God's name is happening? My son throws me to the floor and tries to strangle me. My husband beats my son over something that would not even justify a scolding. Now my husband strikes me, something I would not have believed him capable of doing.

We didn't speak to each other the rest of the evening, and Ron went to bed early. A little after nine o'clock, I sat down at the kitchen table with a notebook. I had decided to begin keeping a daily journal. Too many things I did not understand were happening to me and my family. By writing down my thoughts and feelings, maybe I could make sense out it.

I was physically exhausted and emotionally shredded, like a rat in a maze, forever turning down dead-end paths and running into walls. Some days I would start out full of excitement and faith but in the end I was always whipped.

Ron, I wrote that night, *is one obstacle I must remove.*

"Good morning, hon."

I stared into my coffee and didn't speak to him. Ron's manner was so casual that it infuriated me. *Good morning, hon.* No remorse, no apology, nothing. My lip was still swollen but he didn't seem to notice.

"What's wrong with you?" he asked, joining me at the table after pouring a cup of coffee.

"What's wrong with me?" I tried to stay clam but it was hopeless. "You busted me in the mouth and you want to know what's wrong with me."

"What are you talking about?" he said. "I haven't touched you."

"What in the hell is this?" I said, pointing to my bruised lip. "Do you want to see the bloody blouse I was wearing last night?"

"I would never hit you, Doe," he said. He tried to convince me that I had imagined it or dreamed it, just as he had tried to convince me that I had imagined the apparitions and strange noises in our house. Sometimes I wasn't even sure where the lines were between reality and fantasy. Too much of what had happened in this house made no sense to me, and as often as not, I was convinced that I was slipping over the edge.

Considering my state of mind, he might have persuaded me that nothing happened the previous night. Except for three things: the bloody blouse, my swollen lip, and a witness—our five-year-old daughter. Ashley came into the kitchen while we were arguing.

"Daddy, you did too hit Mommy," she said, as though hoping to settle the argument and restore peace between her parents.

But Ron's continued denials made me angrier. I got up from the table and stood by the kitchen cabinet. "Just admit it, dammit!" I shouted at him.

"I never touched you," he said.

I grabbed the first object I saw on the counter and threw it at him. It was an antique cookie jar, an item I valued greatly. It sailed across the kitchen, bounced off him, and crashed to the floor in a hundred pieces.

He sat still, dazed, for a moment. The cookie jar had left a small slit where it had struck his head. I was completely out of control. Before he could move, I threw coffee cups, ashtrays, anything I could get my hands on.

Ron stood up and started toward me. He is a big man, six-foot-six and 280 pounds. Until the previous night, he had never hit me, but now I was afraid of him. A little voice in my head said, *He's going to hurt you. Protect yourself. KILL HIM.*

I spun around and grabbed a butcher knife out of a wooden holder by the stove. As quickly as I had picked it up, I dropped it. In an instant, my anger drained away and I felt as limp as wet cotton. I heard myself mutter, "What in God's name are we coming to?"

Ron, too, was as serene as if nothing had happened. *Is it possible that he really didn't remember striking me, just as Steven had no memory of his violent behavior toward me?* Whether Ron remembered or not, I wanted him out of the house, not so much now because I feared him, but because I feared myself.

"Do you realize I just thought I should kill you?" I asked him. He stared at me. "I can't live this way anymore. The kids can't live this way. I want you to leave, today, now."

He started to protest but my mind was made up.

"I can't live with violence," I said. "Violence has come into this house and if ending our marriage is the only way to get rid of it, that's what we'll have to do."

He packed some clothes and drove to Louisville that afternoon to stay with his mother. The children cried when he left. They seemed reassured by my promises that their father would return home soon, but I was not so easily able to convince myself.

That night, when Steven and Ashley were asleep, I wrote in my journal again and tried to sort out my feelings toward my husband.

Sitting at the kitchen table, with a cocoon of night closing around the house, I felt alone and unloved. Maybe I was incapable of being loved, by my husband, my children, even God himself. My mother had taught me about love and the foolishness of longing for it. "Goodness is for the weak and dreams are for the stupid," she once told me, "and expecting someone to love you makes you the biggest fool of all."

While I wrote, a strong odor filled my nostrils, the foul body odor we had detected off and on all summer. I looked toward the living room and saw a shadow move past the door. It had the shape of a blurred head and torso floating three feet above the floor. There were no defined features, no suggestion of clothing. Just a shape roughly like that of a man. It paused beyond the doorway and hovered there as though watching me. I closed my eyes, opened them, and the shadow was gone.

After an hour or so, I closed the journal and went into the bathroom to remove my makeup and get ready for bed. I heard someone moving around in Steven's bathroom, which is adjacent to mine.

"Steve, is that you?"

There was no response. *Mice, probably. No, this was too loud to be a mouse.*

I walked to his bedroom, gently nudged the door open, and saw Steven sound asleep. I proceeded to his bathroom and looked inside. The room was dark and empty. But the noises I had heard coming from there had been distinct and unmistakable.

Back in my bathroom, I was brushing my teeth when I heard footsteps in the hallway—loud, heavy footsteps moving from Steven's room down the corridor toward the room Ron and I shared. Even though the hall was carpeted, the sounds of shoe soles on the floor were pronounced. I knew the footsteps of my son, and these were not his.

Still holding my toothbrush, I turned my head toward the partially open door as the footsteps moved past my bathroom. I saw no one. A cold fear prevented me from moving. At length, I summoned the courage to step into the hallway. It was empty. I checked every room in the house and found nothing.

Not sure whether to laugh or cry, I sat on the sofa, ran a hand across my face. *You're going insane, D.J. Absolutely, freaking flat-out insane.*

Chapter 10

Ron's absence had a definite effect. For a few days, there was a peacefulness about the house that I had not felt in a long time. No unexplained odors. No insect attacks. No burned-out appliances. *Maybe it's over. Maybe the blowup with Ron siphoned away whatever hostility the house possessed.* The children missed their father, and before a week had passed, I missed him, too.

We talked daily by telephone. We agreed that we didn't want to be apart. We loved each other. We had spent the last few years working hard at everything—jobs, school, the house—except our marriage. We decided we would seek marriage counseling, and Ron even agreed to try to restore the romance that had been missing from our lives. He came home the next day.

There was no immediate change in the house. Before he left, the air had been charged with angriness, a sullenness that matched Ron's moods and mine. It was as if our efforts to mend our relationship were also mending whatever troubled this place.

Then something odd and unexplainable occurred. It was so bizarre that Ron and I were dumbfounded, so much so that we didn't even try to search for logical explanations as we had done in the past.

We were sitting in the kitchen one evening. I was writing in my journal and Ron was reading the newspaper. We both looked up at the same time and saw an object flutter from the ceiling and alight softly on the table. It appeared to be a rose petal, scorched around the edges. We looked at it, then at each other, then at the ceiling. Could it have blown into the house sometime earlier and stuck to the ceiling? Neither of us knew and we made no effort to explain it to ourselves.

Ron picked up the burnt petal, deposited it in the garbage can, and went back to his newspaper.

*   *   *

Ron stopped after work to buy flowers and wine. He was going to make good on his promise to recapture the romance that had slipped away from us. I had a late accounting class and wouldn't be home until after nine o'clock.

"When Mom gets here," he told the children, "I want you to go to bed early so we can have an evening together." They cheerfully agreed. Steven and Ashley wanted more than anything for their parents to be happy.

When I got home, the children were ready for bed. They kissed me good night and hurried away as Ron poured two glasses of wine. Unknown to me, he had placed fresh flowers in our bedroom and lit two candles, one at each end of the dresser.

We sat in the kitchen, sipping our wine and laughing at a story I had told him about something that happened in class that evening. Everything seemed right.

We were interrupted by a squeal from the smoke alarm in the hallway, just outside our bedroom. When the batteries are low, those alarms will emit a warning sound, a signal that it's time to replace the battery. That was my first thought. I did not know there were candles burning in our bedroom.

After several seconds, it dawned on us that the alarm was not emitting a low-power warning.

"It's not cutting off," Ron said. He darted across the living room. I was right behind him. I saw black smoke rolling up the hallway from our bedroom. Steven's room was to my left, Ashley's to my right.

"Get up! Get up!" I shouted to the children.

Ron, trying to get to the flames, had disappeared into the dense smoke and I heard him yell, "Bring water!"

First, I was going to get the children out of the house. They had only been in bed ten minutes or so and probably had not yet fallen asleep. Ashley's room was closest to the fire and I literally had to feel my way to her door. "Ashley! Get up. Get up, baby." Her room was so full of smoke that I could not see her. But I could hear her coughing and calling out to me, so I followed her voice, scooped her into my arms, and stumbled back into the hall just as Steven opened his door.

The smoke billowed across him and into his room. He dropped to the floor and crawled to the living room, following Ashley and me to the front of the house. I sat Ashley on the porch and propped the front door open. Steven came out with a blanket, wrapped his sister in it, and took her to a lawn chair in the front yard.

Ron was still in the bedroom trying to smother the blaze with blankets. I called the fire department, and Steven and I raced between the bedroom and the kitchen with pots of water. By the time the firemen arrived, the fire was out.

After dousing the smoldering bedding and removing some items to the backyard, one of the firemen approached us.

"The intensity of the fire was tremendous," he said. "How did it happen?"

"I had lit some candles," Ron said, picking up a charred, brass candleholder at one end of the dresser. The other brass holder was untouched and untainted.

The fireman examined the blackened metal. It had a fireproof, lily-shaped glass cover that rose several inches above the wick. We had used them for years and, because they held such small candles, the glass never even got hot.

"The only way this could have started the fire was if it fell off the dresser and ignited something," the fireman said. Yet, the candle had not fallen.

How, the fireman wondered, could the fire, whatever its source, have reached such an intense level before setting off an alarm just a few feet away? If Steven and Ashley had gone to their room only ten minutes before the alarm went off, wouldn't they have seen the flames or smelled the smoke?

We had no answers for him.

The room appeared to have been engulfed in flames in a matter of seconds, as though doused with gasoline or something highly inflammable. Even an electrical cause would not have generated such heat so quickly.

"There are a lot of things about this fire that don't make sense," the fireman said.

Using a large exhaust fan, the firemen cleared the house of smoke and left us to begin the cleanup. A neighbor offered to keep Ashley for the night, so I dropped her off and took Steven to the emergency room. In our scramble to put out the fire, he had stepped on broken glass. We had one piece of good news that night: The cut was not serious.

It was late when we got to bed, and it was not a pleasant night. The house smelled of scorched wood and cold ashes, the wet-soot smell of a fireplace that has been rained into. From the day we moved in, it had been one disaster after another. Trying to fix up this house and keep it fixed had seriously strained our financial resources and strained our patience and tempers even more.

Before falling asleep, I sighed to Ron, "Can our luck get any worse?"

"I dunno," he said.

Of course it could.

With the morning light we could assess the damage more thoroughly. The carpet throughout the house was ruined, either by flames or smoke or water. Our bedroom would have to be completely rebuilt and the wall the firemen had chopped through would have to be repaired. The entire interior of the house would have to be repainted, furniture and drapes would have to be cleaned or replaced. The stench, in all probability, would never leave this place.

We contacted our insurance agent and a construction company that could do the repairs. The contractor said he could get to the job immediately if we picked out carpet and paint that day. We made sure Ashley caught her school bus and, after Steven was also gone, Ron and I began the rounds of paint and carpet stores.

We left the house about nine-thirty and were gone the entire day. At twelve-thirty, Ron left me at the paint store and went to pick Ashley up at school. He brought her back to the store, we had lunch at Burger King and continued shopping. We arrived home at four forty-five. Steven got there fifteen minutes ahead of us.

"Mom," I heard him yell as soon as we walked in the door, "I've got a bone to pick with you."

"What's going on?"

He strolled into the kitchen with a stern, parental look on his face. "I came in a few minutes ago and went into the bathroom . . . the rug was on fire in there."

"We haven't been here all day," I said.

"There was a lit cigarette by the rug," he said.

It didn't make sense. If I had dropped a cigarette before we left the house that morning, it would not have still been burning when Steven got home at four-thirty. Even if one of my cigarettes had fallen and ignited the rug that morning, the whole house probably would have burned while we were gone.

Ron and I talked about the possibility that someone had broken into the house, but we could find no sign of forced entry. Did anyone else have keys to our doors? Not likely. Did we have enemies who would want to burn our house down? That was even more absurd. I had had one minor run-in with the neighbors, the Cyruses, but that was three years ago and we certainly weren't enemies.

We sat the kids down and cautioned them to keep the doors locked and to tell us immediately if they saw strangers parked outside or if anyone they didn't know came to the door.

"Have you seen anybody like that around here?" I asked them. Both shook their heads.

Ashley appeared troubled, as she often did these days.

"Mommy, I have to go to the bathroom," she said, holding out her hand for me to accompany her. When we were alone with the door closed, she looked up at me with sad, oval eyes.

"Mommy, Daddy didn't start the fire," she said.

It was obvious what was bothering her. Ron had taken the blame for starting the bedroom fire with the candles he had lit. Ashley was afraid that if I blamed him for the second fire, I would order him out of the house again. I wanted to hug her and tell her everything was all right.

"Of course he didn't, honey. It was an accident. That's all. I'm not mad at Daddy and I'm not going to send him away."

"No, Mommy, the people in the attic did it," she said with a seriousness and authority that made me shiver. "They're mad and they're going to burn the house down."

"Ashley," I said, "there is no one in the attic."

"There are ghosts up there," she said, almost in tears.

"There are no such things as ghosts," I snapped.

She began to cry. "Yes, there are. They live in our attic. There is a little girl who doesn't have a mommy or a home of her own, and a mean old man. He's the one who set the fire. He's mad at us. He set the bedroom on fire."

"You've got to stop this, Ashley," I scolded. "There is no one in the attic."

"When are you going to listen to me?" she insisted.

I led her to her room and told her I did not want to hear any more about ghosts. She was still crying when I went into the living room. *The child has one hell of an imagination*, I thought. But there was something in her eyes that told me she was not just trying to protect her father. She really believed what she was saying.

I told Ron what she had said, and he laughed.

"Well," he said, "she's always been a creative kid."

Neither of us could accept the concept of ghosts, which, to us, meant the spirits of the departed lingering among the living. When I was a child, my grandmother used to tell me, "The people who have gone to hell can't come back and the people who have gone to heaven don't want to."

"She's just frightened by the fire," Ron said. "This has been a pretty rough time for her."

My mind was racing back over everything that had happened in the past four years, strange things for which we had tried to find logical explanations—not always with comforting success. Perhaps I was mentally and emotionally ready for a supernatural hypothesis.

"What if she's right?" I asked my husband.

"Come on, Doe," he said. "Ghosts?"

"That's the way I feel. But what if we're wrong?"

"Gimme a break."

"Think about everything that has happened here, things we tried to kiss off as coincidence. Everything that could possibly go wrong in this house has gone wrong. What are the odds of that happening?"

The look on his face said everything: He wasn't buying it. I didn't believe in ghosts either, but I was beginning to believe that there was a force, an energy, dwelling in this house and that its purpose was to harm us. Maybe the stress of that summer, punctuated by the violent episodes with my son and my husband and two fires in two days, had made me too susceptible to suggestion. If Ashley had told me Smokey the Bear was stalking us, I probably would have gone looking for paw prints.

We talked into the night about the strange power surges, appliances that burned out inexplicably, car motors blowing up, the animal noises in the attic, Ashley's imaginary friend, the shadowy figures I had seen, the footsteps in the hall, my vision of a little girl at the bedroom door, our chronic health problems. What about the paint and paper that wouldn't stick to the walls? The dead birds, the odd bruises on Steven's body? The image of a woman I saw in the bathtub and the word HELLP scratched in the paneling?

Ron persisted in scoffing at the whole idea of supernatural forces or anything resembling them. I didn't blame him. Neither of us really understood what we were talking about, and I felt a little foolish for bringing it up.

That evening the house became warm and stuffy and we discovered that the nearly new compressor on the air conditioner had gone out.

"Gremlins?" I joked

"I think," Ron sighed, "we have just had the world's longest streak of bad luck. That's all."

Yeah, that's all. Our bedroom was uninhabitable, so we carried a mattress into the living room and bedded down for the night. The smell of smoke was thick around us and the house was as dank as a leaky storm cellar.

"Notice anything?" Ron asked when we awoke the next morning.

Sleep had been fitful last night and I was still groggy and had not had my morning coffee. I looked around and saw nothing out of place.

"No. What?"

"The smell," he said. "The smoke smell is almost gone."

The bedroom was still in ruins, the damaged carpet and furniture had not been removed, and the house was still warm, but the odor from the fire was hardly detectable.

Ron walked to the back of the house and a few minutes later I heard him calling to me from Ashley's room. I approached the door hesitantly, half expecting another disaster.

As soon as I entered, I knew why he had summoned me. The room was cool, much cooler than the rest of the house, and instead of reeking of smoke it held the sweet, vibrant scent of roses.

Chapter 11

Our insurance policy covered the fire damage, so rather than do battle with the walls again, we turned the work over to professionals. The painters met the same resistance we had experienced every time we tried to change the house.

"Damndest thing I ever saw," one of them said on their first day at work. "The paint keeps bubbling up and running down the walls . . . even that new Sheetrock."

"Tell me about it," I laughed. "This house doesn't like to be painted. It has tantrums . . . like a child that doesn't want its ears washed."

New carpet had not been selected, so Ron and I left the painters to fight their battle while we went shopping. When we returned, one of the painters told Ron, "Some woman called from work. Name was Crowley. She wants you to call her."

He cut his eyes toward me. We had had discussions, when my suspicions were rampant, about one of his female coworkers, Crowley. He had denied any involvement with her and assured me he didn't even work with her anymore.

My look telegraphed an unspoken thought: *More of your lies?*

"I swear," he said, "I'm not working with her anymore."

He picked up the phone, dialed his work number, and stood close to me. "I want you to listen to this," he said.

A guy named Barry answered.

"Did someone call my house looking for me?" Ron said, holding the phone where I could hear both ends of the conversation.

"Yeah, just a second."

Bill Crowley, who has a deep voice, came on the line.

"You called?" Ron asked.

"Yeah," Bill said, "I talked to a painter."

"Did you disguise your voice or something?"

"No. What are you talking about?"

"Forget it," Ron said. "What did you need?"

They talked business for a few minutes, and Ron went back to see the painter who had given him the message.

"I just talked to my friend at work . . . Bill Crowley," Ron said.

"Yeah," the painter said, "that was the name . . . Crowley."

"He has a real deep voice," Ron said. "How could you mistake him for a woman?"

"Man, it was no mistake," the guy said. "That was a woman who called here."

Phone problems were chronic and maddening. Friends told us they called and the phone was answered by voices they didn't recognize. Frequently, it would ring and we would pick it up and find the line dead. Pranksters, maybe, or crossed lines somewhere. There wasn't time to figure it out. Things were spinning out of control, spiraling downward. Every day presented a new riddle.

Ashley and I went to the grocery store. It was a warm day with hardly a cloud in the sky. We pulled out of the parking lot and headed toward home, going about thirty miles an hour. From nowhere, a gush of water hit the car with enough force to push it backward and nearly off the street. I slammed on the brakes and wrestled the steering wheel.

"What's happening, Mommy?" Ashley screamed.

I thought the force of the water would crack the windshield. Then it stopped. I looked to my left and saw two men in a brown pickup truck. They saw what happened and, from the looks on their face, it scared them nearly as bad as it had Ashley and me.

Every car around us was dry. Perhaps one of the benign-looking clouds had picked that particular moment to jettison its moisture. There didn't appear to be any other source for such a large volume of water. Another coincidence?

What we found at home did nothing to allay my paranoia. Ashley went into the living room and turned on the television.

"Mommy, it won't come on," she said.

I pressed the On-Off button a few times. I went into the kitchen and turned on the radio. It, too, was dead. I tried a few other appliances and they were as lifeless as the television. In the laundry room, I found black arc marks between the washer and dryer. Everything in the house that had been plugged in was either damaged or destroyed.

Our insurance company sent an adjustor to the house.

"Looks like some kind of power surge," he said. "It probably traveled from room to room and exited through the laundry room."

"What could have caused that kind of surge?" I asked.

"Probably a freak case of lightning," he said, reaching for the most convenient answer.

Freak lightning and a freak cloudburst, I thought. *What are the chances of one person being hit by both, maybe even simultaneously, on a day otherwise free of precipitation and thunderstorms?*

"There hasn't been any lightning anywhere near here today," I said.

"Well, apparently there has been."

What happened on Friday evening, September 13, was a turning point in how we dealt with our problem. That's right, Friday the Thirteenth.

Ron was working late, and Ashley had been invited to spend the night with Kendra and Ericka, Kellie's daughters. Steven and I were alone. The house had been relatively quiet for a day or two and our morale was pretty good. I dropped Ashley off at Kellie's house and stopped at the video store and rented a movie, *Postcards from the Edge*. We had a pizza delivered and put the movie in the VCR.

Steven became bored. He finished his pizza and said, "I'm going to go shave." He went into the hall bathroom and left the door partially open. I stretched out on the floor, surrounded myself with pillows, and felt calm and relaxed for the first time in weeks.

A low rumbling sound permeated the room, the sound of a growl or deep purr of a large animal. It was faint and didn't seem to come from any particular direction. I started to raise up off the floor. *Come on, Doretta, get a grip on yourself. You didn't hear anything.* I relaxed again. I could hear Steven moving around and the water running in the bathroom.

Perhaps ten minutes later, I heard the noise again, this time louder, a definite growl. *Steve's just clearing his throat, or maybe there's a defect in the tape I'm playing.* Of all the unidentifiable noises we had heard in the past, none resembled this. I stopped the movie, rewound it to the scene where I had first heard the noise, and replayed it. There was no audio deformity in the tape.

Steven came back into the living room.

"Were you clearing your throat just now?" I asked him.

"No, why?"

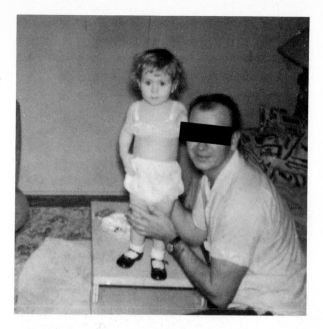

Me at age two with Jimmy Mikos.

Me at age three and a half. I'm on the far left with long blond hair.

On the day of my Baptism.

My mother (left), me (at age five), and my grandmother.

This photo was taken the day after Ashley had awakened in the night being choked by a snake. While there was nothing unusual visible in the room when I took the photo, note the strange light images that appear about her head. In an enlargement of the photo, an image of a snakelike creature appears on the desk behind her.

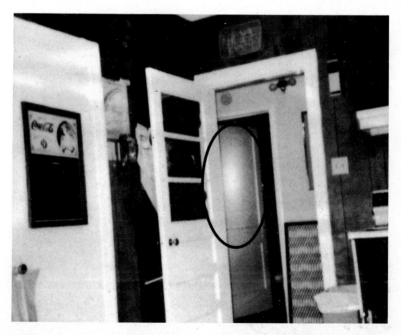

This photo was taken while balls of light were traveling through the house. The ball of light had left the kitchen and I caught it on film as it hit the laundry room door.

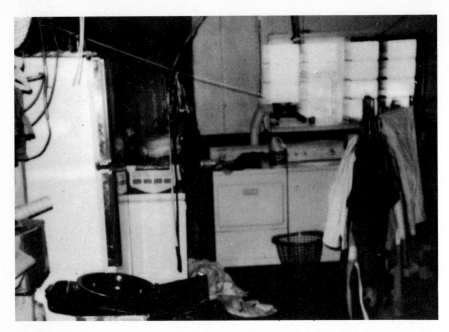

The two windows above the washing machine (upper right corner) are identical but the left window always appeared in photos as multidimensional. The psychics brought in to investigate the house all agreed that this was the porthole through which the entities entered the house.

A current photo of the bedroom that caught fire.

A family photo taken in September 1991 around the time the poltergeist activity began.

A photo taken during poltergeist activity. A facelike apparition appeared on the wall above a collage of autumn scenes.

Ashley sitting in a chair in our apartment in Kent, Indiana. The photo, taken during paranormal activity, was distorted by unexplained light images about her head and to her left. The closet door to her left was open, but there was no natural light source in there that could have caused the light shown emanating from it.

My son Steven's car after the crash caused by an unknown force. I had a frightening premonition that the car would be involved in a fatal crash and tried to stop anyone from driving it. Steven survived but another man was killed in the accident.

Three psychics that "Sightings" brought in to investigate the paranormal activity. From the left: Bill Clema, Patricia Hayes, Marshall Smith.

Dr. William G. Roll during one of his visits to the house. He is holding a scientific meter that he used in his investigation.

A current family photo.

Me at the kitchen table writing in my journal.

"Did you cough?"

"Nope. What's going on?"

"Nothing. I just thought I heard you choking or something."

I climbed onto the sofa and he sat on the floor in front of me. I ran my hands through his hair and teased him about the length. "You need to see your barber," I said.

He started to speak, but a ferocious bellow came from beneath the floor, a roar so thunderous that it shook the entire house. The coffee table actually vibrated and two small vases danced on the top of it. We could feel the floor tremble as we jumped to our feet.

Time seemed frozen. I wanted to run but my legs and feet would not respond. Steven, too, was immobilized. We stared at each other but could neither move nor speak. An eternity seemed to pass before the paralysis broke and we ran to the car. My hand shook uncontrollably as I jiggled the key in the ignition, found reverse, and spun out of the driveway, spewing gravel and dust behind. We crossed Clifty Drive and stopped in the parking lot of the abandoned Park-N-Eat drive-in restaurant. *This is not far enough,* I thought, and pushed the accelerator to the floor.

We were both crying and shaking. The fright had made us physically ill. Half a mile from our house I pulled to the side of the road and we both got out and vomited.

"What did it sound like to you?" I asked Steven.

He was still shaking. "Mom, I've never heard anything like that."

"Where did it come from?" I wanted to know if he had heard the same thing I had heard.

"From the floor in front of the TV," he said. I agreed.

We drove to a convenience store and called Ron's number at work. He had already left. I didn't want him to go to the house alone, so we parked outside a Laundromat and waited. Only a few minutes passed before he drove by. I pulled in behind him and honked the horn and flashed the lights until he pulled over.

We told him what had happened. "I'm not going back in there," I said. "I'll never go back into that house."

Had I been alone, Ron might have tried to brush it off as another of my *episodes,* but Steven was also extremely upset. "Well, we can go to Mom's house and spend the night," Ron said, "but we'll have to go home and get some clothes."

It took all the courage I could muster to enter the house, but I grabbed a change of clothes and an overnight bag as quickly as possible, and we headed for Louisville.

It was nearly one-thirty in the morning when we got to Marge's house.

"What are you doing here at this time of the night?" she asked. We had never told her of the things that had been troubling us and our house. Except for my two sisters and my best friend, Kellie, we had discussed it with no one. How could we explain to someone else what we did not understand? And Marge Johnson was not the kind of woman to whom you would casually tell ghost stories.

But the time had come. She listened patiently as we related as much of the story as we could remember. She wasn't buying much, if any, of it, but she listened. We told her about Ashley and the little girl, and she listened. We described the fire and the odors and the noises, and she listened. She was probably a little overwhelmed by it all. The night wore on and at last she said, "Well, it's late. We'll talk about it in the morning."

I woke up early with the images stuck to my mind like decals. "I just had the weirdest dream I ever had in my life," I told Ron.

"What?"

"I dreamed I left here last night in my nightgown and went to our house . . . just kind of flew there. I walked through the house. It was dark. I walked into the laundry room and the letters CK were painted on the wall. I went out the back door and into the yard. There was a tent, with lights around it, like a carnival. A man was standing there holding some snakes. I thought, *I've got to help him.* But he extended his arms and the snakes coiled around them. He was a snake charmer or something. He had control of them."

Ron said, "Yeah, weird."

We went into the kitchen to eat breakfast, but I wasn't hungry. The dream still raced around in my skull and caused a fluttering sensation in my stomach.

Marge was sitting at the table with phone books in front of her.

"There's just some kind of animal trapped underneath your house," she said. "That's all it is."

"It would have to be a very large animal to make that kind of noise," I said. "How could an animal that big get under there?"

"Oh, you're overreacting," she said. I didn't blame her. If I—and Steven—had not heard the noise, I would have had trouble believing it, too. "Look, we'll call an exterminator and send him to the house . . . have him spray everything. It'll be okay. I'll pay for it."

What we had heard was no animal, but there was no point arguing about it. We would go back home and try to sort it all out later.

Before we left town, I called Nancy. Despite the row we had at Kellie's house, we were still on relatively good terms and I felt the need to confide in someone who would be more believing and sympathetic than my mother-in-law. My house had made Nancy uneasy, as it had Marilee and Kellie, so she was not likely to think I had lost my mind.

I told her about the fires and the singed rose petal omen, about Ashley's insistence that the fires were started by an angry old man who lived in the attic—and about the ferocious roar that had driven Steven and me from the house.

"You've got to do something," she said.

"What am I supposed to do, call Ghost Busters?" I joked. In truth, I had no idea what to do or who to call for help. I may have had occasional questions about my sanity, but I wasn't eager for others to share those suspicions. Ron, I also knew, would be adamantly against involving outsiders. Perhaps these events had become distorted in our minds but were rationally explainable nonetheless. The last thing we needed was to be known as *that nutty Johnson family on Clifty Drive.*

"Well, there must be somebody who deals with this stuff," Nancy said.

"I don't know. . . ."

"Are you going to just sit there until something serious happens?"

"Believe me, if I knew what to do, I'd do it," I said. "I can't take much more of this."

"I'll see if I can help," she said. "I'll look in the phone book and make some calls and get back to you."

Returning to that house was the last thing I wanted to do. It not only frightened me in an eerie sense, but a physical one. I was willing to chalk some things up to bad dreams and licentious imagination, but the fire was real, the family violence was real, the roar from the crawl space was real. Maybe all of it was real and, in some arcane way, connected. The dream replayed in my mind. The face of the snake charmer was as tactile as faces in a dream get. To this day, I could pick it out of a lineup. And what of the writing on the laundry room wall: CK? I searched for an association, recognition, but my memory yielded nothing.

A clump of dread rode in my stomach all the way back to Madison and it swelled like sourdough when we turned into the driveway. Inside the doorway, I lingered for a moment while Steven and Ron carried our bags to the bedroom. I pushed open the laundry-room door, turned on the light, and literally felt the blood drain from my face.

"Ron!" I yelled.

He came up behind me, looked at the letters CK painted in white on the wall.

"Damn," he said.

"Just like the dream," I said.

We checked the house thoroughly. All the doors and windows were locked. There was no sign of forced entry or that anyone had been in the house.

Ron tried to scrape the letters off the wall and then painted over what was still visible. I sat alone in the sunroom, facing the windows that looked out onto the backyard, where, in my dream, I had seen the circus tent and the man with the snakes. *Did I leave Marge's house last night? Did I come here and paint those letters on the wall? That's impossible. Isn't it?*

Nancy called the next day.

"I've got somebody for you," she said.

"Who?"

"His name is Jordan Pitkoff and he's a psychic."

I groaned at the suggestion. Fortune-tellers. The people in turbans who stand outside small tents at county fairs and offer to read your palm for two dollars: scam artists who would have you believe that crystal balls and tea leaves know the future.

"A psychic," I sighed. "Marilee would love this."

Nancy had found him in the phone book under "Psychics and Mediums." He advertised psychic readings, holistic healings, and paranormal investigation and intervention.

"Look, I called him up and told him strange things were going on in your house and asked if he could help," she said. "He just took off. He said, 'Yes, your sister is married and has two children. She's had electrical problems and a fire. There are unusual odors in the house and cold spots.' He talked about things that had actually happened. Sis, I think he's for real. There's no way he could have known those things. I told him you'd call."

"I'll think about it," I said.

She said, "Do it, sis."

As far as I was concerned, this thing was veering off into the ozone. What is a psychic reading? Paranormal intervention? Intervene with what? Against what?

Before going any further, I wanted sane counsel.

Father Jeff, one of the local priests, was the first to come to mind. I had not met him but had heard many nice things about him. Judy Gavin, the principal at Pope John Catholic School, had spoken highly of him when I met with her earlier to discuss Ashley's enrollment.

"Are you in church here?" Judy had asked.

"No, but I've heard you have a really nice young priest . . . Father Jeff," I said. "I've heard that he is open-minded and progressive . . . not as judgmental as some clergymen."

She told me about him, and about Father John, the other young cleric who served the parish. As she described them, both were intelligent and compassionate.

"You know, the Church has come a long way from its narrow views," she said. "A lot of young people are returning to the Church. Father Jeff and Father John are liked very much by the young people here."

It was a subtle invitation to return to the Church, but I neither declined nor accepted. Now the lure of the Church was more powerful.

I drove to the parish house. A small, elderly woman with a pleasant smile led me into a large, ornate room with imposing furnishings. As I sat taking in the beauty around me, a figure appeared at the doorway.

"Hello," he said, "I'm Father Jeff."

His youthful appearance surprised me. I had been told he was young, but I simply thought that meant he wasn't ancient. There were only faint flecks of gray in his medium brown hair and he had a handsome, boyish face that radiated kindness. After a brief introduction, he led me to his office and I sat down in a comfortable, cushioned chair.

"Father, I haven't been to Mass in many years," I said. "I have

been away from the Church for so long . . . I may have no right being
here at all. . . ."

He said, "Doretta, the important thing is that you are here. Tell
me what is troubling you."

"I don't even know where to begin," I said. "So many things have
gone wrong in my life. I have come to doubt so many things I have
believed in."

"What about God? Have you come to doubt Him?"

"No," I said. "I have always believed that God loves us uncon-
ditionally, but lately . . . I don't know . . . I feel like somebody is
trying to tell me something. I need spiritual counseling."

He was exactly as Judy had described. He listened stoically as I
related all the events I could quickly recall. I told him I was exhausted
and on the verge of collapse. He began by asking me questions I had
not anticipated, questions about the house. He wanted to know more
about the electrical problems, the odors, the noises.

"Have there been any changes in temperatures?" he asked.

"Mostly in Ashley's bedroom. Lately it has been much colder than
the rest of the house."

"Has the house ever been blessed?"

"I don't know . . . not since my family's lived there," I said.

"Would you be willing to allow me to bless it?"

I had expected him to offer consolation and sympathy and reas-
surance, certainly a prayer or other spiritual fortification. Instead, he
was suggesting that it was the house, not I, that was in need of divine
mediation. That thought made me uneasy. *Are we talking about a
haunted house here?*

"Sure," I said. "I'll do anything that will help."

"Can I come over now?" There was a definite urgency in his tone.

"Okay."

"I'd like to bring another priest with me."

"Fine."

I wanted to ask what he thought was going on in my house but
before I could speak, he stood and took off through the church,
collecting things he would need for the blessing: a crucifix, Bibles,
holy water, an item or two of ceremonial garb. He summoned Father
John and asked him to accompany us.

Driving home, I rolled down the car windows to let the cool, late-
morning air blow across my face. Soon the hills would be burnished
with the shades of autumn—harvest time, the harvest of hopes
and dreams—and the town would be dressing up for one celebra-

tion after another: Friday-night football, Halloween, Thanksgiving, Christmas. My only hope for this season was that the two young priests, who followed behind me in a church van, could chase away the cloud hanging over my house.

Turning in to the driveway, I checked my watch. Ashley's school bus would not arrive for another hour or so, time enough, I hoped, for the ritual to be completed. There is nothing frightening about a blessing, but it might plant more fears in her young mind.

The two priests were somber and silent as I unlocked the door and let them in. The door opens into a hallway that first passes the kitchen on one side and the laundry room on the other. It continues through the sunroom, which backs up to the living room. Beyond that, the hallway meets another, perpendicular corridor. To the left are a bathroom and Steven's bedroom. To the right are Ashley's room, then mine and Ron's.

Immediately upon entering, the faces of the two priests became flushed and damp. "May we walk through the house?" Father Jeff asked.

"Please do," I said.

As they proceeded toward the sunroom, the house became warmer, and by the time they reached the far corridor, perspiration was pouring down their faces.

Father Jeff turned slowly to face me.

"My God," he said, "who died here?"

The muscles in my throat tightened. "Nobody . . . nobody that I know of," I said.

His gaze drifted over the ceiling and walls of the sunroom and through the windows to the backyard that pushes out to a line of trees. Then he and Father John proceeded down the hall toward the bedroom that had been destroyed by fire.

They had not invited me to accompany them and I was uncertain if I should do so. I knew nothing about the protocol of a house blessing. Maybe the priests required privacy. I stepped into the kitchen to wait. They came back through the living room, praying softly and sprinkling holy water with quick, precise gestures. I went in to meet them.

"Do you know anything about the history of this house?" Father Jeff asked.

"No," I said. "I've met the previous caretakers, but we've never discussed the house. Why?"

"There's a strong feeling of oppression here, a heavy feeling," he said.

Both men seemed apprehensive and their expressions told me they perceived something about this house that they did not want to discuss with me. We walked into the kitchen, toward the back door, and I tried to frame the question I wanted to ask.

The two priests did a final blessing in the kitchen, and as they spoke, an unlit candle in a wrought-iron hanger by the window began to melt and bend. The priests stared at it and continued their ritual. A matching candle, hanging a few feet away, was unaffected by whatever was causing the other to melt.

Behind me, the back door rattled as though someone were trying to force it open. Then it opened and slammed shut, opened and slammed again, again, and again.

The priests closed their Bibles and looked at me. "Is that the wind?" one of them said, almost in a whisper. We all knew it was not. The trees and bushes outside the kitchen window were as calm and still as a photograph.

We stepped out to the porch. "Father Jeff, what the heck has happened here?" I asked. "I don't understand what's going on."

"It's nothing you have to worry about." He smiled. "You're going to be fine."

"Is my family okay here? Are my kids safe here?"

"Your kids will be fine," he said. "But what I'd like for you to do is find out the history of this house. Go to the courthouse and see who the previous owners were."

I was becoming more terrified by the minute. What does he think happened here? Does he think something evil is living here? Spirits? Demons? Not wanting to sound silly or irrational, I didn't ask the questions. Maybe that wasn't what he thought at all.

He hugged me and promised, "We'll be in touch."

Maybe Benny and Dianne Cyrus could tell me something. I knew that when they lived in the house they had sent their daughter, Angela, to live with an aunt in Clarksville. I remembered Benny telling us his family moved out because they *couldn't handle it here anymore,* and how I thought he was talking about the financial burden. Now I was certain money had nothing to do with it. After all, they paid no rent and Jerry Freeman, the owner, would have paid for repairs and upkeep.

Benny was not at home, but Dianne's mother was visiting when I went to see them.

"We're having so many problems with our house," I said, trying to broach the subject innocuously. I certainly wasn't going to start ranting about evil spirits.

"I know you've put a lot of work and money into it," Dianne said.

"When you lived there, did you ever notice anything unusual . . . anything that seemed peculiar to you?" I asked.

She shook her head. "No . . . nothing that I can think of."

"You sent Angela away for a while? Why was that?" She and her husband loved children. They must have had a good reason to part with their daughter.

"Oh, she was just having some problems," Dianne said.

"What kind?"

"Nightmares," Dianne said. "She kept having dreams about planes crashing in her room. She would run down the hall screaming in the middle of the night."

"Which bedroom did she have?"

"The middle one . . . by the bathroom."

It was one we had given to Ashley.

"It was always the same nightmare?"

"Yeah. We thought it might help to get her out of the house . . . in new surroundings. It did help, I guess. She never had those nightmares in Clarksville."

"But there was nothing else unusual while you were there."

"No," she said, showing no curiosity about why I was asking such questions.

Dianne went into the kitchen and I got up to leave. Her mother leaned toward me and, speaking softly enough that Dianne could not hear, said, "Honey, you'd be surprised at the things that happened in that house."

I let the conversation end there. If Benny and Dianne Cyrus had anything to tell me, they would do it in their own good time.

It was time for Ashley to be home and I was going to take her with me to the courthouse. I wanted to be waiting when the bus dropped her off in front of the house, so I went back inside to get my purse and lock up.

As soon as I stepped through the doorway, something I had never experienced before stopped me in my tracks and I blurted out, "Oh, hell." The room was cold and filled with electrical friction so strong it made by hair stand on end and my skin tingle. Only a few minutes earlier, the priests had been perspiring heavily in here, but now every room felt like a walk-in cooler. Since the air conditioner had not been repaired, it could not have accounted for the sudden chill.

Have there been any temperature changes? That was the last question Father Jeff had asked before suggesting that the house be blessed. I grabbed my purse and car keys and hurried outside to meet Ashley's bus. The eerie feeling from the house was still with me, but I tried to act normal when my daughter ran over to the car. I put her inside, leaned over and buckled her seat belt, and reached over my shoulder for my belt.

I pulled, but it wouldn't budge. I pulled again. Nothing. Thinking it was stuck in the car door, I let go of the strap and then opened and closed the door. I reached for the strap again but before I could touch it, the belt made a quick whipping motion and the buckle struck the side of my face, bringing tears to my eyes and causing my cheek to swell and turn pink.

There was the strong sensation that somebody was standing there, somebody who was angry enough to punch me.

Ashley said, "Mommy, what happened?"

"Nothing, honey," I said. "It's okay."

It wasn't okay. The violence that had begun between family members was one thing. This was another. Inanimate objects do not move all by themselves. For a minute or more, I sat in the car staring at the house, firmly convinced that the priests had provoked something in there. I was going to find out what it was and why the presence of men of God would inflame it.

"I'm doing a historical background on my house," I told the young woman in the county clerk's office. "I want to find out about previous owners, things like that. How do I do it?"

"First thing you'll need are the plat numbers," she said.

I handed her the property description I had taken from the warranty deed. *Southeast Quarter of Section 19, Township 4 North, Range 10 East,* Madison Township, Jefferson County, Indiana.

"Now, it depends on how far back you want to go," she said, leading me toward a viewing machine and a stack of microfiche. "Start with these and work your way backward. The older records will be in those bound books over there."

Ron and Doretta Johnson were at the top of the ownership chain. The records showed, correctly, that we had purchased the house from Jerry Freeman in 1987, and that he had purchased it in 1985 from G. Leininger, Jr., and from there the names tumbled back through history. Over the next three days, I moved from the microfiche to the old plat books, peeling away layers of years and owners, names that meant nothing to me. Noble Maddox, George Hand, Merle and Mary Nay, Rufus and Alice Janes, Charles and Caroline Kersey, George and Sara Lee, Haney Trigg, Alexander Smirtha, Annie Simmons, Josephine Higbee, and finally the heirs of Josiah Higbee, who had staked out the original claim before the Civil War.

Nothing in the books looked out of the ordinary. About all I had learned was the land had been undeveloped until Noble Maddox purchased it and built the house in 1943. Even the fact that Jerry Freeman bought the place in 1985, apparently as a business investment, and sold it two years later without ever putting it to work for him raised no flags. Madison's economic slump after the Marble Hill nuclear plant construction was shut down explained his motives pretty well.

Dead end. An ordinary piece of earth with an ordinary history. No recognizable villains from the past in the ownership chain. What had I expected to find among the faded pages and microfiche, a Baron Frankenstein?

"I ran out of names," I told the clerk. "All I learned is that my house has had a lot of owners. Thanks for your help."

"Well, if you want to branch out, you can find out a little more," she said.

"What do you mean?"

"If the original owner parceled it out to his heirs, you can get a copy of the will."

Why not? Somewhere the secrets of that land had to be recorded, if not in hoary legal documents, then in someone's memory. The more I learned, the more names I collected, the better my chances of finding that record. She led me to another bank of bound volumes where wills were recorded. I found Josiah Higbee's name in the index, which directed me to a page number.

Though faded and discolored with age and written in an elegant hand of swirls and serifs that made interpretation difficult, the Higbee testament, dated November 4, 1862, was intact. I made a photocopy and took it home to study.

I read quickly through the preliminary legalese and turned to a page with the heading "Heirs of Josiah Higbee."

A few lines down, my heart climbed into my throat.

I, Josiah Higbee, of Madison township in the County of Jefferson . . . bequeath to my son Japhet L. Higbee the whole of the plantation on which I now live—situated in the township aforesaid—*excepting eighty acres of the S.E. quarter of section nineteen (19) in township four (4) north of range ten (10) east and also embracing the graveyard wherein a part of my family are now buried and the said acres so excepted to be held solely for a burying ground for myself, my children, and their heirs forever.*

Our 1.9 acres of land, unless I misread the document, was part of a parcel Josiah Higbee's will had set aside for a family cemetery.

"Take a look at this," I said when my husband came in from work.

He read the will and looked at the notes I had taken on the ownership history of the house.

"This is a graveyard?" he said. "Are you sure you got the plat number right?"

"They're right here on the warranty deed."

"There has to be a mistake. I'll go to the courthouse tomorrow and double-check," he said.

Walking toward the kitchen the next morning, I heard the clinking of dishes. My husband was standing by the counter with nearly every cup we owned spread out in front of him.

"Were you playing with the dishes last night?" he asked, only half joking.

"Sure," I grumbled. "Anything for a good time."

"I'm serious," he said. "I came in here a minute ago and these cups were stacked up three feet high."

"You're not serious."

"I am serious. It was a stack this high," he said, holding his hand chest high over the counter. "I don't know what kept them from falling."

While he went to the courthouse, I went to the Madison Public Library. Ron came home with his own notes, which confirmed mine. I came home with a book I had checked out. It was *Ghost Hunter* by Ed and Lorraine Warren.

There was a surprising array of books in the section on parapsychology, titles that mentioned poltergeists and ESP and reincarnation and possession, things I knew little about, except what I had seen in movies and on television shows—things I had always assumed existed only in fiction and fairy tales. It was sobering to discover that there was an expansive body of serious literature on research by investigators with degrees from reputable universities.

But the field of the paranormal was confusing and had more tan-gents, more twists and turns, than a switchboard. I picked the War-rens' book because it seemed to be the most direct. I didn't believe in ghosts but it was a concept I could grasp, if not comfortably reconcile, in my mind.

Maybe ghosts could answer our phone, paint on our walls, stack coffee cups three feet high, start fires, make rooms hot or cold, entice hoards of insects, disrupt electricity. . . .

Maybe from the day we moved in, ghosts had been trying to reclaim their territory, and the visit by Father Jeff and Father John had incited them to escalate the war against us.

Ghosts would be the easy answer. I would settle for that.

Chapter 13

On the Saturday after the house was blessed, I straightened up Ashley's room, rearranged things on her dresser, and put her dolls in their places. Ron came in and helped me make her bed. No more than half an hour later, he came into the kitchen.

"Where is Ashley?" he said, visibly annoyed, which was not unusual these days.

"She's around here somewhere, maybe outside," I said. "What's wrong?"

"Come take a look."

We walked to her bedroom and he pushed the door open. The room was in shambles. Toys were scattered all over the floor and the pillows, sheets, and blankets had been pulled from her bed. He went to find our daughter and returned with her a few minutes later.

"Look at this mess," he said in a voice that foretold a scolding.

She surveyed the wreckage as if seeing it for the first time.

"Did you do that?" Ron said.

"No," she said softly.

"Ashley, tell me the truth. No one else has been in this room."

"I didn't do it, Daddy. I haven't been in here, either."

Ron and I looked at each other. We believed our daughter. We sent her back outside to play and we started over again on her room.

Our bedroom had not been rebuilt since the fire, so Ron and I still slept on a mattress on the living-room floor. During the night, we began to be awakened by the sounds of someone moving around in the kitchen a few paces from where we lay. Of course, we never found anyone in there. One night we heard popping noises coming from the microwave oven. We entered the room and the oven was idle and silent.

Like the stacked coffee cups, things were constantly out of place when we got up in the morning. Once the coffeepot was moved to the opposite end of the counter from where I normally kept it.

"Let's make notes of where things are before we go to bed," Ron suggested as we sat up late, talking and drinking coffee at the kitchen table. We weren't yet ready to rule out the possibility that the misplacement of articles was the result of our absentmindedness. We certainly respected the likelihood that, given our states of mind, the smallest coincidences and inconsistencies were easily misinterpreted and amplified beyond their actual significance.

We had barely begun making our notes when we heard scratching beneath the kitchen floor. It was faint at first and grew louder until we thought it would claw through the flooring. An animal, maybe. We pounded on the floor to scare it away but the clawing continued. If it was an animal, it certainly was not intimidated by us.

After half an hour or so, the scratching stopped. We finished noting the location of various utensils and dishes and went to bed. The next morning, a canister of flour had been moved and the microwave was facing in a different direction.

Soon, other objects throughout the house moved on their own—and in our presence. Wall hangings inexplicably crashed to the floor. A chalkboard mounted by the telephone literally flew off the wall and struck me. Bric-a-brac fell from shelves for no apparent reason. Doors slammed, lights went on and off.

Two rooms of the house seemed to be most affected—Ashley's bedroom and the laundry room, which we also used for storage. More than once we came home at the end of the day and found paint, cleaning fluids, soap, and other items knocked from the shelves and strewn about the floor of the laundry room.

Ashley's room often was in disarray or rearranged from the way we had left it. We would find bows tied to her bed and chair and lamp and toys. We were certain the house was not being burglarized. The doors and windows were always locked and nothing was missing, nothing disturbed except those two rooms.

Once again I began to see things, usually late at night or early in the morning after a fitful sleep, times when I was weary and could not trust my mental faculties.

One morning, I opened my eyes and saw a man standing in the doorway of the living room. He was wearing a bow tie and a coat, like something in a period movie, garb from another time. He had a funny little smile and a comical, oval face that reminded me of the Alfred E. Newman character in *Mad* magazine.

"Ron, he's in the door," I said, shaking my husband.

He sat up and looked where I was pointing.

"I don't see anything," he said.

"What do you mean?" I said. Ron had never seen the apparitions that I had described and, for some reason, that angered me. "You've got to see him. He's standing right in front of you. He's not a shadow; he's in color."

The man grinned while Ron stared vacantly in his direction. Then he was gone.

The shadowy apparition I had seen several times also appeared more often. Crossing a room, I caught glimpses of it idling in a corner. While I was reading or watching television, my peripheral vision alerted me that it was lurking in a doorway. The feeling of being watched was more compelling than ever, but I didn't talk about that entity at first. If Ron and the children had not seen it, why burden them with my private ghost? But it was not my exclusive property for long.

Steven started to his room one night, spun around, and came back into the living room, his face siphoned of color.

"There was something in the hall," he said.

"What are you talking about?" Ron asked him.

"I don't know, but I saw it in the hall by Ashley's room. It was kind of a dark blob with a head and arms."

"It's the old man," Ashley volunteered. "He's always around. He doesn't like us."

"Ashley . . ." Ron moaned.

"That's the same figure I've seen," I told Ron. "Could we all be imagining it?"

It occurred to me that the apparitions were of two distinct varieties. Some, like the woman facedown in the bathtub, the little girl at our bedroom door, and the grinning man a couple of mornings ago, were fully shaped human images, like holograms in their own environment, not ours. They did not interact with me but seemed to be moving in their own space and time, posing no danger to those of us in the here and now.

The other apparition, the ill-defined mass of shadow that sometimes appeared full length and sometimes as only a torso, troubled me. As the house grew more malevolent, I was certain that he—

that entity or energy—was responsible. But why was he different from the others (I accepted Ashley's word that it was a "he"), and why were his features obscured?

I got out my copy of *Ghost Hunter*, turned to the copyright page, and jotted down the publisher's address. I wrote a letter to Ed and Lorraine Warren, addressed it to their publisher, and mailed it the next morning.

By late September, the bizarre occurrences increased. Physical attacks against each member of the family were becoming commonplace. Ashley pulled at her clothes and complained that something was squeezing her. Ron woke up in pain one night, rolling around on the mattress. His skin, he said, felt as though it were being pricked by hundreds of needles.

A night or two later, we had just gone to bed and, lying on my back, I felt a pressure across my lower legs, the pressure of someone kneeling on my shins and ankles, holding me firmly to the mattress.

I called out to my husband. He raised up on one elbow beside me.

"I can't move my legs," I said. There was nothing touching me, nothing that we could see. "There's a weight on my legs. I can't move."

My nightgown began to rise, as if lifted by puppet strings. The hem of the garment moved slowly past my knees and over my thighs. It hovered inches above my skin and I could feel hands touching me, icy fingers moving the length of my legs. I was held motionless by fear as much as the weight pressing against me. The room was gray and hushed, a colorless and airless tomb, and it smelled of old and unwashed flesh. If Ron said anything, I didn't hear him. *Is this a nightmare, a wake-dream delusion?*

A minute may have passed, or it may have been ten minutes, but it wasn't until I heard myself exhale that I realized I had been too frightened to breathe. The gown was lying limp across my hips and the pressure on my legs was gone.

"What in the hell was that?" Ron said. He had seen the whole thing and was dumbfounded.

"There is something in this house that doesn't want us here," I said, quivering and drawing my legs up to my breast in a protective, fetal curl.

His eyes spoke for him. He didn't want to hear about ghosts.

"You saw that," I said. "Do you think I did it?"

*   *   *

I lay awake for a long time listening to the night. A soft wind rustled the bushes outside the window. Now and then a car purred along the curve on Clifty Drive and the headlights caused shadows to glide across the ceiling and slide down the walls. I waited to hear footsteps or a tapping at the door. There were none, and at last I slept.

> *The old man's lips are stretched into a tight grin across his face and his breath reeks of whiskey. His eyes are as vacant as an abandoned storefront and his voice is a hollow vibration in a cavernous room, a room with the black air of a coal pit. "I don't want to hurt you." He grins. "I don't want to hurt you." He pulls at my clothes. I try to push him away but my arms are weak and leaden. He grabs at my breasts and legs and holds me down, leaving welts on my naked body where his gaunt fingers had been. I try to scream but no sound comes out. His weight presses down on me, pinning my arms and legs. If I cry out, no one will hear me. "I don't want to hurt you," he says, forcing himself on me, violently and hungrily, like a predator tearing at a dying calf. . . .*

Fragments of the dream were still scrambling around in my brain but I was sitting up in the bed, a booming drumbeat in my chest, breath coming in quick gulps, and the nightgown clinging to my damp skin. Ron was sleeping peacefully and the house was quiet, but I looked and listened, wondering if the ogre I had just encountered would be slipping out a window. *It was a dream, Doretta, wasn't it?* The specter was as vivid as sunlight and I felt the pain in my muscles and a foul film on my skin.

Slipping carefully out of bed to avoid waking my husband, I went into the bathroom, disrobed, and turned on a hot shower, hotter than usual. I wanted to scald away the nightmare, scour away the grime that was on me, wash it out of my mind and down the drain.

For a long time, I stood sobbing under the spray of water, letting it run through my hair and over my face. Fully awake and no longer frightened, I remained nonetheless disturbed by the stark clarity of the dream, a graphic intensity that was diminishing too slowly. Most dreams fade into the recesses of the memory immediately upon awakening. Others linger, in scraps and patches, for months or years. Some leave a permanent imprint, a vague sensation that returns again and again, even when the images do not. This, I was certain,

was such a nightmare, one from which I would not soon be alto-
gether separated.

I stepped from the tub and began to dry myself. The heat of the
shower had turned the room misty and covered the windows and
mirror with a sheen of fog.

"Why is this happening to me?" I sighed.

Words began to appear on the mirror in front of me, one letter at
a time, slowly and deliberately sketched in the steam that covered
the glass. I clutched the towel to my breast as the message was spelled
out.

BECAUSE YOU ARE BAD, it said.

Nancy called again to see if I had contacted the psychic she told me
about. She was insistent that I do so, and with each passing day her
argument was more persuasive. The visit of the priests had not
helped; if anything, it had provoked the wrath of whatever lived in
the walls and the attic and the crawl spaces of this house.

But before calling Jordan Pitkoff, I wanted to know if what was
happening to us could be real and exactly what a psychic, a mediator
of paranormal disturbance, could do about it. My partial reading of
Ghost Hunter had raised as many questions in my mind as it answered.
In fact, it had answered very few, possibly because I was not yet
ready to accept the premise that spirits of the dead and other entities—demons and angels—walked among us, to either torment or
protect us. Even if they did, why me and why this house?

"I've never had any experiences with that, but I know a couple
of people in this department who believe," the man on the phone
said with some amusement. I expected as much. I didn't call the
University of Louisville Psychology Department expecting to find a
nest of ghost busters. I merely wanted to know if there was any
scientific basis for the things my family had experienced. Could it be
real? Could we all be crazy? Was there a group hysteria leading us
all to imagine the same things? "Let me transfer you to one of them,"
he said.

Another man came on the line. I introduced myself and explained
again our situation as briefly as possible. "I don't know anything
about the stuff, but I've read that there are such things as poltergeists," I said. "Can that really happen? Is that real?"

"Oh, yes," he said. "They do happen."

He asked me a few questions before I interrupted. "Do you have somebody there who works with this stuff, a crew or something that investigates them?'' Our house, I thought, would be an ideal lab for anyone who seriously studied such things.

"We have people who do some research in that area,'' he said. "But . . . well . . . this department's resources are spread pretty thin. I'd have to check around and call you back.'' I sensed that I was at another dead end.

"Have you ever heard of Jordan Pitkoff?'' I asked.

"Yes, I have,'' he said. "He has a practice in Louisville and works with the kinds of things you've described.''

Ron followed me into the bathroom and sat dutifully by the tub while I undressed, drew the shower curtain, and turned on the water.

Most of the time, I dreaded just walking into the bathroom. It was as though a stale, dead gas hung over it and Ashley's bedroom, which was adjacent to it. It was in this bathroom that the blow-dryer caught fire in my hand, where Steven had found the burning cigarette, where I had first heard the footsteps pacing about, where I had seen the image of a woman submerged in the tub, where the message had been written on a fogged mirror. In this room, more than any other in the house, I felt suspended in a gloomy, surreal mental zone. Here, I saw things that should be seen only in slumber.

For weeks, Ashley had been insisting that I accompany her to the bathroom, and I well understood her apprehension. By late September, I too was insisting that my husband wait nearby while I showered. He humored me, but I think he was still convinced that most of the things I had been describing to him occurred only in my mind. He had not seen the shadowy apparition and he had not heard the roar that drove Steven and me out of the house. Although he had heard the noises in the attic and beneath the floor, had seen the writing on the laundry-room wall, had found coffee cups stacked three-feet high, and other objects unexplainably relocated in the kitchen, he still clung, more securely than I, to the conviction that there was a rational basis for it all. To a large extent, I believed, he had simply removed himself from it all. Whatever he could not explain, he didn't think about.

Still, he humored me, if for no other reason than to avoid an argument over something he considered preposterous. He sat patiently by the tub while I showered.

I tilted my head back to let the water spray over my face and neck, and the fumes of something dead and decaying filled my nostrils.

I opened my eyes and looked up at the ceiling, which wasn't there. Instead, I saw a clean light, a translucent sky that went on forever. I reached out my hand to steady myself and felt the damp, earthen walls matted with roots as fine as angel hair. It was as though I were in a grave, looking up, and the light was pressing down on me and a chasm was opening in the soil beneath me. I wedged my feet against the sides of the tub to avoid falling into the pit, and I could feel something clutching at my feet, talonlike hands trying to drag me into the abyss.

I must have cried out, because Ron threw back the shower curtain and pulled me from the tub.

"What the hell . . ." he said, looking down at my feet. Blood trickled from deep scratches down the length of each foot. I leaned against the wall with a towel around me while Ron searched for something that could have caused the cuts on my feet. He found nothing but a bar of soap and a washcloth.

I washed the blood from my feet and told him about the *vision*. I suppose it was a vision, but whatever it was, it was inarguable to me. And, for the first time, I think it was real enough to my husband to chip another hairline crack in his skepticism. Could I, in a hallucinatory seizure, have clawed at my own feet? It was possible, but not likely. My fingernails were inadequate to the task. The slits were thin and deep and I had felt absolutely no pain. And my husband was sitting two or three feet away. Surely he would have been aware of self-mutilation occurring on the other side of a shower curtain. Even if he had believed that, there was something else that would have given him pause. When I woke up the next morning, there was no trace of the claw marks on my feet.

Ron's reaction was about what I anticipated. "You did what?" he said.

"Made an appointment with a psychic in Louisville. For tomorrow," I said. "Nancy has talked to him and he knew things about us he couldn't possibly have known . . . if he weren't psychic."

The initial consultation fee would be two hundred and fifty dollars, I informed him.

"I don't believe this."

"Look, we both know things are happening here," I argued. "I think it's time we found out what's behind it. We can't be the only people who have ever had experiences like this." I didn't want to think about the possibility that this nightmare was unique to the Johnson family of Madison, Indiana.

"Come on, Doc. What good is that going to do?"

He was as upset about the money as he was about the idea of traipsing sixty miles into Louisville to talk to someone who practiced a trade that lacked medical or scientific sanction. Ron was even skeptical of psychologists, so a psychic didn't register on his credibility meter. My misgivings were no different. I still wasn't convinced that psychics were not sinister at worst and flaky at best. *This is ridiculous,* I had told myself before calling Pitkoff. *But what if he can help?*

"We've got to do something," I said. "I'm worried about the kids. I'm not going to take chances with them. Suppose we do nothing and one of them is seriously hurt?"

He said, "A psychic?"

I said, "Sounds screwy to me, too."

Chapter 14

Where the psychic lived and worked there were no outward clues to his mystical province. The house was in a solidly middle-class neighborhood of seasoned but well-tended dwellings and tidy lawns, the kind of area where you would expect to find American-made cars, a Weed Eater in every double garage, and a kettle grill on every patio.

The man who opened the door looked far more normal than I had imagined a psychic would look: no transfixed gaze, no exotic accoutrements, no practiced mannerisms. Jordan Pitkoff was portly and had unruly black hair, thick eyebrows, and the blanched complexion of someone who spent a lot of time indoors. He looked more like a jewelry repairman than a practitioner of paranormal intervention. He introduced himself, invited us in, and led us through a foyer with an unoccupied receptionist's desk and through the living room, where a large, black Labrador retriever, secured by a leash, snarled at us.

All of my senses were being bombarded. His house had a distinct odor, the sharp scent of incense or some other chemical. We followed him down a hallway, past an unlighted room with curtains around it. I nearly laughed, because it was what I had always expected to find in the workplace of a psychic or fortune-teller or whatever these people were. I learned later that that room was where séances were held, but, having no yen to communicate with the departed, I never went in there.

Next, we turned right into a sunken office, a room without pretensions. There was a large desk, a couch, and tables and bookcases laden with books and documents and cassette tapes. Jordan sat behind the desk and Ron and I settled on the couch. I watched the psychic closely, studied his face, monitored every move. If any trickery or sleight-of-hand occurred, it was not going to escape my antenna.

For the first couple of minutes, we made small talk but Jordan's eyes were fixed on me, bored into me in a way that made me fidget a little.

"There's one that came in with you," he said.

"One what?" I asked, looking around—for what, I didn't know.

"There's an influence, a nasty character with you," he said, and it was obvious he wasn't talking about my husband. "You've had a lot of electrical problems at your house . . . appliances shorting out or burning up."

We nodded.

"Strange smells . . . cold spots. You've heard voices or footsteps when no one was around."

We nodded.

"I don't know exactly what I'm feeling, what it is I'm picking up," he said, "but I'll walk into that house and within five minutes we'll know precisely what we're dealing with because they don't like me and I don't like them. They'll know I'm there to get rid of them and they may fight back."

"They"? We're back to ghost busters, I thought. *This guy is going to go in like a prizefighter, back them to the wall and throw them out. But who, or what, are they?*

"These can be tough situations," Jordan said. "Of course I won't know until we do the investigation, but I may not be able to handle it. If it's too extreme, I'll back out and find someone else to tackle it."

"You keep talking about *them.* What is in our house?" I asked.

"We'll soon find out."

"Are we safe there? Can anything happen to our children?"

"Don't worry," he said. "People never die in these things. It'll be scary but you're going to survive. You'll be okay."

"I'm concerned about my kids," I pressed him. "Should I remove them from the house?"

"No, no. That's the last thing you want to do," he said. "We want to keep you together as a family. You need the strength of the family to fight this thing. But let me caution you: If you have any secrets, tell each other, because this thing knows everything. It plays on your anger, your fear, all your negative emotions. If you're trying to hide anything, you might as well give it up now. This thing feeds on the energy you throw out when you're angry. It feeds on that and grows, gathers strength, and gobbles you up."

There it was again. This *thing.* If there was a *thing* in my house, how could he be so certain it would not harm anyone? Before I could pursue the issue, he began asking questions about my background, my family, childhood, schooling. He obviously was more interested in me than in the house, and if I was hesitant in answering, it was because I was confused about the significance of the information he was seeking. He soon made clear his point, one which did not endear him to me.

"You're the psychic one," he said, leaning across the desk and pointing a finger at me, a gesture I have always found offensive.

"What?"

"You have a background, yourself, don't you?"

To me, that was the same as saying, "You're the bad one." I became testy and defensive.

"I didn't do any of this," I snapped.

"Of course not," he said. "But in these situations, we almost always find that someone involved has psychic abilities, sensitivities that allow these things to come in. We'll go into that more after I've been to the house."

We had been talking for half an hour or so when a woman joined us. Jordan introduced her as his assistant, Teri. She had contacts "on the other side," he said, and aided in his explorations of hauntings and the spirit world. He suggested that Teri and I talk privately because she had had experiences similar to mine. That fortified my developing sense of guilt. With every word and gesture, he was indicating that I was somehow responsible for my family's ordeal.

Teri—no last name was ever given—explained that she had previously lived in West Virginia and, like me, had suffered poltergeist attacks and other paranormal episodes. Her husband refused to let her get help. She eventually found Jordan Pitkoff, who recognized that she had latent psychic, clairvoyant, and mediumistic abilities. She left her husband, a disbeliever, and joined Pitkoff in Louisville.

"If you think back, you'll probably realize that you've had psychic experiences, maybe when you were a small child, things that you didn't understand and probably didn't think much about at the time," she said.

"What kinds of things?"

"Oh, dreams that coincided with things that happened later," she said, "or powerful intuitions or the feeling that you knew what another person was thinking."

"I don't think so," I said.

"Don't be afraid," she said. "I'm sure we can help you."

Our first meeting lasted an hour. Ron and I were not sure what to make of Jordan Pitkoff and what he had told us. But for some reason—it may have been meeting Teri and learning that I was not alone in this storm of the soul—I was beginning to feel at ease with the psychic and his assistant. No, it was more than just accepting them; I was ready to embrace them.

Even if I did not understand all that they had said, I understood this much: I was not going insane, after all. Besides, we had nothing to lose but another chunk of our bank account, so we agreed to play along for a while. Jordan was coming to our house in five days.

Psychic. Me? What would give him that idea? I didn't particularly like the suggestion, but it was preferable to believing I was losing my mind. Driving back to Madison, I shook my memory crates but what fell out was as garbled and fragmented as graffiti on a wall outside a speeding train.

Grandma came to mind . . . Grandma, the witch healer of neighborhood children . . . Grandma, who could sniff out a runaway grandchild clear across town . . . Grandma, who probably never heard the word "psychic" and, if she had, would have thought it diabolical . . . Grandma, who used to listen to me recount my dreams as though . . .

Watching the hills and farmlands of Indiana roll toward the horizon, I remembered the dream that recurred in the days after my mother's death. In my sleep, Mother would come to me and plead, "Tell me I'm not dead. Why won't they talk to me? Why don't they hear me?" My grandmother wept each time I related the vision.

One night the dream went further. My mother stood at the foot of my bed protesting her own death and when she turned to walk away, I followed, down a long corridor with windows into rooms occupied by sick people. Just before we reached the doors at the end of the hall, I saw a man lying on a bed. I didn't know who he was, but I knew he was related to me, a cousin, someone in the branch of the family tree that had the name Gaddis. He was lying on his back with his stomach grotesquely swollen, flanked by other dying men.

My mother went through the doors at the end of the hall and I tried to follow. She pushed me back and said, "You can't go any further."

I woke up crying and told my grandmother about the dream.

"What did the man look like?" she said.

"Like a Gaddis," I said. The Gaddis men in our family all looked alike and were strikingly handsome.

She took out a photo album and flipped through it, stopping on a page with a picture of one of her sister's sons.

"That's him. He's going to die," I said. At thirteen, I was still young enough to be spooked by nightmares.

Grandma called Aunt Vera a couple of days later. Her son was healthy, she said. Nothing at all wrong with him. A year later, I went to his funeral. He had languished in the hospital for several days with a distended abdomen before dying of colon cancer.

Afterward, Grandma and I never again discussed the dream I had about my cousin, never talked about the possibility of premonition. Was it significant that she took the dream seriously enough to inquire about her nephew? Did Grandma know something about me that even I didn't know?

Jordan had given us instructions, a list of things to do in preparation for his visit. The family was to gather in a circle each night, hold hands, and recite the Lord's Prayer. While doing so, we were to envision a blue light encircling the house and to concentrate on it, pushing everything else out of our minds. The blue light was a protective force, a kind of spiritual razor wire to deter evil from entering.

Evil came in spite of the light. While we prayed and conjured up the protective force, doors slammed in the back of the house, cold spots drifted through the rooms, and odors so foul they made us ill rose from the crawl spaces. Jordan had assured us that poltergeist activity progressed slowly. Ours was rushing at us like a bobsled.

We heard dogs barking at the back door and cats howling at the windows, but, when we looked, there were no animals near our house. We heard sobbing, screaming, singing, and heavy breathing coming from empty rooms. Sometimes at night I went into Ashley's room to check on her. The room would be at least twenty degrees colder than the rest of the house, but she would be sleeping without covers and she never complained about the cold.

Everyone in the family felt the electrical charge that was in the air, and it usually accompanied appearances by the apparitions or the movement of objects or the voices. One day the electric air was extraordinarily intense and seemed to emanate from the bathroom.

Pushing open the door, I saw the man, the same man I had seen in my dream, the one in the backyard with the snakes coiled around his arms. He was sitting on the side of the tub talking to a woman, who was bathing. These were not ghostly apparitions, but holographic figures, fully formed but not quite solid. The man was talking, obviously arguing with the woman, but I could not hear his voice. I could not see the woman's face, only the profile of her head and upper body. She had blond hair and milky skin and long, slender fingers and elegant nails.

The man was about thirty years old and not dressed as men dress today. The tub, too, was from another era. It was a deep oval that stood off the floor on claw feet. It was as if I had walked through a time warp. The sink was an older variety and there was a doorway leading to the adjacent bathroom—a doorway that we had long since closed off.

For some reason, I was not afraid. They behaved like characters on a stage, oblivious of my presence, and vanished after a few seconds.

A day or two later, the characters reappeared in the same positions. This time, the argument was more violent and the man's face was contorted in rage. I stood in the doorway and watched as he stood up, bent over the woman in the tub, and began hitting her. From the adjoining bathroom, I could hear a little girl crying, "Mommy! Mommy!"

The man ignored the girl. He beat the woman and forced her down into the tub and held her head underwater until she stopped breathing. I was mesmerized. This had nothing to do with me. This was a motion picture projected into my space and I was merely a spectator, not a participant in any sense.

The man lifted the woman from the tub, and it was then that I noticed the opening in the bathroom floor. He tugged her toward the hole and was preparing to shove her limp body into it when the little girl ran into the room through the door that no longer existed. She was crying for her mother but before she could reach her, the man picked up a shovel and swung it like a baseball bat into the little girl's face. The blow drove her backward into the wall, and blood splattered toward the ceiling. He first dragged the woman's body into the space beneath the house and then the little girl's.

After they disappeared beneath the floor, the room returned to normal and the electricity was gone from the air.

For the rest of the day, I had the sensation of having peeked through a keyhole into someone's tragic past. Off and on I had been trying to contact previous owners of the house, or their survivors, but had turned up little of interest. The few people I found who were familiar with the property knew of nothing unusual that had happened here.

Then I had looked into the Higbee family and discovered there had been many remarkable deaths among the grandchildren of Josiah Higbee. One of his offspring lost five children under the age of eight, and all were buried in the Higbee graveyard.

A lot of my time was spent trying to make sense of things that were inscrutable. But there had to be a relationship, a wire that bound together what appeared to be random and dissociated acts, whether real or imagined.

Could the little girl who roamed our hallways and played with Ashley be connected to the Higbee family? Was she the little girl I had seen killed with a shovel in my bathroom? But what of the rest of it, the whole catalog of craziness we had lived with for four years? Was it the work of long-dead Higbees trying to drive us from their burial ground? I was ready to believe anything, but there was a glitch in that theory. The Higbee grandchildren probably would have died in the last century. The little girl, as I saw her at our bedroom door, did not seem to be of that era. Neither did the man, woman, and child I saw in the bathroom vision.

Also, we had no proof that anyone was actually buried on our property. It seemed unlikely that the descendants of Josiah Higbee would have sold the family cemetery. We occupied only two acres of the eighty-acre plot set aside in the will for burying family members.

Ron and I decided to scout out the other seventy-eight acres. We drove the streets that gave access to that acreage and walked fields inaccessible by car. Just north of us, across Clifty Drive and behind a row of trees, we found a fenced patch of earth with small markers and tombstones. Nearly all bore the name Higbee.

"Well, I guess we can't blame it on them," I said.

Chapter 15

Before Jordan and Teri arrived, Ron and I talked again about taking care to detect any trickery. We would keep an eye on them every minute. They could go anywhere in the house or on the grounds, but we would accompany them. We did not intend to pay for a magic show.

They arrived on schedule early in the evening. Jordan was carrying a small suitcase, which he placed on the floor in the living room. As the priests had done, Jordan and Teri first wanted to walk through the house. Ron stood in the hallway and watched them closely. I carried Ashley into the living room, where Steven was watching television.

Jordan and Teri took their time, moving unhurriedly from room to room and lingering in each one like prospective buyers searching for defects. I learned later that they were taking a psychic reading.

When they returned to the living room, Jordan asked that we turn off the television, but said little else until he had opened his suitcase. It contained an odd-looking machine, a boxlike device with small windows for gauges—something like an electrical meter. Built into the box was a ball, or flywheel, which he rubbed with his hand, causing it to spin and whir, generating an electrical friction.

Although he was psychic, he explained to us, he did not possess the natural electrical field that heightens the sensitivities of many psychics and sharpens their focus on whatever supernatural forces might be present. The device in the suitcase compensated for that lack.

"There are several entities in this house," Jordan said in a flat monotone after stroking the flywheel of his machine for a couple of minutes. "There is a young girl, three or four women, some men . . . and some you don't want to know about. There was an old man at the door when we came in, but he took off. We saw another man, younger, in the hallway. He had a small mustache . . . like Hitler's."

His mention of the old man was like an ice pick in my chest. The fact that he saw something that all of us, except Ron, had seen gave him credibility. Then he said something else familiar, something Ron and I had known since the day of the fire. Something was different about Ashley's bedroom, the smell of roses, the disarray, the bows, the cold temperatures.

"Ashley's room is badly infested," Jordan said. The machine purred as he spoke. "There are several entities in there. You should just close it off and not use it."

When he had finished relating the results of his psychic reading of the house, Jordan stared at each of us intently.

"I'd like to take some Polaroid pictures of you," he said.

He photographed Ron first, then Steven. There was nothing abnormal about the pictures. He photographed Ashley, then me, on the couch, in the same spot where Ron and Steven had been seated. The lighting was the same. The film was the same. The camera was the same. The pictures were not.

Ashley's face and mine were blank—dim, featureless smudges on the developed photograph.

"The light force of you and Ashley is all gone," the psychic said. "We're going to have to do a lot of work."

He proposed conducting a healing on each member of the family. Each of us has an aura, he said, a field that surrounds us like an invisible barrier. If there is a break in the aura, "they" can enter and attach themselves to us.

Suddenly, I felt weak and fatigued. Jordan didn't use the word *demon*, but I thought that was what he was suggesting. What else would enter our aura and possess our bodies? *Where is this going and where will it end?* I wanted to protest, but whatever disbelief I still possessed was stifled by confusion and curiosity. The priests felt the presence of evil when they walked through the house. The shadowy apparition was the personification of something vile. *If this land is not a burial ground, maybe it is something worse—a portal to hell.*

Remembering the religion of my grandmother, I expected the healing to be like something from a tent revival, a lot of praying and laying on of hands. I was wrong. This was to be a mending of the aura, not the body or the soul.

"I'm going to do Ron first," Jordan said, becoming very animated. "No. Steven, come over here." He appeared indecisive, waffling from one of us to the other as though responding to equivocal voices only he could hear.

He made his decision and asked Steven to sit in a chair. Jordan and Teri held their hands ten or twelve inches from him and moved their palms around his head and shoulders, down his back, sides and chest, never touching him, but smoothing and molding the aura, they said, filling in cracks where spirits might enter.

They worked quietly. Teri's head remained bowed, as in prayer. Jordan occasionally looked around the room, but didn't speak. I watched Ashley's reaction. She was a shy and introverted child and I was uncertain if she could be coaxed into participating in this experiment. Nothing the psychics were doing was especially scary, and she simply watched with childlike indifference.

Ron took the chair after Steven; then it was my turn. I felt no particular sensation, other than a measure of self-consciousness during the healing, but I was not surprised by the diagnosis.

"You have a major break in your aura," Jordan said. "We've got trouble there."

Sure. I was convinced that Jordan was targeting me, determined to make me the broker of the haunting this house was suffering.

He turned to Ashley. With a minimum of cajoling, she climbed into the chair. Jordan and Teri raised their hands and extended them into the zone of Ashley's aura. The atmosphere of the room changed instantly. As it had done many times before, the air became heavy and repressive and charged with electricity. The thought crossed my mind: *Something doesn't want Ashley touched.*

Jordan and Teri ignored the atmospheric anomaly. "That was fine," Jordan said when they were finished. He made no mention of a broken aura. Ashley slid from the chair and sat beside me on the loveseat. Teri sat beside Steven on the sofa.

"Can I use your bathroom?" Jordan asked.

"Sure," Ron said. "It's right across the hall there."

Teri had turned toward me to ask about the house and the events we had experienced. For no apparent reason, Ron jumped from his chair and dashed toward the hallway. I thought he was going to check on Jordan, to see if the psychic was up to something. He looked toward the bathroom and then toward the hallway and I heard him yell, "Oh, shit."

Before I could stand, Jordan came out of the bathroom and Ron was backing into the living room, white as chalk.

"Oh, my God. I just saw it," he said.

"Saw what?" Jordan asked.

"I don't know," Ron stammered. "It was a shadow, a head and arms and torso. It was standing right there . . . in the hall. When I looked at it, it just moved back into the wall . . . disappeared."

I began laughing uncontrollably, jumping up and down like a cheerleader whose team had just won in overtime. Our guests must have been as astonished by my behavior as they were by Ron's sighting of the apparition.

"He saw it! He saw it!" I shouted. I told Jordan and Teri that because Ron had never seen the apparition, it was a source of antagonism between us. Frankly, he usually argued that the "entity" did not exist except in my imagination. "When I see it, I'll believe it," he had said more than once.

Now he had seen it and I was overjoyed.

"That was the old man," Jordan said, cutting short my celebration. "He's angry. He doesn't like this at all. He's going to be the tough one."

As matter-of-factly as a doctor prescribing aspirin and rest for a cold, he gave us a list of dos and don'ts to follow while he organized a strategy against *them*. Play religious music—specifically the Gregorian chants—in the house and in our cars. Control our emotions—the entities were aroused by anger. Maintain contact with the Church. Pray. Sprinkle holy water often throughout the house. Those were the steps of a cleansing, he said, softening the enemy up for the coup de grâce.

"It will try to provoke you," he said. "Ignore it. Don't get upset and under no circumstances should you try to communicate with it."

Try as we did to follow our psychic's instructions, things were happening so fast that it became difficult to concentrate on the battle. We were so busy defending our flanks, we had little time to think about charging the wall. A pane of glass in the kitchen window shattered from no cause that we could determine. Appliances continued to break down. Water and sewer pipes broke and had to be mended.

Our cars also behaved more and more erratically. Radios turned on and off by themselves. Dials and gauges gave erroneous readings. Following Jordan's instruction, I bought Gregorian chants and a cassette of gospel songs by Amy Grant, whose music I have always liked, and the first time I tried to play it in my car the machine chewed up the tape and ejected the cassette.

In the laundry room, I bent over to take some clothes out of a basket and place them in the washing machine. A pair of damp Levis was hanging on a line next to me. As I bent down, I heard a *snap* and the blue jeans fell to the floor.

I jumped back and, without thinking, said, "You are so immature." *What are you doing, Doretta? Talking to your ghosts, scolding them as though they were children.* A part of me believed these *things* were testing me, trying to arouse fear. Being flippant was my way of defying them.

In truth, dread was always within me.

We closed off Ashley's room and she slept in the living room with Ron and me. As the disturbances intensified, Steven also joined us there.

We spent every night huddled like refugees on the living-room floor, robbed of sleep by slamming doors, footsteps, weeping, and tapping on the walls. Everyone in the family became tense and irritable, especially Ron. Our attempt at reconciliation had pretty well fallen apart, and my husband, once again, was brooding and detached. We rarely spoke except in acrimony.

After an argument one evening, I was awakened at four o'clock in the morning by a knocking on a door or wall. When I sat up, the noise stopped. Ron raised up on one elbow and asked, "Is something wrong?"

"No, nothing," I said. "Go back to sleep."

At six o'clock, the same sound woke me up again. Ron was in the kitchen eating cereal. Joining him at the table, I didn't mention hearing the knocking during the night. He was cranky and seemed to be eager to resume last night's argument, but I was determined not to participate. *It feeds on your anger,* Jordan had warned.

After a long silence, Ron stood up and said, "I'm going to be late for work." He looked around and snapped, "Where the hell is my lunch box? What the hell did those sons of bitches do with my lunch box?"

It was the first time he had spoken of *them* in a personal way and I wondered if *they* were finally getting to him the way they had gotten to me.

Ron found his lunch box, tossed some sandwiches in it, and stomped out the door. I sat at the table, drinking coffee and smoking one cigarette after another. The thought began to take shape in my mind: *Give it up. Get the hell out of this house.* Financially, it was not a practical solution. Since I was in accounting school, we had only Ron's salary and the house was devouring it. Our insurance policy covered only a part of the losses we were suffering daily.

I opened my journal and began to write. What had begun as a therapeutic practice now had another purpose—to preserve details of the abnormal episodes, which were occurring so rapidly that I was afraid I would be unable to recall them accurately without notes. After a few minutes, I left the journal open at a blank page and went into the bathroom. When I returned, the page had been written on—four long and slender letters that looked like the scribbling of a dyslexic child: something resembling a backward "E." A broken "T" with the crossbar an inch from the top, or it could have been the fragment of an "H." Another "T" with the bar at the top. An "A."

My hand shook as I picked up the diary and studied the words. "EHTA." *"HATE,"* I thought. Backward, misspelled, rearranged and splintered, but still "HATE." I could come up with no other interpretation.

Could I have written it while in some kind of trance? Dreams and reality had begun to roll together in a confusing glob. Those scratches were not in my hand and not in the handwriting of either of my children. Besides, the kids were still asleep, and one of them could not have gotten up without me knowing it. So, if I didn't write it, who did?

Once again the familiar feeling of being watched came over me. The house was thick with that same awful presence. I prayed and sprinkled holy water in the living room and went back to my journal. *I will remain strong,* I wrote, *because my Lord and savior stands with me.* Through the window to my left, the sun broke over the treetops and flooded the kitchen with a soft yellow glow. My corner of the world was waking up. The children were stirring, and cars rushed by on Clifty Drive.

A sense of normalcy returned to the house, and the strain dissipated. I fixed breakfast and dressed Ashley for school. When she and Steven were gone, I picked up my journal. Maybe I had imagined the alien scribbling. Maybe it was a hallucination induced by weariness and the tension of the previous night. I opened the book and the markings stared back at me: "EHTA."

I slammed it shut, went to the phone, and called Jordan Pitkoff. I told him about the fight with Ron and the letters scrawled in my diary. His voice was comforting and his words reassuring. Continue the prayer vigils, he said, and make certain the whole family participates. Make liberal use of the holy water. "If Ron becomes influenced again, call and I will talk to him," he said.

I felt better. In spite of my many reservations about this unfamiliar realm of psychics and parapsychology, my confidence in Jordan was growing. He had told us that there would be a "disturbance" when he came to our house, and he was correct. It was his presence and his healing that caused "the old man" to show himself to Ron for the first time. We had found no flimflam or hidden tricks in Jordan's act so far, and most of what he told us meshed with our experiences. He might well be the one to lead us out of this wilderness.

"I would like for you to come to my office and bring some photographs of your male relatives, as many photographs as you can find," Jordan said. "We need to start trying to identify these spirits."

Though he had not said so directly, Jordan apparently believed that whatever or whoever was haunting our house was drawn here by me—particularly "the old man." Yet he had said there were at least seven entities—men, women, and children. Who were the others? What were they doing here? Why had we not seen them all? There was too much about all this I could not fathom. I felt foolish whenever I found myself thinking seriously about ghosts or spirits, but the concept was simple enough: a soul trapped between this world and the next. But why here? Why in my house? Even if we lived on a long-forgotten burial ground, none of my male relatives had been buried here. And why had Ashley, at the age of one or two, been the first in our family to "see" the little girl? The layers of unanswerable questions—overlapping, commingled and intertwined riddles—were far beyond the reach of my knowledge and comprehension.

"I'll need some time to get the pictures together," I told Jordan.

"There's no rush," he said. "We have plenty of time."

After we hung up, I sat and brooded about where all this was headed. *Okay, suppose we conclude that my house is infested with ghosts, that this land is, for some reason, a kind of holding tank for lost souls. What do we do about it? How do we dispatch them to the hereafter?*

I spent most of the day looking through photo albums and boxes of pictures I had gathered over the years, some of them passed on to me by my grandmother. There were pictures of one or two of my stepfathers, some uncles, cousins, my three brothers.

I came across an old baby picture of me and Jimmy Mikos. I was about two and a half years old, standing on a table, wearing panties and a tiny bra. Jimmy Mikos had his arm around me and was smiling broadly. I had no real memory of him, just the photograph and things my grandmother had told me about him. I lived with him and my mother only briefly before my heart surgery. He was taken away by the FBI the day after my operation. I set aside the pictures I would take to Jordan, but did not include the one of me with Jimmy Mikos.

A thought occurred to me: This was an opportunity to test Jordan Pitkoff one more time before completely buying into his act. Along with the fifteen or so pictures of my male relatives, I included some of men who were not related to me—friends, Ron's relatives, and the like. It was important to know if my psychic was for real.

Chapter 16

After visiting our house, Jordan was confident that he had things under control. When I went to his office with the photographs, he spent most of the meeting telling me about other cases he had handled and how he would deal with this one. The only outside help he wanted was the Catholic Church. I had not seen the priests since they blessed the house, and Jordan urged me to get back in touch with them.

"We want them close to this situation," he said.

I told him how the house had seemed to react with hostility to the religious men.

"We can handle that," he said. "We're going to need them."

Then I told him that following his visit our house had been in even more turmoil. "We can't even sleep," I said. "Doors slam all night long. The place smells like a sewer. We keep seeing shadows and hearing animals. It feels like a war zone."

"You're not controlling your emotions," he said.

"I'm trying."

He rose out of his chair and leaned on the desk. "You had a fight with your husband. What are you trying to do, rip the whole house apart? You've got to stay calm. You can stop it. You can say no," he said. So far, every conversation with Jordan Pitkoff had the same content: I was the guilty party; I was to blame for the spirits that terrorized my family. Still, I was gradually becoming dependent on him. He was the only hope I had.

"These are the pictures you wanted," I said, handing him an envelope.

Before opening it, he looked at me in such a way that his eyes seemed to bore through my skull. "You had a male relative who hurt you when you were young. Maybe ten or eleven. He's the one who's in your house."

He took out the photographs and thumbed through them quickly. He stopped at one and, with no hesitation, said, "That's him right there."

Jordan's accuracy gave me the creeps. If I had been standing, I probably would have fallen. I sank back into the sofa and stared at the photo . . . and the memory came spilling out of its box.

Uncle Ross was married to my grandmother's sister, who had been rendered an invalid by a severe stroke. They had several children, and Uncle Ross, a pipe fitter, traveled a lot. To my ten-year-old eyes he was very unattractive—an old, bald man with a large bumpy nose. But he seemed nice. He always drove a big car and flashed his money like a high roller. My brothers and sisters and I always were happy to see him when he stopped by Grandma's house. He gave us hugs and kisses and a dollar or two each.

On one of his visits, he and Grandma and I were alone in the house. Grandma went into the kitchen and Uncle Ross asked me to get him another cup of coffee. When I walked over to get his cup, he pulled me close to him and told me what a pretty little girl I was. I was flattered by his attentions, I suppose, until he began running his hands over my body. I tried to pull away but he hooked an arm around my waist and held me against him.

I was confused and embarrassed but couldn't free myself from his grip.

"What's wrong?" he kept asking. "Doesn't it feel good? I just want to make you feel good."

Finally, I broke loose and ran out the door. I stayed away from the house until he was gone. For some reason, I felt responsible for what had happened and I said nothing to Grandma about it.

He stayed away for several months, and when he began coming around again, he acted as though nothing had happened. But I was careful never to be alone with him.

I was appalled when Grandma informed us that Uncle Ross was going to move in with us for a while.

"I don't want him to," I told Grandma.

"Why not, honey?"

"Our house isn't big enough." I couldn't tell her my real reason.

"Well, he's going to pay for his room and board and we need the money," she said.

"No!" I argued.

"Young lady, this is not your house. You don't decide who lives here," she said. "Uncle Ross is family and you better be good to him."

He moved in and for a few weeks things were normal. He gave Grandma a lot of extra money and even bought shoes for all the children. I still tried to avoid him, but it was impossible.

While I was doing homework at the kitchen table one night, Uncle Ross walked up behind me, put his hand on my shoulder, and asked what I was doing. Before I could answer, his hand moved down to my breast. I tried to push him away but he held on to me, breathing heavily down my neck.

"I'm not going to hurt you," he whispered. "I just want to make you feel good."

I continued to resist and he finally let go, probably because he was afraid Grandma would walk into the room.

He didn't bother me for the next few weeks. Then one night I was awakened by someone kneeling beside my bed, slowly raising my nightgown. The house was pitch black and I was aware that my little sister was still asleep on the other side of the bed we shared.

"No," I said, pushing the hand away from me.

"Shhhhh," he said. Uncle Ross pinned both my arms with one hand and held me on the bed, running his free hand over every part of my body. "Doesn't that feel good?" he whispered. "Don't you like it?"

I struggled against his grip.

"Be quiet now or your grandma will find out."

Nancy began to stir and Uncle Ross got up and left our room. For days I tried to sort out what was happening, but the confusion was overwhelming. *Why is he doing this? Uncle Ross always says he loves me. He's not hurting me, not the way I was hurt by the beatings from my mother and stepfathers. But he is doing something wrong to me. Why? What did I do to cause him to do it?*

He came to my room often over the next few months, each time going a little further, touching me over my clothes, then under them, but never attempting intercourse. I would close my eyes tightly and try to pretend I was somewhere else and wait for him to leave. One night, he slid his hand under my panties and forced his finger inside me. I began to cry and he stopped.

A hundred times I tried to find a way to tell Grandma, but she would not have believed me. Around the others, I treated him rudely, shoved him away when he tried to hug me or my little sister, and usually got a scolding from Grandma. "I won't have you treating him like that," she would yell. "He's so good to us."

The last time he came to my room, Nancy was not there. She was sleeping with Grandma and I was alone. When I woke up, Uncle Ross was in my bed, not beside it, and he was rougher than usual. He yanked my panties down to my ankles and harshly told me to shut up when I pleaded with him to stop.

He panted and huffed like an animal and I thought he was going to hurt me. He got up on his knees and then kneeled across my legs and held my hands together with one of his. He pulled my nightgown over my head and tossed it on the floor. I was naked and humiliated. His mouth and hands were all over me but I couldn't move. I could only cry silently. He shifted his weight off of me and pressed his face between my legs. I felt his tongue and the coarse skin of his face and heard the sound of his belt buckle being unfastened. I rolled on my side and kicked him as hard as I could.

I grabbed the headboard, pulled my knees up to my chest, and screamed, "Get out! Get out!"

Early the next morning, I stood under a hot shower and scrubbed my skin as hard as I could.

Jordan held the photograph, waiting for me to acknowledge it. I nodded.

"Okay, that's better," he said. "As we identify these entities, we'll know how to deal with them. This is the bad one. We'll work on him first."

He escorted me to the door and instructed me to call if anything new happened.

Uncle Ross had been one of those painful childhood memories I had put in storage. He was loose in my head now and I wondered if more chaos would visit my house.

"Honey, those things are dangerous," Lorraine Warren said over the phone.

"What things?"

"You've got demons in that house and you have to be very careful."

The authors of *Ghost Hunter* had received the letter I sent via their publisher, and Lorraine had called to find out more. I found myself almost wishing she hadn't. The Warrens were demonologists, I knew from their book, so it was natural that they saw Satanic fiends behind the paranormal activities in our house.

That added a new dimension to the quandary. It occurred to me that Jordan had never used the word "demon." In his mind, we were up against *entities* or *spirits* or some remnant of once-living beings, scraps of the soul or intelligence or personality.

Lorraine's theory was scarier and the ways she told me to handle it conflicted with Jordan's prescriptions.

"Have you done anything about this?" she asked.

"A couple of priests came out and blessed the house," I said, "and I've been talking to a psychic in Louisville."

"How much is he charging you?"

"The visits are eighty dollars an hour."

That seemed to rile her. "You mean to tell me your family is going through all this and that jerk is charging you?"

While I was impressed with her knowledge and grateful for her concern, I also felt defensive about Jordan. He had not missed the target yet, and at least he had been available to us, even if the cost was high.

"What did he tell you to do?"

I ticked off his list of dos (holy water, family prayer, religious music) and don'ts (arguing, communicating with the entities, showing fear).

"Stop playing the religious music," she advised. "That's the worst thing you can do. It only provokes them."

"Should I keep my kids out of the house?"

"I think they're okay right now. I would like to come to your house as soon as I can arrange it."

"Great," I said.

"In the meantime, I need as much information as I can get. Put everything you can remember on a tape and send it to me."

After hanging up, I wondered if I was gaining ground or losing it. *First, I think I'm going insane, and that is hard to deal with. Then Jordan Pitkoff assures me that instead of a loose screw, I have ghosts in my house, and that is harder to deal with. Now, Lorraine Warren tells me I don't have ghosts, I have demons, and I don't think I can deal with that at all.*

Years ago, we have been told, before this strip of Clifty Drive was developed and fill trucked in to level the low-lying areas, the land where our house sits was like a bog, a sponge that held water close to the surface for days after a rain. It is still that way to some extent. Even when the land around us is dry, you can walk across our yard and moisture will slosh up onto your shoes and the air will become so charged with electricity that your hair will stand up and your skin will feel as though it is being brushed with fine silk.

The day after I spoke with Lorraine, the ground was like that and I felt drawn to the backyard. I paced over the area where, in my dream, I had seen the circus tent and the man with the snakes. The air seemed to crack with energy, and a whiff of freshly turned soil, like the grave smell I had experienced in the shower, rose off the lawn. The electricity followed me back into the house and was so strong that I became concerned about another power surge in the wiring and possibly another fire.

I went through the house unplugging everything: the televisions, lamps, computer, kitchen devices, and the radio/tape recorder into which I had been dictating notes to Lorraine.

While ambling through the house pulling plugs, I heard static coming from the kitchen. I walked closer and realized it was coming from the radio/recorder. The power was turned off and the cord dangled from the table well away from the electrical socket. *You're hearing things again, Doretta.*

I was still staring at the radio when I heard the woman speak. "Can you hear me?" The voice was coming from the radio and sounded like a CB transmission. "Can you hear me? Help me. I can't get out of here. I need your help."

It must be a CB signal, but how is it coming over a radio that is turned off and unplugged?

"Help me," the woman said again. "I'm at the Park-N-Eat."

That's it. Somebody's car broke down at the Park-N-Eat and they're radioing for help.

I looked out the window toward the old drive-in that had been closed for at least ten years. No car was parked there.

"Ron!" I yelled. He came from the back of the house. "I think somebody's over there and in trouble."

"Let's take the car," he said. "They might need a jump start."

As soon as we pulled out of the driveway and crossed the road, the electricity again danced on my skin. My whole body stiffened and the hair on my arms stood out. We circled the drive-in and found no stranded motorist. I got out and looked in the windows. The electricity was still strong and Ron was yelling for me to get back in the car. Through the dusty glass, I could see nothing, except an interior that looked as though it had been ripped apart. Everything was torn and broken and strewn about. It reminded me of the way our laundry room had looked on occasion.

"Get back in the car!" Ron demanded again. He was feeling the electricity, too.

We drove back home and sat in the kitchen trying to figure out what was going on. How had we received the radio or CB broadcast, if that's what it was? The air was still electric and both of us were more than a little shaken.

We stopped talking and our mouths hung open. A sphere of light the size of a basketball appeared in the hall near the laundry room. It drifted into the kitchen and floated aimlessly around the room, sliding down the walls and skimming across the ceiling. Smaller balls of light broke off from it and followed the larger ball. One of the lights formed into a kind of outline or silhouette that looked like a Holly Hobbie doll, which is a model of an old-fashioned little girl. She was standing sideways and I could see the bow in her hair and the long dress with a pinafore down the front. Another light sphere formed into the shape of a man and then began whirling around the room. It wrapped itself around a wicker basket hanging on the wall. After a minute or two, the large light moved back toward the laundry room with the smaller orbs in line behind it. There they dimmed, faded, and vanished.

From where I was seated, I could see what appeared to be scratches on the wicker basket. I walked over and examined it.

"Look at this," I said to my husband.

"Looks like writing," he said.

The lettering was crude and nearly illegible. The first letter appeared to be an L but the next three were harder to make out.

"It looks like *Lucy*," I said.

"*Lucy* or *Lacy* or *Luce*," Ron said. "Hell, I don't know."

"Do we know anybody with a name like that . . . anything similar?"

"I don't."

"Me neither . . . I don't think."

The lights were a new phenomenon, but like the noises and apparitions and odors, they seemed to possess an intelligence, a purpose—either to communicate with us or scare the hell out of us. They succeeded in the latter.

"I've been thinking seriously about getting out of this house," I said. "Getting out and staying out."

"Where would we live?" he said. "We probably couldn't sell this place. How would we buy another house?"

"All I know is I'm concerned about the kids," I said. "We don't know what we're dealing with . . . ghosts . . . demons. How do we know what they're capable of? How do we know the kids are safe here?"

"Jordan and Lorraine both said there's no danger."

"Well, Jordan and Lorraine don't even agree on what's in this house. One of them is wrong. Maybe both of them are wrong."

Jordan called that night to see how things were going.

"It's been a weird day," I said.

"In what way?"

"Well, it started out with my radio picking up what sounded like a CB transmission."

He chuckled. "Let me guess, your radio was turned off."

"It certainly was. Off and unplugged."

"That happens. You'll probably be hearing it again."

"What do you mean?"

"You're picking up messages from beyond. You'll probably start picking them up regularly on your radio *and* television."

I told him about the lights and what appeared to be a name scratched on the wicker basket. "Was that something from beyond, too?" I asked, letting my sarcasm ooze out.

He didn't answer right away and in the background I could hear the whirring of the flywheel he stroked to generate a psychic-enhancing electrical field.

"We can explore that later," he said. "Have you talked with the priests again?"

"No."

"Why not? It's important."

"They would think I'm nuts," I said.

"You're wrong," he said. "They need to be involved. You're a Catholic and you need your church. You've heard about exorcisms, haven't you?"

I laughed. "Yeah, I saw the movie."

Chapter 17

My concern for the children intensified. We all slept on the floor in the living room. Ashley was not permitted to go to the bathroom alone, and I kept an ear cocked like a satellite dish whenever one of the children was not in the room with me. Being in this house those first two weeks in October was like being in a small boat slapped around by savage waves and howling winds.

The phone rang and when I went to answer it, a chalkboard flew off the wall and struck me on the head. We heard raspy breathing in the hallway, like the sound of someone being sustained by a respirator. Checking it out, I saw another of those hologram images—an old man with long hair and a white beard reclining in a chair, struggling to breathe. The hallway had the medicinal scent that often lingers around old people.

One morning, Ron left early for work and Steven was getting ready for school. Ashley was still asleep on the floor and I was on the couch beside her, reading. The night before had been clamorous—bumping and knocking and faint laughter—but now the house was quiet. Steven walked past and said good-bye, and I heard the back door slam behind him.

Rarely had the house been this tranquil. I heard footsteps in the hall, the sound of a child running. I stood up to investigate and the steps came toward me, came nearer and nearer until they seemed to pass through me like a cold mist. We saw each other, the little girl and I, and she appeared as surprised as I by the encounter.

In the past, I had found that the apparitions showed themselves mostly at night or in dim lighting. Perhaps light didn't drive them away, but at least I could not see them in sunlight. I stepped to the window and pulled back the curtains to let in the sun's morning glare. Steven was standing out by the road waiting for the school bus, and just as I drew the curtain he turned around and started walking back to the house, as though something had summoned him.

"Don't leave," I told him. "I'm going to drive you to school. Stay here with Ashley while I get dressed. I don't want her to be alone."

When I returned, Steven went into the bathroom.

"Leave the door open," I insisted.

A minute or two later, he yelled for me. "Mom, you gotta come here."

I walked into the room.

"Listen," he said.

Knock, knock. The sound seemed to come from inside the wall.

"Tap the wall, Mom," Steven said.

"No!" Jordan had warned us not to communicate with *them*.

Steven was intrigued enough to ignore me. He tapped three times on the wall and got a three-tap response. He tapped twice and got a two-tap response.

"Stop it," I said. "That's enough. Let's get out of here."

Father John's visit was completely unexpected. I hadn't talked to him for several weeks and assumed he had forgotten us and our problems. He came with an important message.

"I received a call from the archbishop of Lafayette," he said. "Apparently he was contacted by a woman named Lorraine Warren. She told him about your case and a decision was made."

"Decision?"

"The Archbishop took the matter to his superiors and the Church has approved an exorcism," he said.

Good news and bad news, I thought. The Church wants to help me but if the Church has authorized an exorcism it must mean that the Church believes, as Lorraine Warren does, that my house is infested with demons. I had seen the movie and knew that the book it was taken from was based on an actual case of demonic possession. Did the Church think I was possessed? Ashley? The house?

Father John had not been sent to answer all the questions that spilled out of me. He patted my hand and said, "I will be getting another call. The Church is going to bring in a priest who is well versed in these types of rituals. I don't know any more than that."

"What does the ritual consist of?"

"You can discuss that with the other priest," he said. "The Church demands complete privacy in these matters. You are not to tell anyone. I'm only getting information on a need-to-know basis."

*　　*　　*

The next couple of days were pure hell. Ashley woke up at night screaming and complaining that something was biting her. Our ghosts, or demons, clattered around the house at night with such fury that none of us was able to sleep. Both of my children had no appetite and they dragged through their days in a stupor.

"We've got to get the kids out of this house," I told Ron. "Let's see if your mother will keep Ashley for a while. Maybe Steven can stay with Marilee."

"What about his school?"

"I'm more worried about his safety."

Marge agreed to keep Ashley as long as we thought necessary, so we packed her clothes and drove her to Louisville. I signed some papers that essentially gave Marge parental authority over her, empowering her to authorize medical treatment or make other crucial decisions concerning her welfare.

Steven had to stay around a while longer because Marilee was having problems of her own and wasn't able to take him. After one particular incident, though, I was afraid he might run away.

We heard a loud cracking noise in our hall closet. It sounded as though someone had driven a hammer into the wall. Ron yanked the door open and we saw a hole, the size of a fist, in the Sheetrock. From the way the wallboard was bent out, it was apparent that the blow was delivered from the other side of the wall. Closer inspection revealed that the other side of the wall was not damaged. The blow had to have come from *inside* the wall.

Somber and bleary-eyed the next morning, Steven said, "Mom, I love you but I can't take it anymore."

In desperation, I called my cousin, Jenny, in Rineyville, and explained the situation. She didn't hesitate to take him in. We drove Steven over there and signed the same kinds of documents we had signed for Ashley.

"I feel like I've given my kids away," I told Ron on the trip back home.

There was a message on the answering machine from Lorraine Warren. She had picked a date to come to Madison and hunt down our demons. I called her back and we made the plans. Afterward, I didn't know if I should feel relieved or if I should dig a foxhole. *You've got a psychic, a demonologist, and the whole Catholic Church on your team now, Doretta. You'll either win the war or escalate it into Armageddon.*

Father John called the next day. "You'll be getting calls from a Father A," he said.

"Who is he?"

"That's just a code name," he said. "You won't be told any more than that. Be home at nine this evening. That's when he will call."

Something about the voice irritated me. It was haughty and disdainful and rudely authoritarian, the voice of a judge accustomed to handing out stiff sentences.

"I'm Father A," he said.

"I'm so glad you called," I said.

"Well, I see you've gotten yourself in trouble," he said. "How long have you been away from the Church?"

"A long time. Twenty-five years, I guess."

"So you got a problem and you came running back to the Church," he sneered. "A good Catholic wouldn't be in your predicament. Your family is going to pay for your sins."

"My sins?"

"This thing wouldn't be there if you hadn't invited it in, you know."

"I don't know," I said through clinched teeth. Suppressing the urge to lash back at him wasn't easy, but I was completely intimidated. For my kids' sake, I would have done anything, even let him talk to me in this offensive manner. After what we had been through, I could take anything he could throw at me.

"Is your husband a Catholic?"

"No, Baptist."

"Did you marry him in a church?"

"No, a civil ceremony."

"The Church will not recognize your marriage. You've allowed your children to be bastards."

"My children are not bastards. They have a father and I am legally married to him."

"Not in the Church's eyes," he said, the authority in his voice ratcheting upward. "What about your kids? Do they attend church?"

"They have. My son has attended several churches. I encouraged him to attend several until he found one he felt most comfortable with. My daughter has attended Sunday School and children's church, with her grandmother. I have . . ."

"Have you attended church regularly with your children?"

"No . . . I . . ."

"You what?" he interrupted. "You don't think they need a religious grounding, huh?"

Don't let him get to you, Doretta. "Father, I have taught them about God . . . and about right and wrong and good and evil. . . ."

"Why haven't you been in church? It is your duty as a mother to raise your family in the Church."

For a moment I felt eight years old again, being rebuked by the head priest at school for forgetting to bring the lace scarf that was to cover my head during morning Mass. *You feel you do not have to obey God's rule?* the priest had scolded.

"I didn't feel like I could return to the Church. I had been divorced . . ."

"Don't you dare use that for an excuse. You have no right to talk that way. You could have gone back to the Church and repented for your sins. Have you ever been involved in Satanic worship?"

"No, of course not."

"Any occult practices or anything like that?"

"No."

"I understand you are consulting with a psychic."

"Yes."

"You think some charlatan like that can save you?"

"Father, I didn't know who else to turn to."

"He's taking your money and ripping you off," he said.

"But he seems to have an understanding of what's going on. He's dealt with these things many times," I said.

"Well, you don't need him and I don't want any part of him," he said. "The Church is the only thing that can stop what's happening to you. You remember that. I'll have no part of him, or any other interference by anyone. It is time you learned to obey the Church and its rules."

"Listen, I didn't go to the Church for help with this problem," I said, weary of his condemnation. "I went for spiritual guidance. . . ."

"Well, there were one hundred and fifty-seven other cases in line for the Church's help, in similar situations, but the Church moved you to the top of the list," he said. "Somebody thinks you need more than spiritual guidance. You have no idea what you are dealing with. I do. I have spent the last eight years of my life fighting to free families like yours. Only a few priests hold the position I do. I have seen homes, entire families, destroyed. Exorcism is the only way to free your family, so don't think for a minute you don't need the Church's help. Now, let me speak with your husband."

By that time, I was crying and shaking and happy to get off the phone and away from him. I felt as if I had just stepped out of the confessional and God himself had reprimanded me for my disobedience. His verbal lashing left me feeling defenseless, helpless.

He asked Ron a few questions about his family and his background and they hung up.

"We're supposed to be here every night at nine in case he calls," Ron said.

There were two reasons for the trip to Louisville. We were going to visit our daughter, but I also was going to see Jordan Pitkoff for another aura healing. Jordan had cautioned me against missing even one appointment, lest the aura weaken and entities enter and attach themselves to me. Ron avoided the psychic as much as possible, just as he removed himself from me and the problems of the house whenever he could, so I went alone to Jordan's office.

"I've talked with a priest from New York," I told him.

"That's great. That's just what we needed. What are his plans?"

"An exorcism, I suppose. He didn't spend a lot of time detailing his plans. He was too busy chastising me for being a bad Catholic."

Jordan laughed. "Aw, those Catholic priests. That's just the way they are," he said. "I think they are angry at all women and all nonpracticing Catholics."

"Well, I don't know where you fit in but he isn't too crazy about you, either." I said. "He called you a charlatan."

He didn't brush that aside so easily. His face flushed and he snapped forward with enough force to lift his leather-bound chair from its swivels. "Who does he think he is? He has no right to judge me that way."

"I tried to tell him how much you have helped, but he doesn't want you involved."

"Fine, let him handle it himself."

I didn't want Jordan alienated, but I could see that it would be difficult to keep my army intact as the war widened. Along with the ghost and demon front, a political battle was taking shape. The Warrens, Jordan Pitkoff, Father A—all sniping at each other across no-man's-land with me hunkered down in the middle. I had to stay neutral. I could not afford to lose one ally. I didn't know which one could save me.

"How's Ron?" Jordan asked.

"Like a mechanical man," I said. "Things happen and he drifts farther away, pretends everything is fine. He doesn't want to deal with it. I don't think he knows how."

"You're having to fight all by yourself," he said. "Don't you get tired of being alone, fighting all the battles by yourself?"

"Yeah, but that's just Ron's nature. He's never been a fighter," I said. Part of me understood that. In childhood, I dealt with the pain by closing my eyes and pretending to be someone else, somewhere else. Ron was doing the same thing. When a storm passed through our lives, he sort of shut himself up in his private cellar.

"Why do you stay with him?" Jordan asked.

The question irritated me. "Because he's my husband and I love him."

Jordan heard the resentment in my tone and changed the subject. "I'm thinking of starting a psychic circle. Teri, myself, and a couple other gifted psychics. I'd like you to join," he said.

That suggestion also irritated me. Jordan was focusing too much on me, I believed, and not enough on my house. He thought I was psychic and seemed very intrigued by my *abilities,* as he called them. I didn't know if I had *abilities* or not, but I couldn't quite see myself sitting around with a bunch of weirdos reading each other's minds.

"I've got my hands full right now," I said. It was time to go.

For a long time, we drove toward Madison in silence. Jordan was right. I was fighting the battle pretty much alone and I was tired of it. Ron and I never huddled together against the angry wind, possibly because he had not shared everything I had experienced. The demons didn't follow him the way they did me. He was only a skeptical bystander to my visions of snake charmers and doppelgängers and a woman and child murdered in the bathroom. He had seen the apparition in the hallway, heard scratching in the attic and under the floor, but I wasn't sure he believed it was anything but an aberrant mental quirk.

Since we had told his family about our haunting, they essentially shunned us—or me. Maybe Ron, privately, was on their side. Ron was not a fighter because he had never had to be. He grew up in a safe and comfortable home, with a father who gave him love and time and understanding as well as material things. His mother was doting and protective, maybe too much so. Ron had never really lived on his own. He moved from his parents' house when he married his first wife. When that marriage ended, he moved back to his parents and stayed there until he moved in with me shortly before our marriage. He had never had to scuffle with the devil to survive, and for that I both resented and envied him.

My thoughts were interrupted by the familiar feeling of being watched. I turned to my left. Ron's eyes were fixed on me. "I love you," he said. I smiled and turned my head back toward the highway, feeling a little guilty.

A few minutes later, I felt his eyes on me again. I turned toward him. Ron was looking straight ahead but a dark, solid apparition, a male figure, seemed to be sitting on his lap with his head cocked sideways, leering at me, mocking me. Then, it sat down and merged into Ron's body.

"Ron . . . one of them is in the car. . . ."

His face had turned cold and stony and he didn't reply.

"It was staring at me . . . then it sat down . . . inside you."

The knotted muscle in his jaw twitched but otherwise he showed no reaction—until we got home.

He followed me from room to room, ranting and cursing. "I'm so fuckin' tired. It's your fuckin' fault I never get any rest. It's your fuckin' fault I never get any sleep."

Once again I was afraid of him, but I was not going to reach for a knife this time. His mood had changed quickly in the car, as if the apparition that faded into him had taken over his personality. Hitting me last summer was completely out of character, as foreign to his nature as the rampage he was on now. Every time he cursed me, I said, "Ron, I love you." I must have said it a dozen times or more and gradually he began to calm down. He went to bed behaving as though nothing had happened.

*

Father A called nearly every night and we talked anywhere from fifteen minutes to an hour, going over and over the events of the past four years, my family background, my activities, the children. And Jordan Pitkoff. Father A's attitude toward me had mellowed a little since that first conversation—he was still lofty and superior, but without the meanness. His feeling about Jordan had not changed. He wanted me to sever all dealings with my psychic.

He also spent a lot of time talking about himself and his exploits as an exorcist. If he was to be believed, Father A was a man who had on many occasions held the devil in a headlock and kicked his rump halfway across the river Styx. Still, until I was convinced the Church was actually going to do something, I would not let him persuade me to disregard Jordan Pitkoff.

"I'm coming in," Father A said one evening. "You'll be contacted by the local priests with the arrangements."

A gush of air that must have sounded like Hurricane Carla rushed out of my chest. *Finally, something is going to happen.*

"There are some things you'll have to do before I get there," he said. "The children will have to be baptized. Father Jeff will do that. You will have to be married in the Church. Otherwise, the Church does not recognize your marriage and that makes your children illegitimate."

I had to bite my lip. *He's telling me my children are bastards, again.*

"Also, we will have to have a psychological profile done of the whole family. The Church requires that, and it needs to be done within the Church. The local priests will talk to you about these things."

Ron was hardly enthusiastic about Father A's demands but he didn't rebel. He took it with the same stoicism that he took everything else. I was less passive. I had no objection to the psychological profile, provided a qualified Catholic psychologist could be found with reasonable haste in or near Madison (which I doubted). The other demands annoyed me. Did the Church have a right to order children baptized? To order a legally married couple to be married in the Church? No matter. Father A would not come otherwise. He was my best hope.

Within a couple of days, I discovered the value of keeping all options open.

Lorraine Warren called and said she would have to cancel her trip to Madison. Her mother had died the previous day and she would be unable to get away for a few weeks.

Chapter 18

Ashley had been gone just over a week and an eerie silence had settled over the house. Jordan had said the poltergeist activity could leave as quickly as it arrived and we prayed that was the case.

There had been very few disturbances in the few days before Marge called. "Ashley has been crying uncontrollably," she said. "She's crying for her mother, Doe. I can't calm her down."

"Let me talk to her," I said.

Ashley was terribly distraught, nearly in tears when she came on the phone. "Mommy, come and get me. I want my mommy," she pleaded.

Marge took the phone back and said, "I can't handle the situation any longer. You'll have to do something."

"I'm leaving now," I said.

It was late and Ron had to get up early the next morning, so I drove to Louisville alone. Turning in to the driveway, I saw Ashley standing in the doorway, waiting for me. She ran out the door and grabbed me as soon as I got out of the car and never loosened her grip until we were in the car heading home. I had been miserable without her and made myself a promise during the drive home: If our ghosts returned, I would not send my children away. The whole family would flee together.

On her first night back, the house was calm and everything went fine. The second night, it began again.

Ashley had bathed and was getting ready for bed. She followed me into the laundry room to get a clean nightgown, and when we walked through the sunroom she said, "Mommy, I hear a snake hissing."

I stopped and listened but heard nothing. "It was probably just your house shoes scuffing across the carpet," I said.

At two o'clock in the morning, I was awakened by the sound of

Ashley choking and gasping for air. I found her rolling and pulling at something around her neck, something I couldn't see, but could hear. It was the hissing of a snake.

Her face was red and she was breathing with difficulty. I jerked her out of bed and carried her into the kitchen. She coughed and gagged and I held her over the trash can while she vomited.

When she had finished, she said, "The snake was around my neck and I couldn't breathe, Mommy."

I sat up the rest of the night with Ashley asleep in my lap. That was where Ron found us when he got up.

"I'm leaving this house," I said. "I've had enough."

"Doe, I can't take off work today."

"Ashley and I are going to Louisville and stay with Grandpa for a few days. We can figure out what to do later, but I'm not staying here another night."

He left for work and I packed clothes for Ashley and me. When the car was loaded and we were ready to leave, I paused and looked around the house. There was an anomalous air about the place, not the electric feeling I was accustomed to, but something else I couldn't quite identify.

On impulse, I found my Polaroid camera and took pictures throughout the house, but mostly in Ashley's room. I had no idea why I was doing it. I burned one film sheet after another, laying each aside to develop. I photographed the walls, furniture, windows, anything and everything. Once, Ashley jumped in front of the camera just as I made the exposure. When the film was expended, I went back to examine the pictures I had taken and was horrified by them. Strange, spectral images appeared all around Ashley in one photograph. I might have suspected defective film had it not been for the snake. A photo I had taken in her room showed the distinct image of a snake coiled on her dresser. It wasn't in color, like everything else, but gray and translucent, almost like a negative.

I put the camera and photographs in a paper bag, grabbed my daughter, and left the house.

For the next week, Ashley and I lived like refugees. We stayed a couple of days with Grandpa, a night at Marge's, and one night in a seedy hotel. I stayed in touch with Ron by telephone and, to his complete frustration, refused to return home. He finally came to Louisville and we made our plans. We would gather our family and leave the house on Clifty Drive—at least until after Father A had performed the exorcism. If it drove the demons out, we would return. If not, well . . .

We drove to Rineyville to get Steven. Jenny had been very gracious about keeping him but she seemed worried about the course we were on—hopping from camp to camp like a tribe of nomads.

"There's a couple here in town I would like you to meet," she said. "They are pretty religious and people around here believe they have special powers . . . you know . . . for ridding homes of spirits and things like that."

Why not? My army needs all the foot soldiers it can muster.

Jenny invited the couple to her house that evening. They were pleasant and ordinary-looking and seemed knowledgeable on the subject of possessed houses. They held a prayer vigil and ceremonially blessed each family member.

"You should go back to your home and reclaim it with God's power," the man said.

How we wanted to believe that was possible. Steven missed his friends and his school and wanted to go home. Ashley was weary of bounding from grandparent to great-grandparent. Ron and I were just plain weary.

"How about it?" we asked the kids. "Shall we return and try to take our house back?"

"Yeah, let's go back and kick their butts," Steven said.

"Kick 'em out of town," Ashley added.

"That settles it," Ron said. "We go back."

Our courage and our confidence were lofty, but were quickly brought back to ground level. The house began to misbehave as soon as we arrived. The noises, the odors, the cold spots arrived first. We went room to room reciting the Lord's Prayer and ordering the demons out. The air grew fouler and icier. A glass vase slid across the entertainment center and crashed to the floor. A bedroom door slammed shut and we could hear objects pelting the closed door. The ghosts had rested up for our homecoming and were ready to rumble.

"Kevin," I said on the phone, "could we borrow your pickup?"

He said, "Sure."

"We're getting out of this house . . . moving to an apartment in Kent," I said.

Kevin Bradley wasn't surprised. We had become friends after I enrolled at Ivy Tech. He was on the staff and held a masters degree in psychology. Off and on for the past year, particularly during the times when I thought I was losing my mind, I had confided in him a little about the occurrences in my house and the emotional havoc the family had suffered.

Kevin also confided in me about his personal problems. His marriage was falling apart, and when the divorce finally came, his wife got most of their possessions. Ron and I, as well as other friends, donated a few household items to help him out. We had recently bought a new dryer, so we gave Kevin our old one.

"When do you need it?" he asked.

"Tomorrow."

"You can pick it up at my house in the morning," he said.

Kent is a small farm town seven miles west of Madison. We rented quarters there in an old building that probably should have been condemned. The two-story apartment was large and empty and cold and we did little to try to convert it to a home. We fixed up a room for the kids so the place would seem reasonably familiar to them, but, because we only expected to be there until the exorcism was completed, we moved very few household belongings and did not install a telephone. We planned to return to the house in Madison each evening to await our nine-o'clock calls from Father A.

Our advisers—Jordan Pitkoff, the Warrens, Father A—had offered conflicting assumptions about whether or not our demons could, or would, follow us. Jordan was confident they would not, that they were bound somehow to the house. Father A's theory was that the demons were stalking me. My interpretation of Lorraine Warren's analysis led me to believe she tilted toward Jordan's opinion. My belief was that somewhere else, anywhere else, would be safer than the house in Madison.

Our new surroundings were dismal and starkly austere, but at least we felt safe there. We could relax and wait for Father A to purge the house on Clifty Drive.

Kevin wasn't home when we returned the truck, so I parked it in his driveway and left the keys in the ignition. You could still do that in places such as Madison.

Several days later we were at our house awaiting the exorcist's call. The phone rang and it was Kevin.

"When you used the pickup . . . did you have any trouble with it?" he asked.

"No. Thanks, Kevin. We really appreciate the use of it."

"The brakes were okay?"

"Yeah. Why?"

"Well, I backed out of the driveway and ended up in the yard across the street," he said.

I was flabbergasted. "Kevin, it was just fine when I parked it at your house. Why didn't you tell me sooner? Look, I want to pay to have your brakes fixed."

"No," he said. "That's why I hadn't said anything before. I didn't want you to feel responsible."

"You weren't hurt or anything?"

"No, but it was real weird. I had the truck towed to the garage and the mechanic said it was one of the strangest things he had ever seen. Said it looked as though an animal had gnawed and clawed the brakes to pieces. It couldn't have been anything that you did to it."

If I was not at fault, there must be a reason for him telling me about it now, I thought. There was.

"Are you all right?" he asked.

"Yeah, things have been real calm since we moved to Kent," I said.

"I've been kind of concerned," he said. "Not just because of the pickup, but there was something else I never told you."

A little voice whispered to me. *Brace yourself, Doretta, you're not going to like this.*

"Remember the dryer you gave me?" he asked.

"Uh-huh."

"Well, right after I got it, I did some shirts. They came out fine. I buttoned each one at the collar and put them in plastic bags. I took them to my mother's house; she was going to iron them for me. I called her later to see if they were ready and she said, 'What in the world did you do to these shirts?' I asked her what was wrong with them and she said, 'It looks like somebody took a razor blade and shredded them.' One of them had a red stain—it looked like blood—splattered across the front.

"After that, whenever I tried to use the dryer, it yelped and howled like a wounded animal. I took it apart, piece by piece, but couldn't find what was causing the noise."

"Where is the dryer now?"

"In a landfill somewhere, I guess," he said. "I never put it back together. I just thought you should know."

"Thanks."

"Watch yourself."

On a Sunday early in November, Ron, the kids, and I drove back to the house to do some laundry, pick up a few personal items, and make some phone calls.

About seven o'clock, I saw Benny Cyrus walking toward the door. He had not come to our house often, so I sensed it was more than a casual neighborly visit.

Ron invited him in, and while we made small talk Benny fidgeted like a child waiting for a vaccination. It was obvious there was something he wanted to say. I was beyond discretion and diplomacy.

"Benny, did anything strange happen while you lived here?" I said.

Ron glared at me. His face had "Watch out!" written all over it. We had told few outsiders about our problems and were still reluctant—Ron more than I—to do so. Benny looked down at the floor, pondering his answer.

"We need to know, Benny. We've been through hell here," I said.

"I have to be honest with you," he said. "I know you talked to Dianne and I know a lot of things have happened up here. That's why I came over, to tell you what happened when we lived here."

I poured coffee and we all sat down at the kitchen table.

At first, Benny measured his words carefully. Like us, I suppose, he was not anxious to appear a lunatic.

"I was never comfortable in this house," he said. "I always had the feeling somebody was following me around . . . you know? . . . watching me or looking over my shoulder. Sometimes I'd feel somebody tap me on the shoulder and I'd turn around and nobody was there."

"We've felt the same thing," I said.

"And the lights nearly drove me nuts. You could turn on a light and a few minutes later it would go off. I mean the switch would be turned to the off position and there was nobody near it. We thought maybe something was wrong with the switches, especially the one in the bathroom. We'd turn the lights off and go to bed and the bathroom light would turn itself on. I'd have to get up and turn it off. I replaced the switch, but the same thing kept happening. And lightbulbs would start popping all over the house. We couldn't figure it out.

"We had a dog that would bark and howl at empty rooms, like he could see or hear something we couldn't. One day we found that dog dead out on the driveway. We lost three dogs while we lived in this house. They just died. I wouldn't live here again if you gave me the house.

"You know, I would never admit this stuff in front of Dianne. I think the house is haunted, but she doesn't believe in ghosts. It got to where I was afraid to be alone here at night. Dianne used to tease me, said it was her dead grandmother coming back to haunt me because I didn't treat her right.

"But I'll tell you another bizarre thing that happened. A guy checked into one of the rooms out there late one evening. He was polite and well dressed and seemed to be perfectly sober. He came in here and asked for a Big Red. I didn't have one, so I sold him a Coke. He had been back in his room for a little while and the next thing I knew there was a lot of yelling and screaming out there. It scared the kids. They crawled under their beds.

"This guy came running out of his room in his underwear, screaming and babbling. I went out and tried to talk to him. He kept saying he saw something, but I couldn't calm him down. I came in here to call the police and this guy took off running down Clifty Drive in his underwear, pounding on the windshields of parked cars with his fists. Cars would pass by and he'd pound on their windows. The police took him away. I heard later he'd been committed to a mental hospital."

Ron and I tried to keep the conversation going. Benny acted as though there was more to tell, but he suddenly seemed uncomfortable.

"There was another caretaker, a woman, who lived here before us," he said. "She had a real strange fire in the attic, right up there." He pointed toward a corner of the kitchen ceiling. "The fireman couldn't figure out what could have started it. There was no wiring or anything in that area."

"What was her name?" I asked.

"Georgia Jefferies," he said. "She's still here in town. Well, I gotta be going."

Ron and I walked with him to the door, thanked him for the information, and watched until he turned past the motel wing and was out of sight. We gathered up our laundry, put the kids in the car, and drove back to our apartment in Kent.

*   *   : *

On Tuesday morning, while Ashley was still asleep and Steven was getting ready for school, I made detailed notes in my journal about the things Benny Cyrus had told us. The more I learned, the more confused I became. The priest, the psychic, and the demonologist all had convinced me that the ghosts in my house were there at my invitation or in retribution for my sins. But if that were true, why did previous occupants experience similar things? Maybe it had nothing to do with me at all. Maybe demons had lived on that land since Creation or doomed spirits were imprisoned there, awaiting transfer to hell. There was relief, if not solace, in that scenario. At least it did not begin with my family.

Through the window I could see the school bus stop, pick up a young boy, and drive away. My son was still in the shower. I got dressed, bundled up Ashley, and told Steven to warm up the car so I could drive him to school.

"Mom," he said when Ashley and I got into the car, "I was sitting here with the radio on and all of a sudden it just turned itself up, full blast." His face wore that same familiar look of frustration and fear.

"You must have hit the knob without knowing it," I said.

"I wasn't anywhere near the knob," he said.

When Ashley and I got back to the apartment, I helped her out of her coat and boots and she began crying and pulling at her clothing. She dropped to the floor and rolled back and forth, yelling that something was hurting her. Finally, I got her calmed down and went into the kitchen to fix breakfast. I heard her scream again and went back into the living room. She was rolling on the mattress, which was about the only piece of furniture in that room. She pulled at her underpants and cried, "They're squeezing me."

I undressed her and wrapped her in a blanket. She became calm again. I turned on the television and brought her breakfast into the living room. She was smiling and perfectly normal as she ate. Please, God, I prayed silently, stop whatever is tormenting my baby.

Later in the morning, I bathed her and was drying her hair when she became upset again. Trying to distract her, I began playing a word game she always liked. I would say a letter and she would say a word that began with that letter.

"Okay, class," I said, pretending we were in school, "does anyone know a word that begins with A?"

Ashley looked at me, grinned, and said, "Apple."

"How about a B."

"Ball."

It was working. She was immersed in the game and had pushed aside whatever had been troubling her.

"C?"

"Cat."

"D?"

"Dog."

"E?"

"Ear."

"F?"

She paused, thought for a moment and said, "I don't know a word that starts with F."

"How about 'fire'?"

The instant I said the word, sparks flew out of the small electrical heater in the bathroom and dark smoke rolled out from beneath it. I lunged for the wall socket to unplug it and Ashley fled into the kitchen. By the time I got to her, she was pulling and clawing at the door, trying to get out.

"Make it stop, Mommy," she sobbed. "It's happening here. It's happening here."

"It's okay, baby," I said, picking her up. "It's over. It's okay."

She was again calm while I helped her dress for school. But in the car, she again began screaming and kicking and complaining that something was hurting her. She thrashed around the front seat in such a frenzy that I nearly lost control of the car.

Ashley abruptly settled down but the car radio began changing stations. I grabbed a tape and inserted it in the cassette slot but the machine ejected it like a child spitting out a mouthful of broccoli. I turned the radio off and we drove on into Madison.

Just as we started around the bend near our house, the car died and coasted to a stop. Turning the starter switch produced no response, just the stone silence of a dead battery. I became aware of the cold. The power windows and door locks, dependent upon the battery, held us prisoner in a chamber that was getting colder by the minute. I looked around for something I could use to break a window. I prayed and occasionally tried to start the car. I prayed some more and Ashley fought back tears. I reached for the starter once more and the engine purred like a feline.

Driving on to Ashley's school, I thought about what Jordan had said. *They can't follow you.* Maybe not. Maybe the car radio, the battery, the electric heater, and Ashley's spasms were purely coincidental. Maybe not. I decided to contact Father John and see if the exorcism could be speeded up. We had been talking to Father A for nearly a month. It was time to stop talking and act. Ron and I had not remarried in the Church, the children had not been baptized, and the psychological profiles had not been done, but I didn't care. If the Church wouldn't help me, I would find another way. I would keep running until Satan himself couldn't find me.

Jordan Pitkoff was genuinely concerned about the developments in Kent. He said the whole family needed to come in for a healing of auras. We went that evening at seven-thirty.

"Steven brought a man with him," Jordan said immediately after we entered his office. He asked us to join hands and recite the Lord's Prayer as he worked to drive the male presence away. Steven's face was contorted in pain or anger, I couldn't be sure which, when the hour-long ritual began. Jordan sat close to him and, as if molding invisible clay, moved his hands several inches from Steven's head and torso. Eventually Steven relaxed and appeared perfectly peaceful.

Next, Jordan turned to Ashley. "A very ugly presence is trying to get close to her," he said, "but it can't . . . not now." He performed his healing routine on her, and we left.

As we pulled onto the interstate highway, I looked over at my husband and saw something I had not seen since this ordeal began.

He had tears in his eyes.

Chapter 19

"We moved to Kent and now it is starting over there," I said. "Isn't there some way we can speed up the timetable?"

Father John had no control over the exorcist or the procedures of the Catholic Church, but he promised to make some inquiries.

"I'm really scared, Father," I said. "Will you pray for my family?"

"I've been praying for your family since the day I blessed your house," he said.

A few days passed and we had not heard from Father A. Then Father John called. "Father A will arrive on November 21. I will contact you later with the details," he said.

Three more weeks and this will all be over, I thought.

The exorcist began to call more frequently and cautioned on each occasion that the secrecy of his visit was essential. Absolutely no media involvement, no public notice of any kind, or the ritual would be canceled.

"I had a dream about your property," he said, describing my house and the surrounding landscape precisely. "That is not unusual. I frequently have cognitive dreams that help me find the source of the disturbance. In the dream, I saw woods and a snakeskin and an Indian word was spoken to me, the word *Choctaw*. I believe this all may have something to do with Indians who lived on that land two hundred or more years ago."

"Jordan Pitkoff said something similar," I said. "He said the disturbances originated three hundred years ago and the land was affected for three hundred yards around our house and . . ."

"I thought you were going to forget about this psychic of yours."

"There is nothing wrong with Jordan," I said. "He is not a fraud. Many times he has offered his services at no charge. He has offered to let us stay in his home. He has become a friend. Steven really seems to depend on him. I would like for him to be here for the exorcism."

"Well, he can't. If he is there, there won't be an exorcism."

Two weeks before Father A was to arrive, all of the poltergeist activity at the house ceased. There were no odors, no slamming doors, no cold spots. Our daily trips to the house to receive phone calls from him were continuing and I found myself believing that maybe the "thing" that had driven us from here had itself departed. *Maybe it knows Father A is coming and fled in fear.* None of this made sense to me, anyway, so that seemed like a reasonable possibility.

At least it gave me moments of hope, and I was in a hopeful mood when, the day before the exorcist was to arrive, Steven, Ashley, and I drove to Madison to pick up a few things at the house and get Steven's car.

At my insistence, he had not driven the car since he came back from Rineyville. The car had troubled me for weeks, although there was no specific reason, just a gut feeling that was close enough to a premonition to arouse a vague uneasiness. It was a red, 1975 Plymouth Fury and had been running as well as could be expected for a sixteen-year-old car. But even during those periods of peacefulness, I was vigilant to the tugs of intuition, especially where the children were concerned.

Ron had looked the car over and found nothing wrong. He and Steven could not understand why I was adamant about having a mechanic check it out. But, because he had experienced so many inscrutable malfunctions with our automobiles, they bowed to my demands and left the car at Madison Automotive to be examined by a professional.

Our first stop that Tuesday, however, was Kellie's house to pick up Erika and Kendra. Ashley saw her friends less often after we moved, and she missed being with them. We were going to take them with us on the short drive to the garage and the brief stop at the house.

Kellie's mother, Janet, was there. She and Kellie were among the few people who knew of the problems we were having.

"How's the house?" Janet asked.

"It's been real good." I smiled.

"Are you going to invite us over?" she asked.

"No way. Not yet," I said, not really wanting to talk about the house. I was in a good mood and didn't want to dwell on ghosts and demons. The exorcist would deal with them.

Ashley, reunited with her two friends, was also happier than I had seen her in a while, and Steven's day brightened when we got to the garage, which is at the bottom of a hill where Clifty Drive widens to four lanes, not far from our house.

"Couldn't find a thing wrong with it," the mechanic said. "The battery might be a little small for that engine, but other than that, it looks in good shape."

I started back up Clifty Drive and saw Steven pull out of the garage parking lot right behind me. But when I got to the house he was nowhere in sight. I waited. No Steven. I'd often kidded him about how slow he drives, but now I was beginning to worry. Did the mechanic overlook something?

At last, his car topped the hill and turned into the driveway.

"Where have you been?" I said.

"Gosh, Mom, what was your hurry?" he laughed.

"You're supposed to at least drive the speed limit," I said. "How's the car?"

"Running great," he said.

We had not planned to stay long, but since Ron was working late, I decided to do some laundry while I was straightening up the house. The place felt good. We were all weary of the drab, spartan apartment in Kent and longed to be back in our own home. Maybe the time was near. When Father A had chased away the evil, we could return, we hoped. We didn't understand, but we hoped.

"How about if I fix dinner here tonight?" I asked my son.

"That sounds good," he said.

"Run out to the apartment and get a bag of potatoes. I'll bake them while I wash the clothes."

"Okay."

I gave him the apartment key and three dollars to get gas for his car. "I'm going to take Kendra and Ericka home," I said.

Since moving out, we had made a point of not allowing anyone outside the family, particularly someone else's children, to go into the house, and until the problems were resolved, by exorcism or otherwise, I was not going to alter that policy.

I herded the girls into the car and drove the two blocks to Kellie's. Janet was still there, and her uncle, Eugene Shelton, a Madison police officer, had also stopped by.

"You were gone longer than I expected," Janet said.

"It's Steve," I said. "I had to wait ten minutes for him to make it up that hill. I wish that boy would learn to drive faster."

There was no mention of the house until Eugene left, and then Janet's curiosity boiled over again.

"Can't we spend just one night over there," she pleaded. "We'd like to see this stuff before the exorcism puts an end to all of it." ·

"I don't know," I said, wavering a little. Maybe there was no harm in it. Jordan Pitkoff had assured us no one ever dies from encountering a poltergeist. Janet was determined and she could see that I was softening.

"You could stay with us. First time something happens, we'll all come back over here," she insisted.

"The kids can't go," I said. "I won't even let my kids spend the night there."

"We'll work it out," she said. "Maybe Ron could stay with them."

Okay, I thought, *if my husband can tend to the kids, I'll let my best friends have their night in the haunted house.* I called him at work.

"I don't know what time I'll get off," he said, putting an end to the discussion.

"Oh, well, you probably wouldn't see anything, anyway," I told Janet. "It's been so quiet over there. *They* have probably gone away. Well, I'd better be going. Steven may be waiting for me."

Janet walked Ashley and me to the car, still trying to persuade me to reconsider.

Standing at the back door fumbling through my keys, I could hear the phone ringing. As I pushed the door open, the answering machine clicked on and the caller hung up. My first thought was of Steven. He should have been back by now.

I paced back and forth with Ashley on my hip. The phone rang again. It was Ron.

"I just got a call from King's Daughter's Hospital," he said. "Steven was in a car accident."

My heart dropped and I exhaled, "Oh, God."

"No, no, don't get excited," Ron said. "He's fine. What car was he driving?"

He didn't know we had picked up Steven's car from the garage.

"What?" I said.

"Was he driving my car?"

The question may have been related to the concerns I had expressed about the old Plymouth. Perhaps he was thinking that my anxiety had actually been a forewarning, but my immediate thought was that he was concerned only about his car, and that infuriated me.

"No, he was in his own car," I snapped.

"Look, they said it was a serious accident but he's going to be okay. Go on down to the hospital."

After a dash to drop Ashley off at Kellie's house, I drove to the hospital, and the number of ambulances and people outside told me that it was, indeed, serious.

People were everywhere. The first thing I heard when I walked into the crowded emergency room was the terrifying wail of a woman: "My baby, my baby, my baby's dead."

A nurse walked by and I grabbed her arm. "I'm looking for Steven Johnson. I'm his mother," I said.

Without hestitating, she took me by the arm and ushered me through a doorway and down a corridor to a room with X-ray equipment. My son was lying on a back board and had a brace on his neck. He looked at me and said nothing while the technician maneuvered the X-ray machine into place. There was blood all over him and tears streamed down the sides of his face. He seemed so young and helpless. I kissed his cheek and wiped his eyes and tried to tell him everything would be all right.

A nurse escorted me back out to the hallway and asked me to wait up front until the doctor was available to talk to me. They told me nothing, but the scene in the waiting room had said enough. Someone had died and my son was involved.

The minutes slid by like molasses. All around me people were crying and trying to console each other. Some placed phone calls to relatives. A family was grieving for a lost loved one, and I was in the middle of it, a stranger intruding on their anguish. My heart ached for them, but I could do nothing but sit and watch and wait.

I called Ron and told him someone had been killed in the accident and asked him to come to the hospital.

"I have to work late," he said. "I can't leave."

More time passed, hours it seemed. I felt alone, felt trapped and suffocating in the sorrow that filled the emergency room. I called my husband again.

"Look," I said, "somebody died here and it had something to do with Steven's crash. I can't handle this. I want you here."

He assured me he would come right away and I went back to waiting. The doctors still had told me nothing and the nurses would not allow me to go again to my son. But when Ron arrived, he pushed his way past the nurses and returned thirty minutes later with Steven.

"Get in the car," Ron said.

Steven was distraught and confused. He tried to tell us what happened, but he was nearly incoherent.

"Mom, I couldn't stop it," he kept saying. "I couldn't stop the car. The gas pedal went to the floor and I couldn't get it to come back. Mom, I killed a man. He's dead."

"You did not kill a man," I said. "Whatever this thing is that is after our family . . . that thing killed him."

"*It* tried to kill me," Steven nodded. "*It* tried to kill me but that man died instead."

Ron left in his car to go pick up Ashley and take her to our apartment. Steven and I got in my car. I was having trouble calming him down. He cried and talked about seeing the man lying under the pickup truck.

"I want to talk to Jordan Pitkoff," he kept saying. "Mom, something was in that car with me. I tried to stop it but it shoved the gas pedal down and I couldn't pull it back up. Mom, *it* wanted me dead. Not the other man. Me. Why did that man have to die? Why can't somebody stop this thing? Mom, please, I need to talk to Jordan."

We were only a few miles from the apartment, but the urgency of Steven's pleading compelled me to pull into a gas station, walk to a pay phone, and dial Jordan's number in Louisville.

Hanging up the phone, I told my son, "There was no answer. But we'll talk to him soon."

He was pale and partially in shock. Dried blood and slivers of glass were still stuck to him. He was also in a lot of physical pain. At the apartment, I drew a tub of warm water, helped him into it, and held him in my arms while he cried.

My condition was not much better than his. I was ready to fall apart. Besides nearly losing my son, I felt a bone-deep sadness for the other family, and a heart clot of guilt as well. *Did the demons of our house follow us to Kent, follow my son onto a two-lane highway, aim at him, and hit another instead?* I had been led to believe this *thing* could not follow us. There was no doubt in my mind that it had. Somehow I knew there would be no simple mechanical rationale for Steven's crash. *It* had followed us.

Was that possible? What was *it*, anyway? A ghost? A demon? A hallucination? Damn it, I wanted to know.

"Let's drive back over to the house and call Jordan," I said to Ron when he came in. "We need to talk to him."

Before we could place a call to Louisville, the phone rang. The man on the other end identified himself as Officer True, an Indiana state trooper.

"I need to talk to Steve," he said. "Can I come by for a few minutes?"

"Of course," I said.

Steven had on clean clothes and was sitting at the kitchen table when the state trooper knocked at the door. He walked into the kitchen, looked at my son, and said dourly, "You're not sitting here. There's no way you're alive."

Steve was puzzled.

"I just came from the crash site and saw your car," the trooper said. "Son, there's no way you survived that crash. You're a lucky kid."

Steven just nodded.

"Before you say anything," True said, "I have to read you your rights. You could be charged with vehicular homicide."

Holding a small card in his hand, he began to read the Miranda warning, which the Supreme Court has said police officers must give to suspected criminals: *You have a right to remain silent . . . anything you say can and will be used against you in a court of law . . . you have a right to an attorney . . .*

The words, introduction to the criminal justice system, fell on my ears like a claw hammer and I nearly lost control. *There's no way out*, I thought, *no way to stop the things that are happening, no border beyond which these things cannot go.*

Having disposed of Miranda, Trooper True, still incredulous that he was interviewing a survivor of the Plymouth Fury, said, "Son, what happened?"

Steven paused for a second. If he told what he truly believed, our whole family might be carted off to padded cells. He couldn't tell an officer of the law, who was investigating a possible vehicular homicide, that demons were following us, burning our house, wrecking our cars, killing our pets, cracking our windows. . . .

"I don't really know," Steven said. "The gas pedal just went to the floor and wouldn't come back. I kept reaching down and trying to pull it back but it wouldn't move."

True nodded his head. "Well, a couple of witnesses said they saw your head bobbing up and down, like you were reaching for something on the floorboard," he said.

"The car just kept going faster," Steven said. "I couldn't get it to stop."

"Son, I know you did the best you could. The only thing you could have done differently was turn off the ignition. I guess your inexperience went against you."

From what the trooper added to Steven's version, we pretty well pieced together the story. As Steven's car began to accelerate, he swerved from lane to lane dodging other cars, all the while reaching down for the gas pedal. When he finally hit the brakes, the car skidded, flipped three times, and hit a pickup head-on, ripping off one of the truck's doors. The driver was thrown out and killed. His name was Charles Claudel and he was twenty-eight years old. Two passengers in the pickup were not seriously hurt.

Other motorists stopped, True said, but none went to Steven's car. It was crushed like foil, and smoke pouring from it warned of a fire hazard.

"Everybody figured that whoever was driving that Plymouth was dead," he said. Instead, the others rushed to the truck, which was lying on Charles Claudel's chest.

Steven blacked out in the collision and when he woke up, his car was upside down and he was inside on his knees. He crawled out the shattered rear window and staggered over to the truck. No one was doing anything to free Charles Claudel from beneath it. Steven screamed and tried to lift the pickup. A woman pulled him away and insisted that he sit down until the ambulance arrived. "You're injured, too," she said.

Steven did not know the other driver had died until he overheard the doctor telling Ron at the hospital.

"Son, I'll need to talk to you again," Trooper True said. "There'll be an investigation. Until that's done, I don't know if you'll be charged or not."

We were grateful for the way he handled our son. He was as courteous and gentle as possible, but the next meeting might well be more contentious. He could come back with an arrest warrant.

When he was gone, I went into the bathroom and sat in the dark and cried. I talked to God, asking for help for our family and for the family of Charles Claudel.

*   *   *

Ron called Jordan's house again and talked with his son, who promised to have his father call as soon as he returned home. Ron answered when the phone rang half an hour later. He explained to Jordan what had happened. When I took the phone, Jordan was apologetic and seemed genuinely shocked.

"You have to believe me, Doretta," he said. "I never thought this force would grow this strong. You know Lorraine Warren and I were both concerned about Steven, but we never imagined something like this would happen. No matter what I have to do, I will find a way to put a stop to all this. Anything your family needs, I will do. Steven will need a lot of therapy . . . your whole family will."

We had all become dependent on Jordan and the need could be even greater in the months ahead. I thanked him for his concern.

"When is the priest coming to help?" he asked.

"He is supposed to arrive in Cincinnati on Wednesday and be here Thursday."

"There must be no delays in the exorcism," he said. "You must make him understand that. The Church has dragged its feet long enough. There's one other thing. You have to get an attorney for Steven and you have to tell him the truth about what is happening to your family."

"Yes, we've already thought about an attorney," I said.

"Call me after you have met with the priest," he said.

"Okay."

We locked up the house and drove under a cold and joyless night sky toward Kent. The strain of the evening had taken its toll on my body. My legs were nearly too weak to stand, my arms felt like lead, and my mind was numb. I prayed silently as the dark countryside rolled past. *God, please carry me now. Please carry my family.*

Steven and Ashley were quiet in the backseat. Ron stared ahead at the road. His face was drawn and pasty in the glow from the dashboard.

"We didn't run far enough," I said to him. "Next time, we're going where *it* can't find us."

Chapter 20

We were told very little about the whereabouts or movements of the exorcist—only that he was in the area and would meet with us Thursday. Ron had to work and was not planning on attending our first conference.

"Bring the children to the parish house tomorrow afternoon. You can leave your car there and ride in the Jeep with me and Father Jeff," Father John instructed me by telephone Wednesday night.

"Where are we going?"

"I can't tell you now. You'll know when we get there."

We arrived at the appointed time. Ashley, Steven, and I climbed into the back of the Jeep. The two priests sat up front. They still had not revealed our destination. What kind of place would a mysterious exorcist choose for a covert rendezvous? A secret cathedral far back in the hills? A clearing on some remote creek bank? We headed toward the Ohio River, crossed the narrow, timeworn span into Kentucky, hung a left, and followed Highway 36 along the river to a Hardee's restaurant in Carrollton.

We parked and looked around. Since they had not met him, the two priests did not know what Father A looked like. Through the wide glass windows I could see a man sitting inside. He wasn't dressed like a priest, but I was certain he was the exorcist.

When we got out of the car, the man came outside and waited for us to approach him. He extended his hand and said, "I look like Father Karris, don't I? Everybody tells me that."

He was as vain and arrogant as he had been on the telephone during our early conversations. I was in no mood to pander to his egotism.

I studied his face for a moment and said, "No, I don't think you look like him at all."

Actually, he did look a little like Karris, the tormented young priest in the movie *The Exorcist*. He was physically striking and possessed, despite medium height, a powerful presence. He wore black slacks, a light shirt, and black shoes. His clothes appeared to be of good quality and more expensive than the basic priestly attire. He had olive skin, black, wavy hair, and dark eyes with dark circles under them. He appeared to be Mediterranean or Middle Eastern and could have been in his late forties or early fifties, perhaps older; it was difficult for me to judge. There was a certain bearing, a maturity, about him that seemed older than his appearance.

He was the first priest I had ever met who wore gold jewelry.

"Are you possessed by a demon?" he asked. His eyes were like flint.

"Well, my head hasn't spun around today," I said, immediately regretting the flippancy. "I'm sorry, that was sarcastic. But if I were possessed, would I know it?"

We went inside, sat down, and ordered coffee. He peeled a one-hundred-dollar bill off of a wad of one-hundred-dollar bills and paid for the drinks. Fathers John and Jeff looked at the money, then at each other. You could almost hear their eyebrows arching.

"I want to talk to your son alone. Is that all right?" asked Father A. His voice was suddenly kinder, softer, as if he had folded his condescension and tucked it away in his wallet.

"Where are you going with him?"

"We'll just walk outside, only for a few minutes."

"Fine." Later, I would learn that he questioned Steve about his car wreck.

When they returned, Father A sat across the table from me, reached over, and took my hand. He stared at me, silently, almost hypnotically, for a minute or two before letting go of my hand abruptly, as though a spell had been broken. He leaned back and said, "Okay." He had been reading me psychically, exploring for demons within. *Okay* meant there was no possession.

"Look," he said, "I'm not trying to act superior. I'm not God. I'm far from that. But I have to be tough on you and I have to be careful. You could be a witch."

My eyes rolled toward the ceiling and he hastened to elaborate.

"There are good witches and there are bad witches," he said. "A lot of people call me a warlock."

Fathers John and Jeff looked pained.

"There was a witch who put a curse on me and I was in such pain that I could barely walk for days. I woke up at nights screaming in agony. The doctors couldn't find anything wrong with me. One day she called the archbishop and said, 'Father A's pain will end because there will be a sacrifice tonight.' She stole a baby and sacrificed it. My pain ended."

She should have sacrificed Father A and spared the baby, I thought. What kind of story was this for a priest to tell a stranger? Although I wasn't sure I believed him, the tale of a baby being murdered to ease a priest's pain was utterly repulsive.

He rambled on for what seemed like hours, telling stories of his hand-to-hand combat with demons, his out-of-body experiences, psychic healings, ESP—the whole range of the spiritual and the paranormal. He seemed to be trying to impress me with his courage and cunning as much as with his piety. Each story was more far-fetched than the last, and I wanted to interrupt and shout *Okay, dammit, climb into the ring with those things that are in my house. Let's get on with it.*

Late in the afternoon, he said, "I want you to call your husband. I want him here. Just tell him to come but say nothing else. Don't tell him why and don't tell him who is here."

After another round of Father A's war stories, Ron arrived and sat down at our table.

"We have to be careful because of this situation with the car wreck," the exorcist said. "I'm in constant touch with the Church. We're still going to do this, but the accident changed everything. The force is more powerful than I had thought. More precautions will be taken. I want a medical doctor flown in to be at the site when this happens."

Scenes from an old World War II movie flashed through my mind: rockets and mortars and smoke billowing from hills above the beach where bodies were strewn like clam shells.

"I also want a psychologist present and another priest who is more experienced than Father Jeff and Father John," the priest continued. "I know someone in Michigan who will come if I call him."

I pictured a young soldier burrowing into the sand with a field radio calling for reinforcements and more air cover. *We're being butchered down here,* I heard him say.

"I'll be in contact with you after I make these arrangements," he said. "Meanwhile, I want you to take certain steps to minimize the risk of injury. Put tape on all the windows and secure any items that could easily be moved or thrown about."

Ron looked as though he had been jabbed with a cattle prod.

"It could be a violent ritual" the priest said. "I may have to yank this thing right out of your house and it won't go without a fight."

On that cheerful note, the meeting adjourned and Father A drove away, destined, I presumed, for Cincinnati. Ron took the kids with him, and I rode in the Jeep back to the parish house to get my car.

"Excuse me, guys," I said to the local priests, "but I don't understand much of what happened back there. He was always asking me if I was part of a Satanic group or something but he sounds pretty occult, himself . . . talking about witches and baby sacrifices."

They agreed. "I can't believe that guy," Father Jeff said. "I can't believe some of the things he said."

Before I left the parish house, both priests hugged me, and Father Jeff said, "Hang in there. I know it's tough but everything's going to be all right."

Lying in bed that night—a mattress on the living-room floor of the apartment still served as our bed—Ron and I heard an odd noise coming from the ceiling. It wasn't a tapping, but more like bumping, the way a moth might sound fluttering against a window screen, an irregular thumping with a vague suggestion of wings.

"Insect?" I said.

"Probably."

"It sounds too big to be an insect," I said.

"Yeah."

"This isn't exactly the season for flying bugs," I said.

Ron was already asleep.

The kids and I went Christmas shopping in Clarksville the next day and stopped by the house on our way back to check for phone messages and pick up some laundry. We had been there only a few minutes when Ashley screamed out that something was biting her. She grabbed at her neck and back. I found a swollen red mark on her shoulder, but no sign of a spider or anything else.

She settled down in front of the television. Less than ten minutes passed before she yelled again, "Something is biting me."

I pulled her shirt off and found another red, puffy area on her lower back. We gathered the laundry and got out of the house. Two miles down the road, Ashley again started crying that something was biting her arm. Steven pulled her coat off and we saw two welts on her arm.

"What did it feel like was biting you?" I asked.

"Like a cat, Mommy. It felt like a cat was biting me."

The attack continued back at the apartment. I lay on the mattress, holding her in my arms, but she squirmed and moaned and new welts arose on her arms and legs. Ron and I prayed and tried to perform the ritual Jordan Pitkoff had recommended—imagining the protective blue light around us. After several minutes, Ashley relaxed and soon fell asleep.

We sat by the phone waiting to hear from the exorcist. He had promised to let us know when he had arranged for a medical doctor, a psychologist, and backup priest, so we weren't expecting anything to happen immediately. But when the call came that night, we certainly weren't expecting what we got.

"He left. He flew out this afternoon. The archbishop pulled him out," Father John said.

"He's gone?"

"I'm really sorry." He said the Church apparently had feared publicity because of Steven's accident and postponed the exorcism until that issue was settled.

The feeling of abandonment was overwhelming, and a hard knot of outrage squeezed my insides. It was still there when Ron answered the phone the next day.

"Father A," he said, offering the phone to me.

"I don't want to talk to him," I said, knowing I would not be able to control myself. I didn't want to alienate him or the Church—I still needed them—and, under the circumstances, congeniality was a long shot.

Ron and the priest talked for a couple of minutes and, just from hearing one side of the conversation, I knew the song and dance the priest was performing.

"Give me the phone," I said on impulse.

"You don't owe us an explanation," I said. "I understand your fear."

"Fear?" he snarled. "I'm not afraid. I have God on my side. I don't have to be afraid. Look, I want psychological testing done on you and your family, that's the reason. You talk in a monotone. . . ."

"I talk like a zombie because I've been told to control my emotions. You want emotion? I'll give you emotion. Let me tell you about your damned archbishop. . . ." That was highly impolitic. One does not curse the Church hierarchy, but I was losing control again. He probably thought the demon in me had been awakened. "I'm glad I left the Church. I can't believe the Church would sacrifice the lives of children and people because it doesn't want publicity. I think you're afraid of what's in this house."

I handed the phone back to my husband. Father A promised to stay in touch but I had no interest in talking to him again. Ron could come back and await his calls if he chose to, but my only intention was to stay out of this house, permanently if necessary.

My nerves were shot on Saturday morning. So much had happened in five days—Steven's accident, the meeting with the exorcist and his subsequent departure, the biting attacks on Ashley, the new stirrings in our apartment—that my circuits were seriously overloaded.

I sat with my journal and brooded about my children. Both had been changed by this ordeal. Ashley rarely smiled anymore and Steven's accident, I knew, would haunt him for the rest of his life. I felt powerless to protect them or myself and the futility and despair spilled onto the pages of my diary:

> *It's nine o'clock A.M. and a very cold morning. I'm shivering to the bone. I have the heat turned on but considering the age and condition of the baseboard heaters and the fact that this huge apartment should have been condemned long ago, I do not expect to be warm.*
>
> *I did not want to get up early because right now sleep is my safety zone, my only escape. Every day I wake up and pray that someone will tell me it was all just a long nightmare, that everything is fine.*
>
> *Ashley seems to be unable to find escape anywhere. She rolls, tosses, cries out and is tormented even in her sleep. Steven sleeps, but the nightmare has affected him physically. He has a nervous twitch that distorts his handsome face. My heart bleeds for my children. I am angry that their lives have been torn apart.*
>
> *Ron seems to be like a mechanical man. He just wants to shut emotion out, as though he is not programmed to have it. Maybe that is his safety valve. Twelve hours a day he is gone, gone to work, gone to a world that hasn't changed. Sometimes he comes home and tries to talk about things that happened during the day. I smile and pretend to listen but a part of me wants to shout, "What about us? What about your daughter's nightmares, her*

uncontrollable crying. What about the pain in your son's neck? What about the heartsickness that eats at me like a cancer?''

I feel as though I'm standing in a blizzard naked and Ron is beside me in a warm coat. Maybe it is unfair to him but I feel that he is insulated from the cold but I am not. I am resentful because he has escaped and I have not.

Sorting out my thoughts on paper did not always bring about the understanding I sought, but now and then it brought me to a difficult decision.

"I'm leaving," I said when Ron came into the kitchen that cold morning. "If I can scrape some money together, I'm going to rent an apartment in Louisville."

He groaned.

"Look," I said, "the Warrens were coming to help us and a death kept them away. The Church sent an exorcist to help us and a death drove him away. Maybe this thing is more powerful than anybody thought. Is somebody going to die every time we are about to get help?"

"Father A may come back," he said.

"Don't hold your breath. I think he's terrified of what's in that house. I think he's afraid to come back."

"He's supposed to call tonight. I'll try to make him understand how important this is to us."

That night, Ron came home disgusted. "I'm sick of his war stories. I heard all about a thirteen-year-old girl he recently liberated from her demon."

"What about us?"

"He wanted to know where things stood with the investigation . . . if charges were going to be filed against Steven. I told him it didn't look like it, that we had not been contacted by the state trooper since the night of the accident, but he seems to think that because a man died, the police will have to do something. I think we can forget about Father A."

We were back to where we were four months earlier. The psychic from Louisville was all that was left of my army.

"I've contacted some people to help with this," Jordan Pitkoff said. "We can do what's called a lay exorcism, but I want these other people involved."

"Jordan, how much is this going to cost . . . bringing people in from out of town and all?"

"They have agreed to pay their own expenses. All I'll charge you is two hundred and fifty dollars. That will cover the cost of the ritual supplies. I'll have to buy candles, Bibles, and other things. I won't charge you anything except my out-of-pocket expenses."

This is the man called a charlatan by the priest who abandoned us, I thought. *If not for him we would be completely alone now. If the Church had acted sooner,* I told myself, *Steven's accident would not have happened and a young man would not have died. I would not be sitting up night after night listening to my daughter scream and watching sorrow pulling at my son like quicksand.*

"We will be at your house on Sunday," Jordan said.

Chapter 21

At three o'clock, Jordan and Teri arrived with two men who would assist in the ritual. One was a psychic whose name I don't remember, but the other was Ted Andrews, a spiritualist from Cincinnati. While I retained some of my skepticism of the whole psychic shtick, I was impressed by Andrews. He was in his late thirties or early forties, looked Indian, and had a genial, self-assured manner. He had written books on spiritualism and there was no mumbo jumbo in his style or technique.

Jordan brought some of the materials to be used in the ceremony: two sixteen-inch white candles, several clay pots, several plastic pots, four glass containers, a dozen sage sticks, sand, water, salt, a rosary, a sterling-silver medallion, four crosses, prayer books, Bibles, and a cassette tape of Bach's compositions. He asked me to provide a white linen tablecloth, some matches, a round table, and plastic drinking cups.

He also brought a copy of the Catholic rite of exorcism and copies of eight prayers to be recited in a specific sequence. The ritual, he informed us, would begin outside and would be repeated at five sites, including the car, which he felt were infested with spirits.

We proceeded to the backyard. A cow that belonged to the Cyruses stood in a pasture forty yards away and watched our somber entourage cluster around the spot where I had seen the snake charmer in my dream. There we recited two prayers, one in Latin and one in English.

Tantum ergo Sacramentum
Veneremur cernui:
Et antiquum documentum
Nove cedat ritui:

Praestet fides supplementum
Sensuum defectui.
Genitori Genitoque
Laus et jubilato,
Salus, honor, virtus quoque
Sit en benedicto;
Procedenti ab utroque
Comar sit laudatio. Amen

Soul of Christ, sanctify me.
Body of Christ, save me.
Blood of Christ, exalt me.
Water from the side of Christ,
   wash me.
My Good Jesus, hear me.
Within your wounds hide me.
Never permit me to be separated
   from you.
At the hour of death, call me
And bid me come to you
So that with the angels and saints
   I may worship you.
Forever and ever. Amen.

How many times had I tried prayer to purge this place of its curse? Would God hear these psychics and spiritualists if He would not hear me? This was an intensely religious liturgy, and as I recited the lines, I longed for the presence of a priest.

Ted Andrews carried what looked like a small bowl. It was some sort of drum or gong, which he struck with a metallic rod. The cow in the field lifted its head, bellowed a long "mooooooooo," and ran away. A sign? Perhaps in that faint drumbeat it heard the ancient thunder of hooves or the summons of a tall and grizzled man in black with snakes coiled around his arms. Whatever the reason for the cow's anxiety, it imparted to me a fleeting twinge of encouragement and hope.

We moved from location to location, circling the house and repeating the prayers at each stop, and then paused at the back door. Before entering, we recited six other prayers, each with a specific invocation:

For God's protection and Christ's presence—

. . . May the power of God uphold me, the wisdom of God guide me . . . the eye of God look before me, the ear of God hear me. May the hand of God protect me, the way of God lie before me, the shield of God defend me, the host of God save me.

For divine assistance—

Heed my call for help, my king and my God. For you, O God, delight not in wickedness; no evil remains with you, the arrogant may not stand in your sight. You hate all evildoers; you destroy all who speak falsehood; the bloodthirsty and the deceitful the Lord abhors.

For deliverance from fear—

The Lord is my light and my salvation; whom should I fear? The Lord is my life's refuge; of whom should I be afraid? When evildoers come at me and devour my flesh, my foes and my enemies themselves stumble and fall.

For comfort in distress—

Like Christ on the cross when he said, "My God, My God, why have you forsaken me?" we cry out to you, O Lord.

For spiritual fulfillment—

As the eyes of the servants are on the hands of their masters, as the eyes of a maid are on the hands of her mistress, so are our eyes on the Lord, our God, till he have pity on us.

For serenity—

Grant that we may lie down to rest with a quiet mind, and rise again in health and strength. Spread your shelter of peace over us and direct us with your wise guidance. Dilute the power of the wicked instigation that assails us on every side and take it away from us. Shelter us in the shadow of your wings. For you are God, our guardian and deliverer from every evil and from fear in the darkness of night.

Inside the house, we repeated each of the prayers. After Ted Andrews performed some kind of Indian ritual, we said the prayers again and the individual exorcisms began. It was a long and tiring afternoon and at each step of the procedure, I expected the house to rise up in protest, loosing its poltergeists with a rush of wind and fire.

But the house was singularly serene. These things are not afraid of Jordan, I thought. They are not intimidated by him; they are going to sleep right through his frontal assault. My head was bowed, as was everyone else's—except Ron's.

"Lights, lights," he gasped.

Globes of light, like the ones we first saw in the kitchen after hearing the woman's voice pleading for help from the Park-N-Eat, drifted into the living room, swirled around randomly and then left.

Jordan looked at me and asked, "Didn't your grandmother just die?"

"My stepgrandmother," I said. "My grandmother died eight years ago."

Jordan finished the ritual and we drove to Kent and repeated it in our apartment. When it was over, I was frazzled by the anticipation and the uncertainty. Had we accomplished anything? Had I expected too much? We had not seen the hand of God clutch our demons and spirits and drag them kicking and screaming to their rightful place—wherever that was.

"We've weakened it, but we haven't removed it," Jordan said. He urged me not to send my children to school the next day.

Everything was quiet for a couple of days. Too quiet, I thought. Such a stillness is always followed by an outburst.

I was beginning to form some opinions about this house and this land, the belief that people had died or were murdered here and their spirits were trapped here. Not just Indians from two or three hundred years ago, but others, such as the little girl, the woman in the bathtub, maybe even the "old man" whose identity was never revealed. But why would their souls be impounded on this land?

Jordan's psychic readings and aura healings were not answering my questions and I wanted more than his counsel. I wanted Lorraine Warren. I wanted the Church, but, while it was becoming apparent there would be no charges filed against Steven, I had concluded that Father A had no intention of returning.

For three or four more days, the tranquillity rubbed against me like sandpaper. *It is laying back, gaining strength, waiting to spring when our guard is down.* It was a war of nerves and I was losing.

Driving into Madison to shop for groceries, I drove by the house and parked in front. The place was dark and still but I felt the presence of the spirit, felt it sneering at me from behind the curtains.

I went inside and turned on the light. The quiet was all-consuming and I stood there, cold to the core, and looked at the photographs on the antique table: my happy, smiling children. *This is their home. This is where they belong.* Tears ran down my face, and an ache swelled in my chest like an inflated balloon.

"Show yourself, you bastard," I heard myself scream, "and tell me what you want! Leave my family alone, you bastard! Leave us alone!"

Ron and I lay in bed and talked about our plans. I wanted to leave the apartment as soon as possible.

"Why can't we take out a loan and rent an apartment in Louisville?" I asked. "I can't take any more of this."

"Suppose this *thing* isn't after us," he said. "Suppose *it* is after this Father A. If he's the demon slayer, maybe it is using us to get to him."

"Well, *it* is going to fail. He's not coming back. I think he is frightened and that's why he left. I don't believe that the Church pulled him out so suddenly."

We massaged that theory into the night: The *thing* had been fairly quiet for a couple of weeks leading up to the exorcist's arrival. Then, the day before we were to meet with him, Steven's car malfunctioned horribly and the result was the death of an innocent young man. Father A claimed to know *it,* said he had faced *it* many times before. The car wreck was a message from hell that was not lost on the priest from New York.

We had the theory pretty well molded into shape when we heard scratching on the ceiling, then voices. It was Steven and Ashley talking. They had been in bed for hours. We listened.

Steven said, "Dad? Is that you?"

We jumped up and ran to their room. Steven was sitting up in bed. "Dad, it was at the door," he said.

"What was, son?"

"I thought it was you, but then I saw another man. He had on a straw hat and bib overalls."

On my next visit to Jordan Pitkoff's office I informed him that I was getting the hell out of Indiana.

"The exorcism didn't work," I said. "Everything that happened in Madison is starting to happen in Kent."

"One exorcism isn't always enough," he said. "We may have to try another time or two."

"Maybe so," I said, "but I'm not taking any more chances with my children."

As he had done more and more often, Jordan turned the conversation away from the house and toward me and what he believed were my psychic abilities. I felt that he was trying to draw me into his circle, a sphere of influence that I was determined to resist. His strategy, it seemed, was to drive a wedge between my husband and me. A chasm already existed between us and the agitation of outsiders served no constructive purpose that I could fathom.

He pressured me again about Ron, chastised the "weakness" that kept me married to a man who lacked the courage to fight this battle with me.

I blew up. "You have no right to talk like that," I said, rising to my feet with full intentions of either punching him or beating a hasty exit. "No matter what he's like, he's my husband and you are not going to be disrespectful of him."

He stood and backed away from me. "Calm down. Calm down," he said. "Take deep breaths."

That exchange probably marked the beginning of the difficult process of disconnecting from Jordan Pitkoff, who had been my only ally, the only light along the dark coastline. But I felt he was manipulating me and I wouldn't permit that, even if it meant I had to go this thing alone.

With that eventuality in mind, I decided it was time to educate myself. From the Warrens' book, I had concluded that the study of ghosts and demons and paranormal events was a wide and long field that I needed to explore further. At a bookstore, a clerk directed me to a confusingly abundant section of books on parapsychology.

I selected *Psychic Self-Defense,* because the title seemed tailored to my immediate need. I debated between two books by Loyd Auerbach, *ESP, Hauntings and Poltergeists* and *Reincarnation, Channeling and Possession.* Each had the same subtitle: *A Parapsychologist's Handbook.* After thumbing through them, I elected to buy both.

None was light reading. Many of the terms were vaguely familiar. *Clairvoyance. Precognition. Teleportation.* Others were completely foreign. *Psychometry. Psychokinesis* and its baffling relative, *recurrent spontaneous psychokinesis.*

But I found solace in the opening chapter of Auerbach's book on hauntings and poltergeists.

Over the past hundred years or so, ever since the field of science dealing with experiences and abilities that seem to lie outside the "normal" range began as "psychical research" (now known as parapsychology) one thing has become clear to parapsychologists: whether or not you believe that there are or might be psychic occurrences, whether or not you think such claims are absurd or even crazy, people all over the world are having experiences they describe as psychic (or paranormal, anomalous, even supernatural). The unfortunate thing about these experiences is that in many cultures, when they do occur, they generally evoke reactions of unease, fear, terror, or simply forgetting, due to a lack of understanding or familiarity. In any case, few people know what to do about them.

Parapsychology, or psychical research, may lie well outside the purview of mainstream science, but it is approached with a measure of scholarship by learned men and women who could just as easily have applied their degrees in higher education to pursuits that would have earned them greater professional acceptance. If they do not believe the paranormal enigma is ultimately explainable, materially interpretable, what draws them to the investigation of it?

Even before digesting the books, I turned to the back of each one, to the indexes and appendixes and bibliographies, and made a short list of experts. Some could be contacted through their publishers, some were at universities, and others were affiliated with paranormal research organizations.

There was no harm in telling my story to as many professionals as possible, so I began writing letters. One went to Loyd Auerbach; another to Dr. Arthur Hastings, of the California Institute for Transpersonal Psychology; another to Dr. Julian Isaacs, of John F. Kennedy University, in Orinda, California; another to Dr. Elizabeth McAdams, of the Southern California Society for Psychical Research, in Los Angeles; and the last to Dr. William G. Roll, of the West Georgia College psychology department, in Carrollton, Georgia.

Dr. Roll was a man of impressive credentials—University of California, Oxford University, and the University of Lund, Sweden, and the author of several books and hundreds of papers on parapsychology. He was quoted liberally in Auerbach's text, and I was especially hopeful of getting a response from him. In a chapter on psychokinesis (PK), which Auerbach defined as "true mind over matter," Dr. Roll's name was mentioned in connection with poltergeist experiences remarkably similar to ours. Though I didn't understand it fully, it seemed that the context was far different from the ghosts-and-demons theory I had been hearing for six months:

> We come to the PK-related phenomenon that will receive most of our attention throughout this book: the poltergeist experience. In German the word literally means "noisy ghost," but parapsychologists link the experience to a living person or persons, and to a stress-related situation. In a poltergeist case, objects are generally reported to move about under their own power, things break by themselves, sounds are heard, and perhaps some vague forms may be seen lurking about. Most of the events follow a pattern, occurring when a certain person is around (we call that central person the "agent"), although the timing of the happenings is generally spontaneous. Because the events tend to recur, William G. Roll, of the Psychical Research Foundation, Chapel Hill, North Carolina, coined the phrase "Recurrent Spontaneous Psychokinesis" to cover this kind of paranormal event.

While I felt uneasy with the suggestion that someone in the family—me? Ashley?—was, in some way, responsible, Auerbach's explanation was less accusatory than Jordan Pitkoff's and Father A's had been. In Jordan's indictment, my unrestrained emotions had invited the spirits in and fed them like transient hoboes. To the priest, the demons came calling in retribution for my sins.

All along I had been searching for a scientific rationale behind the things that had happened to us. *Psychokinesis* may be something less than high-grade science, but it was worth exploring. Surely, when I understood it well enough, it would make as much sense as anything else I had come across.

Chapter 22

Ron didn't approve of the apartment I found in Louisville and I didn't blame him. It was in the impoverished neighborhood where I had lived after my first marriage, when I was broke and struggling to survive with an infant son. But the $300-a-month rent was about as painless as rents got. He got some apartment-locator books, found a place on the other side of town for $800 a month. It was more like a town house, and the complex had enticing amenities, such as a club room, a swimming pool, and spacious playgrounds. The kids loved it. We planned to move in the first week in January.

Christmas was approaching and, knowing we would soon be back in Louisville, I was able to get into the spirit of the holidays. A new beginning was ahead and my elation showed in the journal entry I made after the decision to move had been made.

> I can finally see the light at the end of the tunnel. We can start our lives over again. We won't have to drive by that house every day. We won't have to drive down the road where the accident happened. We can begin getting the help this family needs to heal the wounds we all have obtained. I look forward to the simple things: helping my children fix up their new rooms, going to PTA meetings. I will have control of my life again. There will still be some problems, but there will be hope—the one thing I nearly ran out of.

Jordan came back to perform another exorcism, and Ron, who was not eager to move away, tried to convince me, and himself, that it had been successful, that there was no reason now to abandon our home.

Any inclination I might have had to waver was removed the afternoon Ashley and I drove into Madison and my car began to overheat as soon as we turned onto Clifty Drive. Though I had vowed never to return to that house, the car was running so hot that I had to stop there and figure out what to do. Ron was forty-five minutes away, so I called Kellie. She was not at home. Neither was Janet. I called a cab and sat down by the kitchen window to watch for it.

"Mommy," Ashley said, "your head has a light."

I shrugged. *Light from the window,* I thought.

"Mommy," she said, "your head glows."

I stared out the window, watching for the cab that never came. I called Ron and he left work to come and get us. He replaced the thermostat in the car and we all went back to Kent.

At dinner that evening, Ron looked across the table at me and said, "I'll be damned." His eyes were as round as silver dollars. He was muttering something about a light around me.

"What the hell is wrong with you," I said.

"Stand up," he said, "and move away from the light."

I thought he had finally cracked, but I got up and walked a couple of steps into a dimmer area of the kitchen.

Ashley said, "It's that light again, Mommy."

Ron said, "I've never seen anything like it. You have a glowing light around your whole body."

I went into the bathroom and looked in the mirror. I could see it, too, a kind of smoky, translucent glow three inches from my head and body.

Steven came home from a friend's house about an hour later.

"Do you see anything different about me?" I asked him.

He blinked and stared at me for a second. "Yeah, you're glowing. I can see your aura."

The glow remained with me for the next twenty-four hours. Rather than being frightened, I felt strangely heartened by it, as though I were safe and protected by it.

At the same time, I could not be sure it did not foretell another disaster.

Compared to the seasons that preceded it, that winter in Louisville was close to blissful. It was marred mostly by the scars we had brought with us, but I was confident they would soon heal.

"We're going to put everything behind us," I told the children. "We're not even going to talk about what happened."

We had moved most of our furniture from Madison and closed up the house completely. The windows were nailed shut, the drapes closed, and the utilities turned off. Our plan was to continue making payments on the house until we could sell it or figure out some other use for it.

For a couple of months, our lives returned almost to normal, but I was naive to believe that positive thinking was enough to put the ordeal behind us. After a few weeks, the children began to ask questions: Is it over? Is it going to be okay?

As spring approached, Steven slid into a serious depression. Though he had tried to conceal it, his accident and Charles Claudel's death had weighed silently and heavily on his mind. He stopped eating, lost weight, and developed a nervous twitch around his eye that sometimes made his face look distorted. If I asked, he would deny that anything was troubling him. But he began to talk about death, what happens to people when they die. One day he asked me, "Do you think Charles is a ghost now?"

I tried to console him and assure him the accident had not been his fault but my efforts were futile. He broke down. "Mom, I can't handle it anymore," he sobbed.

We had been back to Jordan Pitkoff's office a few times for counseling and psychic healing, but I knew that was not enough.

"We're going to get some help," I told Ron. "We're all going to do this together."

I took Steven out of school and checked him into Tenbrook, a psychiatric hospital. Reluctantly I told them the whole story. *They may think Steven and I are both crazy,* I thought, *but it is time to deal the whole deck.* To my surprise, the hospital staff was not unfamiliar with poltergeists and other things paranormal.

Ashley was having trouble sleeping. Her nightmares had returned and she complained that something was watching her. She said she saw moving shadows in the hall and described one of them as a two-headed monster. To convince us, she drew pictures of it.

I contacted the psychology department at the University of Louisville and asked if someone there could recommend the best child psychologist in town. "Clara Maddox," I was told.

"It will take a while," Clara told me. "She may even have nightmares for a while, but eventually she will open up and work through it."

Again, I breathed easier. The children were getting the therapy they needed. Our demons had not followed us, and Jordan Pitkoff was certain they would not. We were on our way back to the real world. Or so I thought.

When things were at their worst in the house on Clifty Drive, a lot of items turned up missing or misplaced. One of my favorite earrings was among them. It disappeared sometime in late 1990 or early 1991. I kept the matching earring in hopes the mate would turn up again, but after a year or more I had given up on finding it.

Three or four months after we moved into the apartment in Louisville, I walked into the bedroom and saw the earring lying on the dresser. Thinking it was the one I had saved, I picked it up to return it to my jewelry box. When I opened the lid, the other earring was lying there, just where I had left it.

"Funny how that thing turned up after being missing all this time," I told Ron.

It wasn't really funny. We had tried to convince ourselves we had left the spirits or demons behind, but by the end of April we could not deny that what happened in Madison and Kent was recurring in Louisville.

The television turned itself on and off. A large, gold-trimmed mirror I had owned for years fell to the floor, and the hanging brackets looked as though they had been pulled from the wall. Cracks appeared in the apartment walls. We heard scratching behind the plaster. Our cat would snap awake from its nap and stare at the ceiling or an empty corner of the room. We would return home and find the apartment in a mess, furniture turned over and things knocked off the tables or shelves.

Jordan told us not to be concerned about those things. Our own psychic abilities could have caused some of them, he said. My mind wanted to believe him, but my heart wouldn't go along.

Steven seemed to be making good progress, but Ashley's therapy inched along at first. She was uncomfortable talking with Clara Maddox about the house in Madison and the little girl who came to her room at night. At home, though, her moods made sudden, sharp turns. One minute she would seem genuinely afraid of the shadows she saw, and the next minute she would be calmly watching television. Sometimes, while eating dinner or playing in the living room, she would suddenly point in one direction or another and say, "They're watching us."

Ron and I attended counseling sessions with her and she became more open with Clara Maddox, first telling her how much she missed her friends, Ericka and Kendra, and how sad it had made her to leave her home. "I want to go back," she said. Then she talked about the house in Madison and, for the first time, mentioned the little girl.

"What is her name?" Clara asked.

"Lisa," Ashley said without hesitation.

Ron and I were astonished. She had always told us she didn't know the little girl's name and didn't know anything about her except that she lived in the attic and didn't have a mommy.

Lisa. We said nothing to Dr. Maddox but Ron and I were thinking the same thing. *Lisa . . .* the name scratched on the wicker basket the first time the globes of light circled through our house in Madison.

Ashley's birthday was coming up on May 3. We decided to make a big production of it. Kellie and her girls came down from Madison, and we invited a few other friends and family members. We had helium-filled balloons, banners, and lots of food and games. The apartment was filled with birthday presents.

Kellie and I had not seen much of each other in the past few months, and being together again brought out a mood of levity I hadn't felt in a long time. I persuaded her to spend the night so we could catch up on each other's lives.

Ron and Steven turned in early, and we got the girls to bed not long afterward. Kellie and I settled down to talk. She filled me in on what had been happening in Madison and then asked me about our situation.

"Is it over?" she said.

"Yes," I said. "Everything is great. It's all behind us."

I talked about my renewed interest in religion and how my faith and prayers had helped me through some scary times, despite my recent "falling out" with the Catholic Church. Kellie seemed cynical.

"This isn't about God," she said. "I don't care what they say."

The words had scarcely passed her lips when five or six balloons, which had been hugging the ceiling, descended and floated across the room and paused near my head.

Kellie said, "D.J., are you doing that?"

I burst out laughing. "Did you see me touch those balloons?" I said. Obviously, the balloons had merely lost some of their helium.

We were still laughing when we heard a clicking sound, like plastic snapping together, on the table near the television. It was the video-tape rewinder. The lid had closed by itself and there was no tape inside. The machine switched on and hummed at full speed. Kellie leaned forward and turned her head to the side.

"Oh, hell," she said.

"What's the matter?"

"D.J., it's not even plugged in."

"Maybe it's . . ." I was interrupted by a piercing scream just outside the balcony doors. It did not sound human and it did not sound like any animal I had ever heard. It was shrill and came from deep in the lungs and cut through the night like jagged metal.

I jumped to my feet and for an instant my blood turned to ice. "My God," I gasped, "it's a banshee."

We went out onto the balcony. The howling was coming from a wooded area across a small lawn from the apartment. It was dark and we could see nothing, but we heard movement in the brush, something running. Branches and twigs cracked around it, marking its progress through the darkness. In a matter of seconds it covered perhaps one hundred yards. No human could have traveled that fast; for all I knew, no animal either.

Kellie looked like she had swallowed toxic waste. "You said it was a banshee?" she said, her eyes searching for clarification.

"I don't know why I said that. I don't even know what the hell a banshee is."

No sooner had we sat down again than the brass plate on the mail slot in the front door began to open and slam shut. I checked to see if someone was outside. The plate slammed a few more times and Kellie said, "D.J., you weren't telling me the truth. It's not over. *It* has come home to you. *It* followed you here."

"No, no, no. *It* hasn't followed us."

"D.J., you're lying. You can say what you want to say but it is happening again. When are you going to accept it?"

Kellie and the girls left the next morning, and I worked on the apartment, straightening up from the party and making space in Ashley's room for her new toys. I tried to push last night out of my mind but couldn't. *Banshee,* I thought. *What is a banshee, anyway?*

I found a dictionary and looked it up. *"A female spirit in Gaelic folklore believed to presage a death in the family by wailing outside the house."*

* * *

"Running hasn't gotten us anywhere," I told Marilee that afternoon when she arrived in Louisville. "I've got to draw the line somewhere. I've got to find a way to fight this thing and beat it."

Marilee and I had not talked at length in the three years since she left my house after the Ouija board incident and refused to return. She had married and moved to Salem. Her son, Jimmy, now lived in Henryville, near Louisville, with his girlfriend. Marilee had come to town to visit them.

"You won't believe what's been happening for the past two years," I said. "Well, maybe you will believe it—you basically warned me." I gave her a full rundown.

"Well, I knew after our Ouija board experiment that something was wrong in that house," Marilee said. She thought for a moment and said, "Did you ever figure out what those initials meant—CK."

CLICK! The collision in my head was like two billiard balls.

"Marilee, those initials were painted on our laundry-room wall while we were away one weekend."

"You mean somebody broke into your house?"

"No. We were at Marge's house and I dreamed I went back to Madison. In the dream, I saw some people in the backyard. One was a man, some kind of snake charmer. In the laundry room, I saw the initials CK painted on the wall. I told Ron about it the next morning. When we got home, there it was. CK painted on the wall. All the doors and windows were locked. Nobody could have gotten in there."

"That's bizarre, sis."

"Look, Marilee, I haven't been back to that house since we moved to Louisville, but Ron has. He's been checking on the history of it and the previous owners, so he has stopped by a few times. He says Ashley's room is still cold, a lot colder than the other rooms. Let's go up there and just look around. I'd like to know what you think."

"I can tell you right now. I think you should stay away from that place."

"I've been thinking . . . if whatever this thing is can follow us wherever we go, we might as well go back to Madison, to our home, and fight it out there. Just go up there and look around and tell me what you feel."

We made plans to drop Ashley off at Jimmy's house in Henryville the next day and travel on to Madison.

*   *   *

It seemed that my daughter and Marilee's son tried to keep us away from the house. First, Ashley woke up with such severe abdominal pains that I thought we would have to cancel the trip. I thought of calling Ron to see if he could come home and stay with her, but before I could make that decision he walked in the door. He was also having stomach pains.

When I got to Jimmy's house, he was pleading with Marilee not to go. "Mom, I beg you," he said. "That house is evil."

"My sister needs me," Marilee said. "I'm going. I'm not worried about any of this."

As we got close to Madison, my anxiety was hard to conceal.

"Relax," Marilee said.

Exchanging nervous glances, we went through the back door and were greeted by the warm, musty odor of vacancy. We had no game plan.

"Just walk around," I told her. "Tell me anything you see or feel or think."

She walked through the sunroom, turned down the other hallway, and entered Ashley's bedroom, and stood at the foot of the bed. "It smells like roses in here," she said. "And it's cold, too. My toes feel like I'm standing on a block of ice."

She stepped a couple of paces to her left. "It's warm here . . . not cold at all."

In the master bedroom, she wrinkled her nose. "It smells like dirty socks or something . . . body odor maybe."

I nodded.

She tilted her head back, sniffed, and said, "It's coming from the ceiling."

We stopped in the bathroom, Steven's room, and the living room and ended up in the kitchen. Marilee went around one end of the table and stood beside a window facing Clifty Drive. "I smell fire," she said. "Do you smell it?"

"No," I said. "But one of the previous owners had a fire in that corner of the attic . . . right above your head. That was many years ago."

"Interesting," she said, her hand gripping a crucifix so tightly that her knuckles were white.

"Let's go out back," I said. "Just walk around and see if you feel anything." I did not direct her to any particular location.

Marilee meandered around the yard and suddenly stopped on the spot where I had seen the circus tent and snake charmer in my dream. The back door, which I had left opened, slammed shut. Marilee looked at the door, then down at the ground, and her eyes widened.

"There's something wrong with this spot," she said. "I feel like I'm standing in quicksand."

"Just tell me anything you think."

She shuffled her feet a little. "I don't know, Doretta. I've been on soft ground before, but this is a weird softness. It's almost like there's nothing under me. I feel like I'm standing over a pit. I can almost feel myself sinking."

She quickly moved a few steps away. "Doretta, there is something wrong with that spot. I don't know if it's a pit to hell or a grave or what, but I don't like it. I felt like I was about to be sucked into the earth."

We went back inside, and I told her she had been standing on a spot where I had often felt the same strange sensation of being over a pit or a grave. "I think somebody is buried there," I said.

"Maybe we ought to leave," she said.

The back door, which I had closed behind us when we came in, slammed one more time.

On the drive back to Henryville, Marilee was as tense as a banjo string. "I felt evil," she said. "I felt evil. I felt evil was watching me."

Chapter 23

"Do you remember anything about Jimmy Mikos?" Marilee asked.

"Not really," I said. "I have some pictures of me with him, and Grandma told me a little about him, but I was pretty young when Mother was married to him. Why?"

Her gaze moved past me, to some long-ago point, some fleck on the time continuum out on the edge of space. Marilee and I had never talked much about our childhoods. Those years were as brutal for her as they were for me and, as adults, we had never dredged up the details. But that night, the excursion to Madison still fresh on our minds, we talked more intimately than we ever had.

"I've always wanted to apologize for leaving you with him," she said of the stepfather I barely remembered.

I had lived with my mother and Jimmy Mikos for less than a year while I was gathering strength to have open-heart surgery. I turned three years old during that time. Marilee wasn't there and neither were my brothers.

"Apologize for what?" I asked.

"Did he ever hurt you?"

"No."

"Did he ever touch you . . . do anything to you?"

"No, never," I said. "Grandma always told me he loved me and was very good to me."

"He molested me, Doretta," she said. "You were living with Grandma, but Larry and Patrick and Billy and me lived with Mother and Jimmy. I never told anybody what he did, but I called my dad in Michigan and told him to come and get me. I took the boys and we left."

"Well, the FBI took him away the day after my surgery," I said, "so I really wasn't around him very long, I guess. I don't remember much."

"I always felt guilty after I found out you were living with him and Mother," she said.

Guilty. Did all of my siblings suffer that complex? I had assumed I was the only one. When my stepfathers beat me, I felt guilt, as though I had done something to deserve it. When Uncle Ross fondled and tried to rape me, I felt guilt. When my mother cursed me, I felt guilt. When my grandmother preached and whipped me with a belt, I felt guilt. When the cockroaches crawled on my plate or I was locked in a closet or strange men came into the bed I shared with my mother, I felt guilt. *I must have been very bad to deserve such treatment.*

But the worst guilt I had ever known visited me after Mother's death. I had never told anyone, but the burden was always somewhere in the back of my mind, like a body hidden in the trunk of a car. Marilee had bared her soul to me and I had an overpowering urge to reciprocate, to get this one great load off my chest. It gushed out of me like air from a punctured tire.

"I think I killed our mother," I blurted out.

She blinked and her jaw dropped.

"It was after she had the cancer operation," I said. "I was dating Ray Holmes, the guy I later married. We went to the hospital to see her, and before we got to her room one of the nurses stopped us. She said Mother was very sick and might ask me to give her something to drink. She told me there were ice chips beside the bed and I could feed her those. Under no circumstances was I to give her anything else to drink.

"Well, we walked in the room and it was scary. It smelled awful. There was a large bottle, like the kind used in bottled-water machines, and a long hose was threaded into its top. A dark, nasty-looking liquid was dripping into it. The liquid was coming from Mother's stomach. She was swollen like she was nine-months pregnant. I walked over to the bed and she asked me to get her a drink of water.

"I said, 'I'll get some ice and rub it on your lips.' She said, 'No, I want water.' I told her I couldn't give her water. I started to feed her the ice chips. She couldn't move but she could talk well enough. She said, 'Get me a fuckin' drink of water.' I was always afraid of her, Marilee. There she was, lying in bed with tubes running in and out of her and I was still scared of her. I got weak inside and started to tremble, just like I did when I was little. She ordered me to go into the bathroom and fill up a cup with water.

"I held her head up and she sipped the water. God, her lips were so dry and cracked. She was like a dying woman in the desert. After she drank the water, she seemed so at peace. She moaned a little and smiled and drifted off to sleep."

Marilee had not taken her eyes off of me.

"Ray came over and took my hand and we left. We didn't talk much until we were on the bus headed home. He said, 'If my mom had wanted water, I would have given it to her, too. But you probably shouldn't tell anyone you gave it to her.' It hadn't occurred to me until then that giving her the water might make her sicker.

"That evening, Grandma and Grandpa went to the hospital. Grandpa came home and Grandma stayed with Mother. Later, Grandma called and Grandpa went again. Several hours must have passed before they came home. Grandma was crying and Patrick and I were trying to find out what was going on. Grandma was nearly hysterical and started blurting out the horrible details. She said she was sitting beside Mom's bed and Mom's stomach burst open and blood and pieces of her insides gushed onto the floor. Grandma screamed and the nurse ran over, grabbed a blanket, and threw it over Mom's blood and entrails.

"I was seeing all of this in my mind when it hit me: *The water. My God, the water must have made Mom's stomach explode.* I ran to my bed and buried my face in a pillow. I kept saying to myself, 'Oh, God, I've killed her. I've killed my mother.' I never told anybody about giving her the water, but I've always believed that was what killed her."

Marilee said, "Doretta, that's crazy. She had cancer. She had half her abdomen cut away. You didn't have anything to do with it."

"There were times when I thought I hated her enough to kill her," I said. "Maybe, subconsciously, I was glad to give her the water."

"Get that out of your head," Marilee said. "Cancer is what killed her. Cancer and booze and drugs."

I nodded but it was an empty gesture.

Ashley's stomach pains got worse over the next few days. First she had diarrhea and then began vomiting and was unable to keep food down. The doctor said it was a viral infection, but she was not running a fever. The doctor gave her medicine, and it stopped the vomiting but not the diarrhea. I kept taking her back to the doctor, and each time his diagnosis seemed a little more tentative. The howling banshee was still on my mind, and I shivered every time Ashley threw up or cried out in pain.

"It's okay, Mom, calm down," the doctor kept telling me. "It's just a bug of some kind."

I wanted to put Ashley in the hospital but the doctor did not think it was necessary. Maybe it wasn't, but I wanted to get her away from the apartment, away from the foreboding of the banshee.

When Ron came home that afternoon, I was packing boxes.

"What's going on?" he asked.

"I'm going to Grandpa's house."

"Doretta, we can't keep doing this. . . ."

"I can. I'll just keep moving if I have to. I had a few weeks of peace in Kent," I said. "I had a couple of months of peace after we moved here. If I move again, maybe I'll have a couple of months of peace there."

"This is ridiculous," he said.

"Maybe, but I'm going to Grandpa's."

He went upstairs to take a nap. Ashley came into the room.

"Mommy, I feel better," she said. "Can I go outside and sit on the steps?"

The day was radiant and warm and I thought the sunshine would be good for her.

"Okay, but don't go off the steps."

I continued packing and, about ten minutes later, went to the door to check on her. She was sitting on the stoop in her rocker with her doll in her lap. She seemed perfectly well and contented. I returned to my packing.

No more than five or six minutes had passed when I heard the door open. I looked around and saw Ashley falling forward into the apartment. There was blood on her neck and shirt and she was struggling to breathe.

I picked her up and ran toward the kitchen, screaming for Ron to wake up. Ashley's throat looked as though it had been cut from one side to the other. I doused her with water and could see the cut was not deep.

Ron came into the kitchen, looked at her neck, and said, "What happened?"

"I don't know, Daddy."

"Tell me what happened, Ashley."

Between sobs and gasps, she finally told us she had hung from a tree. Ron took off outside and I changed Ashley's shirt and got her ready to go to the hospital.

Ron went to a large tree in the middle of the courtyard and found a slender nylon cord dangling from one of the branches. The end was cleanly severed, as if by a knife.

"Are you the little girl's father?" asked a man who had come from another apartment.

"Yeah," Ron said. "Did you see what happened here?"

"Well, sort of," the man said. He turned and pointed to an apartment near the tree. "I was in there watching television and had the balcony doors open. I heard something that sounded like a cat scream. I walked over to the door and looked out and saw this long hair swinging from the tree. I realized it was a little kid hanging out there. I jumped off the balcony and yelled for my wife to bring a knife.

"I lifted the little girl up to take the pressure off her neck and tried to untangle the rope, but I couldn't get my finger underneath it. Man, it beat anything I've ever seen."

Ron asked, "What do you mean?"

"I'm not just talking about a cord wrapped around a kid's neck. I'm talking about a cord wrapped around and around and around the neck. My wife came out with a knife and I cut the kid loose."

"Was anybody else out here?"

"Nah, the courtyard was empty . . . nobody else around."

On the way to Humana Hospital, I questioned Ashley but was unable to find out anything. She insisted she could remember nothing. At the emergency room, we got everyone's attention very quickly.

I told the nurses as much as I knew and told them Ashley had given no explanation.

A nurse turned to Ashley and said, "I want to know what happened. You don't have to be afraid of anybody but you have to tell me the truth."

Ashley seemed frightened by the severity of the nurse's tone. "I was standing under the tree and then I was hanging from the tree," she said. "I don't know what happened."

"We've got to call the child protection agency," one nurse said to me.

"Call anyone you want," I said. "Just take care of her."

She turned back to Ashley. "You do know what happened," she said. "You're going to have to tell me."

Ashley began to cry. "I don't know. I can't remember."

"Honey, you do remember," the nurse said.

I stood by silently. If I had tried to interfere, or said anything at all, they would have thought I was trying to coach my daughter. They carried Ashley into an examining room, and a doctor checked her over and talked to Ron and me, questioning us about the circumstances of the hanging.

"Look, I was not there," I said. "There was a man who cut her down. I will show you where he lives. You can talk to him."

"I'm sorry," he said, "but we have to report this."

The frustration was maddening. I couldn't tell him what I really believed happened, couldn't tell him anything about what had happened to us. If I began ranting about banshees and demons and poltergeists, I would have risked having my kids taken away from me.

Ashley's neck was X-rayed and while we waited for the results, Ron and I talked more with the doctor and nurses. They appeared to be convinced we had no part in hanging our daughter, but they were impatient with Ashley's reticence.

One particular nurse persisted to the point of badgering her. "You're not telling the truth. You're going to have to tell me everything if you want to go home."

At that point I nearly lost my temper, but I felt Ashley needed to hear from me. "She's going home," I said. "She's not lying to you. She's telling you what she can."

Ashley's eyes shifted back and forth, from me to the nurse. "I was just playing in the tree," she said, "and I got tied up in the rope. That's all."

The X ray did not indicate a fracture or other serious problem and Ashley was released. I was told to bring her back in a week for a checkup.

At six o'clock the next morning the phone rang. "This is Dr. Steele," the voice said. "I don't want to alarm you but I need for you to bring Ashley back to the hospital. Be very careful when you put her in the car. How is she this morning?"

"Well, she's still asleep. I slept with her and she didn't cry or anything. What's wrong?"

"I think her neck is broken."

"How could you have missed that last night?"

"Well, breaks are hard to see in that area. You have to look really close."

I propped pillows around Ashley and drove very slowly to the hospital. A sudden stop or turn, a bump or pothole, anything that could cause sudden movement in her neck could be disastrous.

More X rays were taken, then blood tests. Ashley kicked and squirmed at the sight of the needles. One of the nurses brought her a large stuffed animal.

"Where is Josey Wales?" the doctor smiled when he entered the room. He was referring to the movie outlaw who survived a hanging and had rope scars around his neck. *God,* I thought, *is Ashley going to look like that?*

"Mom, I think we're going to be okay," the doctor said. "It's not a crack, just some blood that collected there."

"Is she going to be scarred?"

"Just like Josey Wales," he said. "I'd get her some pretty scarves to wear around her neck. Don't let the sunlight get to it and keep some lotion on the skin when it begins to heal. In six to eight months it will begin to fade. By the time she's a young girl and really worried about her looks, the scar will hardly be visible."

Less than a week later, I was helping Ashley dress for school and as I buttoned her dress, I noticed that the marks from the hanging were virtually gone. Was that extraordinary? I had a chance to find out a few days later when Grandpa got sick and had to be taken to Humana Hospital. Ashley and I went down to see him. On our way to the snack bar, we walked over to the emergency room and saw one of the nurses who had been kind to Ashley and helpful to all of us. Ashley walked up to her and smiled.

"How are you doing, sweetie?" the nurse asked her.

I said, "Look at her neck."

She leaned over and examined Ashley's skin. "My God, honey, you done took her to a faith healer or what?"

"Nope. It's just gone."

Once again we were back on the run and it broke my heart to see how it affected Ashley. Her life had been almost constant turmoil for two years—pain, nightmares, doctors, therapy, living out of boxes, never knowing what the next day would bring. Ron was taking her to Marge's to stay while we packed boxes. A few of our belongings would go to Grandpa's house; the rest would be put in storage.

"Where will we sleep tonight?" she asked.

I wanted to hug her and tell her everything was all right. I wanted to scream. I wanted to kick, pound the walls, and make all the hurt go away.

Instead, I said, "Don't worry, honey, we'll sleep at Grandpa's. But we're going to go back home soon. We're going to get our home back."

That night, Ron went to his mom's house to get Ashley and he was extremely upset when he got home.

"I got into it with my mother," he said. "She started asking me questions about why we were moving and about Ashley's accident. I told her the demons had followed us and we believed they had tried to kill Ashley. She said it was all in our heads . . . there's no such things as ghosts and demons. She said we're just crazy. She also told me Ashley's hanging was a warning from God, because we're not good Christians."

His voice broke and he almost cried. "How could my mother think God is doing this? You know what else? She said my father had suffered before he died because he had offended God. God made him pay for his sins."

I could accept that Marge did not believe in ghosts and did not understand what was happening to us. Even we did not understand. But I was outraged that she could be so cold, so nonsupportive of her son, could accuse him of being crazy.

Fear of being called crazy was what kept us from discussing our ordeal with anyone but those we had to confide in, such as Ashley's and Steven's counselors, the lawyer we had consulted after Steven's accident, a couple of close friends and relatives, and, of course, Jordan Pitkoff, Lorraine Warren, and the Church.

"You know," Ron said, "I got in a conversation with a couple of guys at work . . . about supernatural stuff. I didn't tell them anything about us, but I found out they don't think this stuff is crazy. One guy brought in a picture taken at a house in Prestonville and you could see this bizarre image shaped like a man. He told me about a lot of strange things that happened in that house. The other guy said he had similar experiences, you know, hearing noises or seeing images in his house."

He was relieved that if our story ever became public, he would not be ridiculed by his friends and coworkers. That was important, because our story was about to become public in a big way.

Chapter 24

Journal entry, May 26, 1992:

*Today we finished moving out of the apartment. All the furniture
has been put in storage. All we took to Grandpa's was clothes and
personal items. Steven complained of pain in his back and of not
feeling good. He was extremely irritable. He fell down the steps
while carrying a couple of empty dresser drawers. We heard him
scream and found him leaning against the apartment holding his
legs, which were swollen and bruised. He said it felt like someone
had grabbed his feet and pulled them from under him. We could
smell that familiar, horrible odor at the top of the steps.*

*Florida keeps crossing my mind. Steven loves the ocean and the
palm trees. Ashley has fantasized about going to Disney World. I
told Ron we should take the children to Florida but the suggestion
had a macabre ring to it, as though I were saying, ''Let's do it
before it's too late.'' Is that what we've come to, living each day
in grim anticipation, wondering if a freak accident or peculiar
illness will claim one of us?*

*In front of my children, I try to keep a very positive attitude. If
they knew how afraid I really am, they would be terrified. They
need to feel that Mom's in control and that she's not worried. Ron
depends on me just as much. ''What do we do now?'' he always
asked. ''Where do we go from here?''*

*I pray every night to God: Please make me strong. I tell myself
this nightmare will soon be over and our lives will be better than
before. I close my eyes and I see us in a beautiful home. We're
together and happy. If I see it in my mind, see it hard, see it often
enough, maybe it will become a reality.*

*   *   *

Moving in with Grandpa was a mistake. He was getting old and cantankerous. After my stepgrandmother died, he began drinking a lot and had just gotten out of a detox program when we showed up at his door. The children irritated him and it showed. Ron and I bought all the food, but Grandpa grumbled about all these new mouths to feed. After only a few days there it was apparent that we would have to move on. But where? It was not a decision easily made.

Imagine that your mooring lines have been cut and you have been set adrift. How do you pick your next port? Open up a Zip Code directory and pick a place at random? Throw a dart at a map? Given a continent on which to make your nest, the choices are ludicrously narrow: Invariably, you are drawn to accustomed turf.

Ron and I talked about returning to Madison, possibly renting an apartment or house trailer until we could make a decision about the house—whether to sell it or reclaim it from the spirits. We desperately wanted the house back, but I feared for my children's safety.

We decided to spend a night there and test the house for disturbances or demonic presences. We left Ashley with Nancy and drove to Madison with a video camera, sage sticks, and candles. We also took a generator for electrical power. We put the camera on a tripod in Ashley's bedroom, turned it on, and left the house. For an hour or so, we just drove around aimlessly, hoping the video recorder would tell if ghosts still walked about.

When we returned about eleven o'clock that night, the house was quiet. We moved the camera to the living room, lit some candles, and pulled the mattress to the middle of the room. Ron and I were sitting on the mattress, talking, when we heard the generator motor strain and pull, as though it had been drained of power. Just as quickly, it returned to normal.

We got ready for bed. Ron set candles in front of the fireplace, lit the kerosene heater to keep us warm, and turned off the generator. The house was peaceful and quiet and we quickly fell asleep.

Twice during the night we were awakened—first by the sound of the video camera shutting itself off and later by a loud *pop* that sounded like an exploding lightbulb. Otherwise, the night was uneventful.

Back in Louisville the next day, I replayed the tape. While we were away and the camera was in Ashley's room, it picked up nothing: no movement, no ghostly images, nothing. Then the tape reached the segment where it watched over the living room while we slept. First the microphone picked up a *click,* the sound of something tapping the camera. The lens refocused and sat idle for several minutes. That happened a few more times and then the camera panned from side to side.

I replayed the tape for Ron when he got home that evening. "Something is still there," I said.

By the tenth day with Grandpa, Ashley was pleading for us to return to our home, and Steven became her strongest ally. "It's time to go back and fight," he said. It did not require a lengthy family discussion to arrive at a consensus.

On Saturday, Ron and I headed back to Madison. Before leaving Louisville, I looked up the address of a mystic shop someone—Jordan or Teri or Nancy—had told me about. It was supposed to be a kind of voodoo store run by two women. I went there to buy sage and incense and anything else that might ward off the evil in my house.

The outside of the shop was painted in zebra stripes. Inside the door, I found embroidered cotton, candles, jewelry, and an array of mysterious knickknacks. Three women watched me through a beaded curtain from the back room.

One of them came out and asked, "May I help you?" She was large but attractive. For the first time, I recited my tale of ghosts and demons to a complete stranger. She invited me to sit down and I continued to pour out my tale. She seemed to hang on every word. "Come back here," she said, rising and moving toward the beaded curtain.

She gave her sister a brief version of what I had told her. They asked questions about my house and my family.

"This all happened in Louisville?" the first woman asked.

"Oh, no. In Madison, Indiana."

She leaned back and rolled her eyes. "Girl, that town is full of witches and Satan worshipers."

She went back through the store, talking about dragon's blood and garlic cloves. She gathered protective charms and frankincense and scented candles and a few things I didn't recognize.

"Take these," she said.

I paid for the items and left the store, bound for Madison and a house that Father A, the demon-slayer, feared to enter: a house that could not be cleansed by Jordan Pitkoff and his band of spiritualists and mystics, a house that spat fire and trembled and sent forth visions to reveal its loathsome secrets. I was going back with a sack of gris-gris. I was not exactly brimming with confidence.

There was an unmistakable presence in the house. The hallway reeked of sweet perfume and rose petals. I stepped into Ashley's room and was certain I saw a slight shadow move across the wall. The room was as cold as a meat locker and a kind of sleepy dizziness came over me. I sat on the bed and heard Ron calling my name. His voice was weak and distant, as though he were summoning me from across a great chasm.

"Let's go," he said.

"I'm too sleepy to move."

"Get up," he demanded, "and let's get out of here."

That night, Ron and I took the kids outside to keep them out of Grandpa's way. He was complaining about everything—our kids, our clothes, our cat.

We sat on the porch and talked until well past the children's bedtimes.

"I would rather go back to the house than be treated this way," I told my husband.

"First thing in the morning," he said, "I'll start taking our stuff back to Madison."

Nothing went right. Halfway to Louisville, a tire on the truck blew out. Ron and Steven had to unload everything to get to the spare tire and then reload the truck. I spent part of the day packing some materials to send to Ed and Lorraine Warren, but mostly I tried to keep Ashley and Grandpa away from each other. They argued over control of the television, so I took Ashley outside to play. The cat bit her on the hand and Grandpa went into a rage; he was angry with Ashley, not the cat.

Ron and Steven returned with more bad news. The water heater at the house was busted and would have to be replaced before we could move in. Things broke even when the place was empty.

"It'll take a few days to get it ready," Ron said.

"Well, I can't stay here any longer," I said. "I'm going to Marilee's for a week."

We agreed that I would take Ashley and Steven would stay behind to help Ron get the house fixed up and livable again.

Four birds squawking just outside the window kept me awake

until after one o'clock. At five-thirty, I was awakened by Ron leaving for work. I walked into the bathroom, flipped on the light, and—POP!—the bulb exploded and I got a strong whiff of men's cologne, the same cologne I had smelled often in the house on Clifty Drive. I turned, half expecting to see the apparition of the old man in the hallway. *If you followed me here, you bastard, you made the trip for nothing. Now you'll just have to follow me back to Madison.* No one, nothing, was behind me.

If all of this had happened to Marilee, she probably would have handled it better than I. She was more intellectually receptive to the paranormal and more emotionally plugged in to her own intuitions and premonitions. When she befriended a psychic a few years earlier, she embraced the supernatural without the impediment of skepticism I brought to such matters. Marilee believed in God, not ghosts, but she also was comfortable with the notion that the hard, empirical, physical reality did not preclude all other actualities.

As soon as Ashley and I arrived at her house just outside Salem, she said, "Sis, I've got something I *have* to show you. I found this book at our library. I don't know why, but I'm *supposed* to give it to you. Don't ask me how I know that. I can't explain it. I only know I'm *supposed* to show it to you."

She went into the bedroom and returned with a small volume titled *Beyond Coincidence*, written by a man named Alex Tanous, described on the dust jacket as a renowned psychic. I thumbed through the book for a second, closed it, and looked again at the cover. Behind the title print, the face of a man peered out of the dark background, a face I was certain I had seen before. I turned to the inside back flap of the dust jacket and there was another photo, sharper and better lighted, of Alex Tanous.

It couldn't be. I showed the photographs to Ashley and asked, "Have you ever seen this man before?"

She said, "Uh-huh, it's Father A."

A as in Alex, I thought.

I had never seen or heard of the book, but reading it was, as someone once said, "like déjà vu all over again." I had been over that material before. Alex Tanous's stories were identical to the personal tales Father A had related to me in our many telephone conversations and our one personal encounter. Alex Tanous boasted of spectacular ESP and telepathic powers. He had been used by the police to find lost children. He had performed psychic healings and expelled demons and spirits from possessed people. He did battle with spells cast over him by witches. He had strong ties to the Catholic Church and wanted to become an ordained priest, but he was an outcast until the Church softened its position on psychic practices.

Alex Tanous and the elusive Father A were one in the same, I was certain. But something didn't square up. Tanous was sixty years old when his book was published in 1976. He would have been well past seventy-five in 1991, when I met Father A, who appeared to be, at most, in his early fifties.

"Nothing ever makes sense anymore," I told Marilee. "But if this guy is Father A, I'm going to find him."

The next day I placed a phone call to the Parapsychological Association in Research Triangle Park, North Carolina. I had read in Loyd Auerbach's books that it was the only professional organization of parapsychologists in the world. Even if Alex Tanous was not a member, someone there surely would know of him and, possibly, his whereabouts.

The woman who answered the phone responded tersely to my inquiry. "Alex Tanous is dead," she said.

"When did he die?"

"He died several years ago. That's all I can tell you."

"Do you know . . . ?"

"I can't discuss anything more with you," she said, and brusquely hung up the phone.

Marilee had been the first to encourage me to move out of the house in Madison, and she was even more insistent that I not move back in until something was done, until I had located someone who could be of help. I had remained in contact with Jordan Pitkoff, but his methods had not been very successful and I had no reason to believe they would be any more effective in the future.

"What about the people you wrote to?" Marilee asked.

"I never heard from any of them."

"Then call them."

I got several of the numbers from directory assistance and had no luck until I came to Dr. William Roll at West Georgia College.

"Why do you want him?" asked the woman who answered in the psychology department.

"I need help and can't get anyone to respond."

"He has retired," she said, "but give me your name and number and I'll forward it to him."

Dr. Roll called the next morning. "You're the one who wrote the letter, aren't you?"

"Yes, and nothing has changed. In fact, it's gotten worse."

After we had talked for a while, he said, "I would like to come right away."

"How much will it cost?"

"I would guess about two thousand dollars," he said. "I would need two hundred dollars a day, plus expenses."

"It might as well be a million," I said. "I'm broke. I guess I could try to get a loan."

"Wait a minute," he said. "Maybe we can do something else. Maybe I can find private financing. I might be able to get a television production company or network to finance it."

"No!" I said. "I don't want any publicity. I can't do that."

He paused and said, "Well, I'll check around and see if there are any other possibilities . . . foundations or something."

As soon as I hung up the phone, Marilee came at me like a cruise missile. "What are you doing?" she said. "I don't believe this. You're so damned ashamed of what's happened to you that you'll turn down help? What are you going to do, drag this thing out until one of your kids is killed?"

I called Dr. Roll back and told him to pursue a television deal if necessary.

"Ron and Steven are in the process of moving back into the house, right?"

"Right."

"Would it be all right for you and Ashley to stay where you are for about a week?"

"Yes."

"I think you need to be in a place where you really feel safe."

We talked again three days later. He mentioned a few television shows that dealt with the paranormal and said he would contact them. I didn't object but I was clearly unenthusiastic about the prospect of making a theatrical spectacle of something that was deadly serious to me.

Again, Dr. Roll was understanding of my recalcitrance, and we ruminated over other possible sources of financing. It was then that I got the first inkling that his assessment of our situation would likely be radically different from anything we had heard so far.

"There's always the possibility we might receive some help through the ministry," I said.

"Don't count on it," he said. "I wish you wouldn't even think about it, because it doesn't have anything to do with stuff like that. No, I'm just . . . Don't move into the house at the present time, okay, Doretta? Okay?"

Here we go again, I thought. *Another leg of the endless guilt trip.*

"I don't understand. I mean, what do you think the possibilities are?" I asked. "Do you think we, to a point, are responsible, and it's going to be activated once we go back, and terrible things are going to happen?"

"It's not a question of being responsible," he said. "It is much more complex than that. Let me ask you—is your house located near power lines?"

"Yes."

"I would have guessed that. You see, the picture is something like this: Truly creative people—artists, engineers, physicists, musicians, and so forth, people such as yourself, perhaps—have a certain kind of mind. And if that mind gets into a certain configuration, such as electromagnetic radiation interacting with the brain, the result can be straightforward stuff that's sort of created accidentally and the people don't even know they are doing it.

"We don't know what the process is. This is not fact, this is still in the area of theory and we're still trying to figure it out, but under the right conditions a person with psychic abilities—that is, sensitive temporal lobes—is able to experience what most people would recognize only as subjective dreams. In such a case, the dream world, the psychical world, melds with the physical world. Something, tectonic stress or high-tension wires, acts as a catalyst for the unconscious to become conscious and projected into the environment and observed by other individuals. You see, the mind would function like a television transmitter."

What he was saying was still outside my grasp. "I've picked up radio transmissions before," I said, referring to the woman's voice calling for help from the Park-N-Eat. He was talking about something entirely different.

"But you are also a transmitter," he said.

"So *they* can use me as a conduit to travel through?"

"It is not a 'they,' not in the sense of a being or entity apart from yourself. But you transmit things and they are out in the open and other people can see them and hear them. Do you understand?"

"I'm not sure."

"What I'm saying is that what happens in these cases is an expression of our own internal world. This is more in the realm of clinical psychology. It is not occult. These entities or apparitions are not the ghosts of dead people, but an expression of ourselves—a side of ourselves that has been hidden somewhat. We all carry the baggage of our childhood with us as we go through life. If we had unpleasant experiences, if we were hurt, we may try to put that out of our minds. But it stays there, even if it is in the subconscious mind, and can affect us in real ways."

He seemed to be telling me that my subconscious mind had *dreamed* up everything that had happened to us and projected the dream like a three-dimensional movie into our environment.

"But a lot of people had documented experiences in that house long before we moved in," I said, thinking of the Cyrus family.

"And people are going to continue having those experiences in that house if strong magnetic fields are there. But what I'm saying is that you have this extra psychic kick in your mind, this extra sensitivity."

"It's just so complicated."

"Not so complicated once you understand it," he said.

"Well, I would rather believe your theory. I don't much care for the ghost stuff."

That was not really true. I didn't care much for either theory. Under both scenarios, I was the guilty party. Either I was the agent for the poltergeist or my brain had written and orchestrated the whole show. If I ever found out that my psychic abilities were responsible for the terrible things that had happened to my family, I would leave and stay as far away as possible from the people I loved.

Chapter 25

How I wished my grandmother had talked to me more about some things. Jordan Pitkoff had not convinced me that I was psychic or, if I was, that it had anything to do with anything. But Dr. Roll also raised that issue. *Sensitive temporal lobes,* he called it. I tried to picture it in my mind: a third eye that could see into places the mind was not meant to see, lightless dungeons where hideous creatures dwelled and unthinkable things occurred.

More and more I was becoming convinced that Grandma knew or suspected things she never told me. After Mother died and I told Grandma of the dreams I had—dreams of my mother standing at the foot of my bed, of leading me down a long corridor, of seeing the dying in cubicles along the way, of seeing one of my Gaddis cousins with a distended abdomen—she took those visions seriously.

While I had never believed my mother actually stood beside my bed, Grandma apparently did. She had pumped me for details. How was Mom dressed? Was she crying? As I related what I could re-member, she bawled like a baby and begged God to have mercy on her departed daughter.

After talking with Dr. Roll, I remembered another incident, where I was eight years old. Patrick was playing basketball with a boy who lived near us, and I had stopped to watch them. A picture, as ephem-eral as a strobe light, flashed into my head. My brother and the boy were slugging each other. Then I saw a third person holding a gun.

Later I told Patrick, "You're going to get in a bad fight with that boy and somebody is going to pull a gun."

"How do you know that?"

"I saw a picture . . . inside my head."

He laughed and said, "You're a fruitcake, kid."

At dinner that evening Patrick told Grandma she should take me to a shrink. "She's seeing things in her head," he laughed.

Grandma wasn't amused. "What kinds of things?" she asked me.

Grandpa interrupted. "Honey, I don't want to hear any more of this. You stop this stuff right now," he said to Grandma. "It's the devil's work."

He looked across the table at me and said, "It's the devil talking to you."

Grandma didn't argue with him, but after he was in the living room and settled in front of the television, she took me aside and asked again about what I had seen. Worry was etched on her face. "You've got to be careful about what you say in front of people," she said. "People used to get burned as witches for talking like that. When you see things, don't tell your grandpa, you come and tell me."

A day or two later, Patrick and the boy got into a terrible fight and the boy's father showed up at our house with a shotgun in his hand. He was half crazy with anger and threatened to shoot Patrick for beating up his son.

Dr. Roll called to tell me he had been in touch with some people with the Fox Television Network. They wanted to send a producer and camera crew to Madison to film a segment for a show called "Sightings," which dealt with a broad range of paranormal, supernatural, and unexplained events—everything from ghosts to UFO abductions. The network would pay for his expenses for the trip to Madison to take part in the filming, he said. There would be no dramatic reenactments, just interviews, footage of the house and property—anything the camera or crew saw.

Reluctantly, I agreed. We had been unable to find funding that wasn't commercial in some sense. If going public was the only way to get Dr. Roll involved in our case, then we would have to do it.

"They want to come pretty soon, probably within a couple of weeks. I'm going to bring some people with me."

"Who?"

"Patricia Hayes and some people from the Delphi School of Inner Sense Development in McCaysville, Georgia," he said. "She's the founder. She has a degree in behavioral science and has done a lot of work in this area."

"Sightings" would pay her expenses, as well as those of Bill Clema and Marshall Smith, who worked with Patricia at her center and its companion institute, the Delphi College of Parapsychology, which conducts workshops in such things as mediumship training, automatic writing, psychic readings, channeling, psychometry, and haunting investigation.

In short, they were psychics. That surprised me, because my earlier conversation with Dr. Roll had led me to conclude that he did not approach cases such as mine from that particular angle. In fact, he seemed to reject the psychic's notion that paranormal events involved external entities.

"Psychics can be valuable in these investigations," he said, "but I wish they were not so entity-oriented. They come from spiritualistic religions and believe that after death we are the same as before. But it is useful to have their reading of a house and the occupants. It helps us to focus on what is behind the activities."

With so many learned souls convinced that I possessed latent psychic prowess, I wondered why I had not discovered it, why it had not been pointed out to me earlier. A few childhood premonitions and intuitions did not prove I was capable of bringing this reign of terror upon my family. Whether *entities* exist or are dreamed up in the mind was not the question. The question was: Why me?

Ron and I went to Grandpa's house. I had racked my brain for clues, anything that would help me understand all this. I wanted to know what Grandpa knew. He reacted very badly to my questions. At first he was stolid and reticent.

"Grandpa, I just want to know if anything happened. . . ."

He burst into a rage. "Don't you dare start doing those things again," he said.

"Doing what things? Tell me what I did."

"I don't want to talk to you. You're not going to start that stuff again."

"If I did something bad, tell me what it was."

He began to shake and back away from me. I had never seen him behave that way. Ron, too, was shocked. Grandpa was always quiet, always in control. Now he acted as though he were facing Satan himself.

"You're evil, child," he said. "This is evil stuff you're talking about."

He looked at Ron, whose mouth was hanging open, and said, "Her grandmother was a part of that. I don't want to hear any more of it."

*   *   *

Steven, Ashley, and I drove to Madison on June 25, when the crew of "Sightings" was scheduled to arrive. Ron was working but would join us later, as would Marilee, who was driving in from Salem. I was eager to meet Dr. Roll, but, truthfully, I was not overly sanguine. *Curious* would be a more apt description of my feelings. *Is he really a scientist? Is he just in this for the television exposure? Are we getting back on the same old merry-go-round with a new roster of passengers?*

Dr. Roll and the "Sightings" crew were staying at the Hillside Inn, so I checked in also and went into the dining room, where we had arranged to meet at one o'clock.

We took a table overlooking the center of Madison and the Ohio River and settled in to discuss the plans for the next few days. Dr. Roll was pretty much as I had imagined, based on a few brief telephone conversations. He wore a casual jacket and open collar and spoke with a vague accent that seemed to be a mingling of European influences. With his thick glasses and slightly tousled hair, he had the harried look of a pediatrician with too many kids in the waiting room. His voice was soft and had a scholarly quality that I found reassuring.

He was anything but an alarmist, and it was during that first discussion that I began to appreciate some of the nuances of parapsychology and its distinction from the dogma and methodology of the psychics, demonologists, and exorcists with whom we had dealt.

It was apparent from the beginning that he was more interested in me than the house. Most of his questions were about my background. It was surprisingly easy to talk to him about the difficult parts of my childhood that I had tried to forget and had rarely discussed with anyone. We talked until nearly six o'clock.

Ron arrived, and then Marilee. Dr. Roll talked with each of them separately. He was very precise in the kinds of information he tried to elicit, and I began to feel confident that he knew exactly where he was going.

While Dr. Roll and Marilee were off having a private chat, Father John got off the hotel elevator near where we were sitting. He walked over and asked us how things were going.

"Well, we're meeting with a parapsychologist and a television film crew," I told him. "They're going to do a show about our situation. It was the only way we could get the help we thought we needed."

If he found the impending publicity objectionable, he didn't show it.

"It was very unfortunate that the Church turned its back on you," he said.

"I agree," I said.

"Father Jeff and I tried to find out more about Father A," he said. "We were sent home and told to mind our own business and not to try to investigate further."

When Marilee and Dr. Roll returned, she took Ashley up to our room. Steven left for the movies with a friend, so Ron and I were alone with Dr. Roll. He asked us to go over once again the unusual occurrences and the dates and how they coincided with the Church's involvement with us.

"I felt like this thing gained power when the Church got involved," I said. "First after the house was blessed and then after we began talking to Father A."

"When the Church called it demonic, it became demonic?" he asked. "That's how it sounds."

"Right," I said, still unsure of the point he was trying to make. "It made it more frightening. By then I was like a robot. Jordan Pitkoff had taken all the emotion out of me. If I cried, I was yelled at and told I was feeding it."

"Who said that?"

"Jordan Pitkoff. Everything was laid on me. I'm an emotional mother and I could not see things happen to my children and not cry. But I was told I couldn't cry, that it was wrong."

"Because if you showed emotion, it would feed the demon, is that it?" he asked.

"That's it."

He reminded me of our earlier phone conversation in which he told me he did not deal in demons and spirits, but in the mind and the melding of the mental and physical worlds, a phenomenon made possible by some catalyst, or a combination of them—in my case, an electromagnetic field working on my psychic powers like jumper cables.

"If you get slightly annoyed or upset with someone it can trigger this psychic reaction, projecting your feelings and emotions into your environment. It isn't a question of demons feeding on your anger. It is a matter of your anger taking a certain form in the physical world around you."

"Do you believe this . . . this effect can cause machinery to tear up and car engines to blow?"

"Well, it can," he said. "I've seen things . . . some really massive stuff happen."

"We've had spontaneous fires. . . ."

"I know. It's like two energies are coming together—this electromagnetic constellation around that house, which is going to produce strange phenomena, plus your psychic ability. You see, you don't know enough about this energy, Doretta. You know something about it but you don't know enough."

"So, I don't know how to control it, if it is me . . .?"

"You don't know how to control it and you don't know what is bringing it on, because it's something you don't feel. If you get annoyed at somebody and something happens to them, you don't know whether it's you or not."

"But a lot of times when something happened to somebody, I was miles and miles away. Surely I could never have that much energy."

"Usually, things happen close to a person, in the psychical space of a person, you know? But not always, as in the case of psychic healing. We've done research and we know it exists without regard to distance. And the other thing probably exists also: psychic harming. And one doesn't necessarily have to be conscious of these things for them to have an influence. What I'm saying is that you don't have to be aware of them for them to work."

"My God," I said, "my kids have almost been killed by this thing. You're not suggesting that I . . . even subconsciously . . ."

He smiled. "Of course not. A lot of things have happened to you, Doretta. It is not at all clear that *all* of them were related to what we're talking about. Steven's accident could have been nothing more than a mechanical failure in the car. There are a lot of things to sort out. We'll get to them in time."

With his tape recorder running, Dr. Roll asked question after question—about my childhood, my marriage, my children—and he listened patiently, allowing me to do most of the talking. I told him the whole story of our years in the house on Clifty Drive, bits and pieces of my abusive childhood and my relationship with my mother.

He asked if I had ever consulted a psychologist.

"Once," I said.

In the fourth month of my pregnancy with Steven, my health began to deteriorate. I gained huge amounts of weight each week, and my face and hands were bloated and swollen, and my body expanded like the Goodyear blimp. By my seventh month, the doctors at Louisville General Hospital diagnosed the problem as toxemia, or preeclampsia, a rare condition in which the mother's blood pressure rises dangerously and her body retains fluids for no known reason. When it came time to deliver, the nurse checked my blood pressure and said, "This can't be right." She summoned a doctor and there was a brief discussion about a C-section. But the baby wouldn't wait. From my bed, I could hear two doctors talking outside my door. One suggested that a priest be called in.

The delivery was pure agony, and when it was over I bled and convulsed so violently that I had to be held to the bed. I was in intensive care for ten days and remember virtually nothing of that time.

When I finally came around and met Dr. Cash, who had delivered my son, I had no idea what had happened.

"You almost died on me," he said. Later, just before I was discharged, we talked at greater length and he told me, in no uncertain terms, that I should never again become pregnant. "The next time," he said, "you *and* the baby would likely die."

He asked for permission to sterilize me and I consented. But he could not persuade two other doctors, the required number to sign off on such a procedure. I was only sixteen years old and had only one child, they argued, and therefore such an operation might be premature. But as I left the hospital, Dr. Cash warned me again, "Please, don't get pregnant again."

I did. It was about two years later. Ray Holmes and I had divorced and I had a boyfriend, whom I had met through my brother Patrick. I was eighteen and he was an older man—twenty-nine. Everyone in my family loved him. He had a prison record and a violent temper but he was also smart and charming. He read a lot and knew a lot and his knowledge of the world made him seem downright debonair. I was sufficiently taken by him to live with him for a short time before his beatings and drunken tirades drove me away. I was pregnant when I moved back to Grandma's house.

By the twelfth week, I had gained fifteen pounds and was having seizures.

"You have to have an abortion," the doctor told me.

To me, that was not even an option and I told him so.

"You'll die and the baby will die," he said.

Grandma sided with him and insisted I terminate the pregnancy. After a few days, I caved in, but knowing I had destroyed a child growing inside of me was almost more than I could bear. I went through periods of stark depression, anxiety, and nightmares. But, in time, that ordeal was pushed into the crates where I had been storing unpleasant memories all of my life.

Nearly three years passed before it broke free again. I had met and married Ron and for the first time was living what most people would consider a normal life. Unlike most of the men I had known, Ron was gentle, ambitious, and rooted in the Ozzie-and-Harriet lifestyle I had longed for. He had a family, a sense of purpose, and no prison record. Together, we had a future.

Then Grandma died and my old life seemed to wash over me like raw sewage. Her death was traumatic and I spent hours brooding over the loss. I thought of the sacrifices she had made to rear the children of her daughter, the heartaches and the poverty she had endured, the needs that were never filled. She was the person who had held me together. Without her I would not have survived.

One morning several months after she died, I sat at the kitchen table and read the Bible. I thought of the baby I had aborted and wondered if God was punishing me by taking the person who had been dearest to me. I tried to find peace in the Scriptures, but it was futile. It was a few minutes before nine o'clock when something drew my attention to the microwave oven. I looked over and saw a male face in the tinted glass front. The face didn't move. Beside it appeared a little girl, a beautiful little girl with dark curly hair and a sweet smile across her tiny face.

The faces were frozen in the microwave glass for what seemed like no more than five minutes, and they disappeared. I looked at my watch and it was two o'clock. Five hours had passed.

"That's it," I said, talking to myself. I got in my car, drove to a psychiatric hospital in Louisville, walked in, and said, "Look, I'm crazy."

I was admitted to the hospital but Ron came to get me the same day. He insisted that I leave. For a week, I stayed in bed with blankets over my head, which made my husband furious. "Get up and get yourself together," he demanded. "Handle this thing." That was Ron's way of dealing with problems. Handle them yourself without some nutty headshrinker.

Later, I made an appointment with a psychiatrist, Carolyn Peters, and saw her regularly until I was convinced I was not crazy. The hallucination was the result of pent-up guilt and anger, she said, and I needed to rid myself of both.

* * *

Dr. Roll, obviously intrigued, had been leaning toward me as I related the story.

"So, did anything happen?" he asked. "Just a picture?"

"They were like bright lights."

"Was the microwave like a television?"

"Exactly. Just like a television screen with the faces being shown on it."

"Who did you think the man was?"

"I don't know. God, maybe. I thought the baby girl was the baby I had aborted. And she had a peaceful smile on her face."

"How did you feel later?"

"A little confused. After I got over thinking I was crazy, I felt really good," I said. "It was like something very big had been lifted off my shoulders. I had hundreds of nightmares following the abortion, but I never had another one after that day. I was at peace with myself. But, my grandfather said if I told anybody about the vision, they were going to have me locked away."

"It seems to me," Dr. Roll said, "that this vision was a very positive thing. Why was everybody so upset?"

"Because I saw it."

"And you're not supposed to see things."

Chapter 26

As the producer, Joe Day's mission for "Sightings" was to capture ghosts on film, but my apparitions had never behaved so cooperatively in the past and I was not optimistic that on this occasion they would parade themselves before the klieg lights, cameras, and a house full of strangers. Outside of my family, only Jordan Pitkoff and Teri had seen them and, if I correctly understand psychic sight, it is not vision as most people infer. Psychics, Jordan had explained to me, do not see into supernatural dimensions with their eyes, but with their minds. Unless Joe Day's cameras were psychic, they might not record anything, even if my ghosts appeared before them in Day-Glo tuxedos.

Then, again, they might. My little Polaroid camera had picked up what I was certain was the wan specter of a snake just before we moved out of the house. Maybe Joe would get lucky. I hoped so. I wanted concrete evidence as much as he did.

Ron and I had resumed our talks with Dr. Roll on Saturday morning and were discussing Jordan Pitkoff when Joe Day joined us. I had become disenchanted with Jordan and made no secret of it. I had begun to feel he was using my family and stringing us along without results. He kept insisting his exorcism had been successful, but I knew better. At the same time, he used fear tactics by suggesting that the danger had not completely passed. On my last visit to his office, I had told him, "No more. I'm not coming in for any more counseling."

He said, "Well, you had better be careful, because I see some real ugly things hanging around Ashley."

We debated whether Jordan should participate in the television program. Joe preferred to exclude him and I was undecided, mostly because I thought it would be difficult to keep Jordan away. Dr. Roll suggested that Joe interview him, but that he be gone before Patricia Hayes and the other psychics from Delphi arrived.

Joe was more interested in what provoked the poltergeists, what incited them to appear, move objects, create sounds, and flaunt their derision of things mortal.

"Painting," Ron said. "You can open a bucket of paint and, boom!, it's like the atmosphere will change."

"Do you have paint at the house?" Joe said.

"We have plenty."

I mentioned that the Gregorian chants had the same effect, but we did not have the tapes with us.

"Why don't I send my production assistant out to the record store to buy some?" Joe said. "Is that a good idea?"

Dr. Roll nodded his approval.

"What else?" I mused. "Oh, emotions play a part in it."

"Are you gonna try to get angry about something while you're there, or should I try to get angry?" Joe asked.

I shrugged. "It doesn't take a lot."

We talked for a while about the house, scheduling interviews for the television segments, experiments to provoke the spirits. Then Joe began to relate a dream he had the night before.

"I was walking along and at the hotel door there were towels, one or two towels wrapped around the door. The door was shut, closed on the towels. I thought I was with someone. I said, 'Those towels are there to keep the door from locking. There must be a burglar or something in there.' And then behind me there was this steep narrow stairwell going down and I remember feeling that I was half awake and half asleep. I kind of gently floated down the staircase. As I got closer to the bottom, it got light . . . not blinding light . . . and all of a sudden I thought, *Uh-oh, I shouldn't be doing this. I want to wake up. I want to wake up.*

"I got the feeling there was something at the bottom of the stairwell and it was no longer safe just because it was a dream. Usually, when I'm dreaming lucidly I'm not afraid of anything because I know I'm dreaming. But all of a sudden I felt like this was not as safe as I thought it was. Something wasn't right and I wanted to wake up. I didn't wake up terrified, but I just felt like I should leave now. I remember thinking, *Am I going to have nightmares about all this stuff?*"

Joe was startled by my reaction. "I've definitely had a feeling that a lot of the answers for me lie beneath the ground, beneath the house."

"Literally?" he said.

"Literally." I told him about my vision of the snake charmer in the backyard and what Marilee had felt when she stood over that spot. I told him about the vision of the man killing a woman and little girl in the bathroom and dragging their bodies through a trapdoor. "The only thing that's stopped me from digging is that I haven't quite had the guts to do it."

Dr. Roll said, "Okay, we'll get four tapes, two shovels, and a spade."

Joe's eyes brightened. "If you guys want to dig, 'Sightings' would probably pay for a bulldozer."

Ron said, "If the other psychics feel that there's something there, I'll have it done. I want to know what's down there."

"Do you have any sense of how long ago these people were alive . . . like the little girl, you know, a hundred years . . .?" Joe asked.

"Not that long ago," I said. "I'm thinking it happened in the late nineteen-fifties, early nineteen-sixties. That's just my feeling."

Dr. Roll said, "Does Ashley still experience the little girl?"

"She says she's still in the house. When I told her people were coming to try to help us with the house she said, 'Are they going to hurt the little girl? Can they tell her to go into the light? That's why she's here. She was afraid of the light, so she ran away from it and got stuck here.' "

"Where does she get that about the light?" Dr. Roll said.

"I told her once that when you die, there is a beautiful light and you go into it and there is nothing to be afraid of," I said.

Patricia Hayes, Bill Clema, and Marshall Smith arrived that afternoon and went directly to the house. At Dr. Roll's insistence, we were not to meet them until after they had explored the property and conducted a psychic reading. A psi session was scheduled for seven o'clock that evening, and only my immediate family, Dr. Roll, and the necessary members of the "Sightings" crew would be permitted to attend.

The others were already there when Ron and I arrived. In spite of all the television equipment strewn about, the house seemed hollow and glum, like an empty silo surrounded by barren fields. But everyone was more or less in a jovial mood. Joe Day and the cameraman and technicians cracked jokes and made lighthearted banter, the kind of humor, I suspected, employed to vent nervousness. Patricia Hayes and her colleagues were not what I expected. They were cheerful and outgoing and exuded none of the detachment or the murky mysticism I had anticipated.

They explained what they had detected from their psychic reading of the house and grounds and I was floored. Everything they had picked up in each room matched precisely what we had seen and heard. However, each did not always see the same thing.

Patricia saw the little girl, but the two men did not. All had detected the presence we referred to as "the old man." Patricia and one of the men had seen the blond woman. Still the doubting Thomas, I wondered if Dr. Roll had briefed them earlier. But as they read from their notes, I realized they were speaking of things I had not yet told Dr. Roll.

"The blond woman is here to protect the little girl," Patricia told me. "It isn't her mother, though. The man is chasing the female entity. He had chased her through life and is now chasing her through death. The woman can leave and go on, but she won't until she knows the child is safe."

To prepare for the psi session, which essentially is a séance, folding chairs were placed in a semicircle, one chair for each participant and one empty chair for the *entity* that would be summoned.

"There is nothing to be afraid of," Patricia said, taking her place at one end of the arc. "We're just going to deal with love and light."

We were merely going to communicate with the beyond, she said, without referring to ghosts or spirits or demons. Strength and love radiated from her, and for the first time in a long time I was not afraid in that house.

We sat down, joined hands, and closed our eyes. Silence crawled over the room with the stealth of a leopard. I felt my flesh tingle just a little.

Patricia began to speak. It was more like a meditation than like a ritual. She instructed us to "breathe in healing energy from the universe . . . as you exhale feel the circle filling with the healing energy."

We were instructed to repeat:

> *I ask that healing love flow through me.*
> *I ask to be a channel of healing.*
> *I ask to be protected in the white light.*

"Visualize a large white column of light in the center of the circle," she said. "Each one project your energy into this column of light and say, 'Okay.' Breathe in and imagine feeling lighter and freer, and lighter as you lift into the column of light."

She summoned the little blond girl, implored her to take the empty chair. "Come into the circle and make your presence known," she said. "We surround you in love and light and ask that you use any one of us to identify yourself. We welcome you in love and we wish to be used as channels of healing to mentally transfer any messages you have. We need to talk to you. We need to learn what's going on."

A warm wave built in my chest, a great slumberous current that swelled into my throat and crashed and spread through my arms and legs. I felt limp and sleepy and heard my own voice, faint and distant, responding to Patricia. It was as though I were there and speaking, but not there, but a spectator high above the arena.

The little girl spoke through me directly to Patricia and tried to explain why she was there. "I'm trapped," she said. "I can't go."

"You must," Patricia said. "You need to go on. There is no peace for you here."

Once again, the air seemed to shift and become charged with electricity, and I heard one of the male psychics say, "He's here. He just walked in." It was the old man, the evil entity.

"Why are you here?" one of the psychics said.

"Speak to us," another said. "Tell us what you want. Tell us who you are."

I began coughing and choking, which was common when the old man came around. He never communicated with the psychics, and the session ended.

Joe Day was determined to draw out the entity that had intruded into the séance, if not to photograph, at least to see it for himself. He went into the laundry room, opened a can of paint, and sketched a peace sign on the wall. It didn't work, but he paced around the house consumed by his mission. "I want to see it," he kept saying.

Patricia Hayes and I talked for a long time, mostly about her school in Georgia and how people with psychic abilities can recognize and develop them. It was late when she and the other two psychics went back to the hotel. I, too, was tired and wanted to sleep, but Joe Day was wired like a smart bomb.

When the paint and the Gregorian music failed to lure the entity into the open, Joe stormed through the house shouting invectives, insulting it the way he would insult a mortal man.

"Show yourself, you pencil-dick bastard!" he yelled. "Come out and face me if you've got the guts."

His eyes were large and strained, like those of a child up far past his bedtime. Dr. Roll confronted him, admonished him to calm down. "This isn't funny," he said. "This is not something you want to play with."

At four o'clock in the morning the cameramen were still wandering around the house, filming randomly, and Joe was scurrying from room to room, cursing the ghost. I just wanted to avoid it all.

There was no furniture in the kitchen, just a bench against the wall by a window. All the lights were off in there, so I wandered in and sat down on the bench, exhausted, and tried to close off the clatter from the other rooms.

I had been there only a couple of minutes, staring blankly ahead, when the male entity appeared in the doorway across the kitchen. It moved toward me, a dusky, shifting mass of shadow, and angled to my right and stood against a paneled wall.

My first reaction was fear. The energy of the room changed and I knew this thing was capable of hurting people. Then I felt anger and defiance. "I'm so sick of you, you son of a bitch," I said, barely above a whisper. "You've wrecked my life, but you're not even brave enough to show yourself to the cameras."

As if responding to my insolence, my provocation, the apparition began to glow, to turn from shadow to light. I was alone with this thing and it was responding to me. Mentally, I had my dukes up and waited to see what its next move would be.

At that instant, Steven started to enter the kitchen through the doorway from the living room. I raised my hand, signaling him to stop. He saw the thing glowing against the paneled wall and backed away, motioning at the same time for Craig Highberger, one of the cameramen.

Craig stepped to the door and said, "Oh, shit." He had just come in from outside and did not have a camera with him, but seemed too transfixed by the apparition to think about photographs. The entity was like a ball of energy, translucent and glowing with a kind of pale gas around it. Craig's eyes were bugged out as he stepped toward the wall. It appeared that the entity was reacting to him, or that they were interacting with each other.

Suddenly, Joe Day barged into the room with a camera and bright lights and the entity vanished.

"Where is it?" Joe shouted. "Where is it?"

Craig was visibly upset, nearly in tears. He seemed shocked, awed.

"My God," he said, "I can't believe it. I can't believe what my eyes have just seen."

That infuriated Joe. "What the hell was it?" he said. "Where did it go?"

Craig said, "I can't believe you ran in here with a camera."

Indeed, if Joe had approached quietly and stood outside the door, he might have caught everything on film. Everyone seemed to sense there would not be another opportunity that night. We all wanted to leave, but Joe insisted on taping an interview with Craig for the segment. He wanted to stay the rest of the night, but I told him he would have to stay alone, because the rest of us were leaving.

He seemed partly frightened of the house and partly frustrated that the ghost had eluded him.

"I've got to go to the bathroom," he said. *Why is he telling me this? He knows where the bathroom is.*

He looked toward the hallway, turned to me, and said, "I'm not going in there alone."

I laughed. "Well, I'm not going with you. Find somebody else."

After a few seconds of thought, he went to the back door and relieved himself on the lawn.

The "Sightings" crew stayed around for a couple of more days in hopes of getting something conclusive on film. They dug a little in the backyard, but the spirits would not be provoked. Ron pointed out the three high-power lines that form a triangle around our property, and Dr. Roll used an instrument he had brought with him to measure electromagnetic currents near them. The readings were strong near the power lines, but weak near the house. If magnetic fields were a factor in my psychic excursions, he concluded, they were transient and their effects would not be constant. He wandered around and talked to a couple of neighbors. He contacted and interviewed some people who had lived in our house previously.

It was a tiring and seemingly unproductive time, wholly uneventful but for my clash with Jordan Pitkoff. He drove up from Louisville to be interviewed for the show. For months he had talked to me about spirits, entities, and infestations, but when the camera was turned on, he moderated his verbiage considerably. He talked about "spiritlike" activity, as if he was skeptical of its existence, except in the imagination. I felt manipulated, conned. He took my money, led me along with stories of malevolent beings stalking my family, but on camera, he waffled.

My blood started to boil and I couldn't restrain myself. I walked over and sat down across from Jordan. "Mr. Pitkoff," I said in a trembling voice, "let's talk about you and your infestations. I haven't heard you use the word spirits. I haven't heard you talk about the evil entities that are hanging around me and my family."

Joe Day was loving it, but Jordan's face was florid and damp with perspiration.

"Calm down," he said, rising from his chair. "Calm down. Stop the camera. Calm down."

"No, you calm down," I said. The camera continued to run. "Do you know what you did to my family? You were playing with our lives and now you come in here and act like it was something else."

"Calm down," he said again. "It's not what you think."

"There never were any demons in this house, were there? Tell me there were no demons. What the hell was it?"

He stammered, but didn't answer my questions. I ordered him to leave and followed him to the door.

After the television crew and the psychics and Dr. Roll had left town, we moved back into the house but left most of our furniture in storage in Louisville. Once again, we were living like itinerants, sleeping on mattresses on the floor and shuffling our belongings around in boxes. The first night we were alone, the whole family was relaxed and unafraid and we all fell asleep easily.

About one o'clock, I was awakened from a deep, heavy sleep. My entire body was tingling in a pleasant sort of way. Then I realized I was almost paralyzed. I couldn't move my hands or legs, not even my lips. I tried to say "Ron" but couldn't form the word with my mouth.

The next thing I was aware of was more frightening. I was not touching the mattress, but hovering above it, floating slowly away from it. I strained with every muscle to speak. In panic, I closed my eyes and tried to will my lips to speak. At last, the word "Ron" came out and I fell back onto the mattress as though I had been dropped.

"It's just your powers," my husband said. "You were levitating."

I burst into tears. He may have meant it or he may have been patronizing me, but he had no idea how scared I was. Maybe Dr. Roll and Jordan Pitkoff and Patricia Hayes had convinced him I had psychic abilities, but for me, for reasons I was only beginning to understand, the possibility was too awful to contemplate.

Chapter 27

Although I didn't realize it at the time, the filming of our story by a television crew was both cathartic and catalytic. Dr. Roll had caused me to look at what had happened in a different light. Craig Highberger's confrontation with my ghost was sweet vindication. Word of what was going on began to circulate around town, so I no longer felt the necessity to conceal anything. I could approach people honestly and they could react in any way they chose.

Georgia Jefferies was one I definitely would have to approach. Benny Cyrus had first mentioned her name to me. She had lived in my house several years earlier, before the Cyruses, when it was still the Wind Drift Motel. According to Benny, she had had an unusual and unexplainable fire in the attic over the kitchen.

When Joe Day asked for names of anyone in town who might have knowledge of the house, I gave him hers, and the producers contacted her, along with a few others, for interviews. Dr. Roll also talked with her for his files and sent a transcript of that conversation to me. It indicated that she knew much more than Benny had told me.

At my request, Georgia came by for a visit and we became friends almost immediately. She had no hesitancy in sharing what she knew about the house. Her three children were away at college most of the time she lived in the house, she said, but her son, during the brief times he was at home, often felt someone was watching him and he frequently had chills for no apparent reason.

Like us, she had applied new wallpaper, only to find it lying on the floor the next morning. She would lock her cat in the laundry room and the next morning it would be roaming the house or lying in bed with her. She also told me there had been another fire, besides the one in the attic.

"When we first moved in the furnace wasn't working," she said, "so I had the fireplace going. I was alone that morning and everything was just fine. Then smoke came billowing out of the fireplace. I got up and was almost asphyxiated. I fell on the floor and blacked out. The dog woke me up by scratching on my face. I managed to get to the phone and call my daughter at work. When she got there, the house was full of smoke and I was nearly unconscious. She put out the fire, opened all the windows, and took me to the hospital. We never really knew what happened. Somehow the damper in the flue had closed. We checked the damper and it was working fine. It just seemed to have closed by itself."

"Did you know anybody else who lived here?"

"A lady . . . the one who was supposed to have died here. Her name was Caroline Kersey."

"She died here?"

"They say she committed suicide. She took an overdose of pills or something like that. She was not in good health, a bad heart or something. I don't know any of this for sure, but from what I've heard, she took an overdose of pills and died in the bathtub."

Caroline Kersey. Of couse, I had seen the name on the old plat records, but never made the connection. Caroline Kersey. CK—the initials the Ouija board had pointed to when Marilee first visited my house. CK—the letters printed on the laundry-room wall while we were in Louisville.

"Did she have blond hair?" I asked.

"No," Georgia said, "it was dark and cut real short. There was one other person who died in that house that I know of. An old man. Grandpa Kersey. He was Caroline's father-in-law. He and Caroline didn't get along, and she supposedly treated him pretty mean."

"Did she have any children?"

"A daughter. She was retarded or something . . . never went to school. It seems like she had a lot of broken bones."

Journal entry, July 31, 1992:

> *Today seemed like the longest day of my life. The "Sightings" show will be on at nine, Louisville time, eight ours. We have seen the segment and it is powerful. We are pleased with the show. It was presented well and showed our family in a good light. I was much relieved. . . .*

The ridicule I had feared never showed itself. Our last names were not used on the show and our house was not photographed from the front. Even the town was not identified. But Ron and I were interviewed without disguise, so it was no secret in Madison. People I knew casually seemed to look at me a little differently, but if there was mockery, it was well concealed.

Initially, in fact, the opposite was true. People I had never met called and volunteered information about the house. One man knew Noble Maddox, who built the house, and he told me it had burned to the ground during construction. Another caller said he had heard many years ago that a man had burned to death in the house not long after it was built. The local newspaper ran a story about us, and reporters from Louisville called. Our story always was told in a straightforward manner and, consequently, I became less leery of publicity. A London tabloid carried an article, a Japanese television station scheduled a reporter and camera crew to visit us in September, and we agreed for our story to be dramatized for the television show "Haunted Lives." We even had calls from people who wanted to rent the house for a weekend on the chance they might get to experience a haunting.

The most negative fallout was at the bank. We were nearly broke and looking for ways to cut our overhead. After the "Sightings" show was taped—but before it was aired—we applied for an equity loan against our property. An independent appraiser set the value of the property at nearly twice what we had paid for it—the hard work we had put into the house was not totally lost—so the risk to the lender was small. The bank was agreeable on the condition that we make a few specific changes to the house. Although we were strapped for money and behind in some of our bills, we made the repairs believing we could pay for them with the loan proceeds. We received the loan papers in the mail, along with a letter advising us when to be at the bank for the closing.

On August 4, a few days after the "Sightings" segment was shown, a vice president of the bank came to visit us.

"The bank is withdrawing its offer of a loan," he said.

"Why?" Ron asked.

He glanced down, around, and then said, "Because your house is haunted."

The main benefit to the attention we were getting was that it enabled me to stay in contact with Dr. Roll. He did not charge us for his time and the expenses for his trips to Madison usually were paid by the television production companies.

We spoke frequently by phone and, as always, I did most of the talking. He listened and asked questions but didn't lecture or preach. Rather than trying to put ideas or instruction into my head, he was trying to draw something out. He had assured me my ghosts came from within, so he let me talk. If I talked enough, maybe he could discern their origins, their natures and identities. He held firmly to his notion that this haunting was enlaced with my psychic powers and encouraged me to experiment with them, test them in ways that seemed strange to me.

I resisted. "If my psyche is projecting these things into my environment, how does that explain the visions—the snake charmer, the blond woman in the bathtub, the people I've seen who have nothing to do with me? They seem to be of another time."

"Not just people have memories, Doretta," he said. "Places and objects also have memories. With your psychic gifts, which may be enhanced by periodic surges in the electromagnetic field around your house, you are receiving those place and object memories."

It all seemed too far-fetched, so abstract, that I had difficulty grasping it. Dr. Roll sent me a paper he had written entitled "Psi, Psychology and Physics."

> Psychic perception, like the familiar senses, may depend on a sense organ adapted to its own sensory field. The temporal lobes of the brain may function as a sense organ for psi. Until recently, however, no sensory field was known that this hypothetical sense organ might respond to. With the recent verification of the existence of gravitational waves, the medium through which they travel, space-time, has also been verified. The temporal lobes seem well-adapted to this field because of their orientation to the past. While the familiar senses place the body in space, the temporal lobes place it in time. Space-time may also be the medium for psi interactions.

He posed interesting questions. Do we see the past? Of course. Maybe, in a sense, that is all we see. When we look at an object on a desk, we don't see it in the present, but in the past, as it was one ten-millionth of a second ago—the time required for the brain to process the light signals. When we look at the moon, we see it as it was two seconds ago—the time it takes for the image, or the light from the object, to reach our eyes. When astronomers look through telescopes at a distant star, they are seeing it as it was millions, perhaps billions, of years ago.

What prevents one brain, through enhanced temporal lobes or some other variation, from perceiving more than another brain? Maybe it's possible. After all, the other senses in humans vary. Some of us have stronger senses of smell, keener senses of taste and touch, stronger vision and hearing. Among all animals, the degree of sensory development is more diverse. Dogs can hear sounds we cannot, but because we don't hear it does the sound not exist? A cat's eye requires only a fraction of the light needed by the human eye to see an object.

Okay, if I possessed this psychic sensitivity, I might see into the past of this house or perceive bits and pieces of the memories it held. But of all the things that had occurred in this house and in our lives in the past four or five years, those visions were the least horrible, the least significant.

The poltergeists, the apparitions, the odors and cold spots and broken windows, the light balls and fires and noises in the attic and the objects that moved by themselves, the paint and wallpaper that would not adhere, and the stain on the fireplace that could not be scrubbed away—those things were not so easily explained. They were, are, in Dr. Roll's analysis, products of my subconscious, something entombed in my head and leaking into the physical world through tender precincts of my brain.

"Very often," he said, "we find these psychic disturbances in adolescents who are going through that emotional passage into adulthood. If we look deep into the past of such individuals, we normally find a troubled childhood, episodes of violence or abandonment or sexual abuse."

Certainly, I fit the profile to a large extent.

Generally, the psychic disturbances, the merging of the mental and physical worlds, are brought on by stress or emotional upheaval, he said.

Again, I was in compliance. We had moved into the house on Clifty Drive at a time when there was stress in my marriage and, worse, I was going through the trauma of getting my sister paroled from prison to a mental hospital and confronting, through her therapy, things about our childhood and our mother that were deeply disturbing.

Psychokinesis is the term for the so-called poltergeist activity. Mind over matter. Solid objects of virtually any weight moved by the strength of the subconscious mind without the awareness or cooperation of the conscious mind, moved about even while the conscious mind sleeps.

Still it was unfathomable to me that the mind could possess such power. Yet Dr. Roll and Patricia Hayes and Jordan Pitkoff had encouraged me to experiment with that power, to develop it and, thereby, control it. Something about that frightened me, squeezed at my heart, and forced me to rebel against it.

Whenever I was tempted to toy with such things, that fear held me back . . . a picture from long ago . . . a lonely little girl peeking through the bars of a hospital crib at a little boy surrounded by toys, stuffed animals, and doting parents . . . the boy's father bringing a teddy bear to the little girl . . . the little girl's mother angrily taking it away from her . . . the stuffed bear lying in shreds and tatters on the floor.

Could the rage of a three-year-old child recruit unseen beasts for such destructive work? Did I possess that capability?

Yes, there were still times when I preferred the conjectures of the psychics and the demonologists to the rationalizations of the scholars, times when I preferred to believe that the ghosts and devils were real and I was just an innocent bystander, a random victim.

After the Japanese came and went, I was more amenable to psychic experimentation. It was the photograph, or, more precisely, the two photographs, that changed my mind. They showed one of two things: an apparition or one of my subconscious projections. Whichever it was, it was recorded photographically and it was time for me to learn, once and for all, its origins.

The crew of seven, a motor coach, and more electronic equipment then I had ever seen outside of a Radio Shack, from On-Air, Ltd., in Tokyo, arrived early in September. They set up a computer and monitoring devices in the sunroom to measure beta, alpha, and other waves in the house. Gadgets and instruments were strewn everywhere. Video cameras were placed throughout the house and connected to monitors in the RV. Cables crisscrossed the floors, and the crew photographed every square inch of the house.

Early in their stay, the house was as quiet as I had ever seen it, and they were obviously disappointed because their best electronic wizardry produced nothing of consequence.

But during the second day, one crew member, a young woman, wandered through the house taking Polaroid pictures, mostly of empty rooms. In Steven's bedroom, she stood in a corner and pointed her camera toward the doorway. The room was dim. The curtains were drawn and there was no light source from the hallway. When the picture developed, though, it revealed a large, spiral light across the wooden door that was opened against a white wall.

She looked at the picture carefully and then summoned one of her colleagues, who suggested she take another picture from the same location. In that photograph, the light was missing. All the other pictures taken from that film pack were perfectly normal, so they ruled out defective film as a cause of the peculiar photograph. Suddenly, they were excited by the prospect that their journey had not been in vain.

But the most inscrutable photograph was taken a few minutes later. I wanted a copy of the photo with the light, but since Polaroid film does not produce negatives from which copies can be made, the only option was to take a photograph of the original.

We taped the photo to a door in the kitchen and held the same camera as close as the automatic focus would allow, and made the exposure. I watched the new picture slowly develop, concerned mostly about whether a copy would show the light, the apparition, in sufficient detail.

Having lived with the ghosts of this house for so long, I thought nothing could truly amaze me anymore. But as the picture developed, it was clear it was not the same picture. The spiral light that filled a large area of the original was, in the copy, a straight beam of light cutting across the open door. And in the lower right corner there was a blurred image of two people—a man, tall, with dark hair and a mustache, wearing a dark jacket and open-collar white shirt, and a woman, much shorter, with billowing dark hair and a white dress.

The Japanese studied the two photographs, but were unable to explain the variations. They agreed that the image in the foreground was of two people and that the shape of the light had changed and was more intense in the copy. Nothing they could imagine—defective film, malfunctioning camera, fluke light waves—could have produced those results.

"Is there an unhealed soul walking around this place?" the narrator would ask when the show was broadcast a few weeks later. The photographs were displayed and the narrator asked, "Was it done by an unseen ghost?"

Or was it done by the subconscious mind of Doretta Johnson?

Watching a tape of the show some weeks later, a realization came to me. Why I had not recognized it earlier is a mystery, but I found the Polaroid copy and carried it into the bedroom and held it beside a picture in a heart-shaped framed hanging above the bed—our wedding picture of Ron with long, dark hair, a mustache, a dark jacket and white shirt with no tie, and me in a white dress. The wedding picture somehow became superimposed on a Polaroid snapshot taken in another room.

Chapter 28

One evening while writing a letter to Marilee, I paused for a moment and searched for a thought or word. The pen rested limply in my hand, still touching the paper. I felt a pressure on my hand and the pen began to move, propelled by an invisible force, pulling my hand along with it. It moved more rapidly than I could possibly write and then it became still again at the end of a sentence that was not in my handwriting: "Under the bathroom floor."

We had moved our furniture back in and had the house in pretty good shape, but I was inclined to heed the message and tear things up once again. I had read about so-called automatic writing and had discussed it briefly with Dr. Roll. Of course, there were two schools of thought about its meaning. One theory held that it was the way spirits communicated, by channeling their thoughts through a mortal medium. The other suggested that it was the subconscious communicating with the conscious. I had read about authors and songwriters and inventors and others, who claimed their best works often occurred during trancelike states. They would work in frenzied spurts only later to be amazed by their own creative output, mystified by what they had conjured up.

I had not settled into either camp in the debate over the source of automatic writing. Despite the more rational alternative, a part of me could not deny that there is communication past death. That, together with my belief that the secrets of this house were still buried here, gave enough credibility to the message that I insisted my husband open up the bathroom floor and dig beneath it.

There was a time when he would have strenuously objected, perhaps even refused. Not now. The message, I was certain, was from the blond woman, and it had arrived at a time when she was a greater presence in the house than ever before. I had seen her in the bathtub murder vision. Ashley may have seen her, as did the psychics who had visited the house.

But that September, she began to appear to others as well. It almost seemed that she was asserting herself for reasons of her own.

Ron was working on the house, putting siding over a window we had boarded up at the urging of the psychics, who believed it was an entryway for spirits. He sensed that someone was watching him, and when he turned around, there stood an attractive young woman with long blond hair. She had pale, almost translucent skin and was wearing a peach-colored dress. Ron thought she had stopped to ask directions. He started to speak to her and she vanished.

Not long after that, we hired Greg Jefferies, Georgia's son, to baby-sit while we went out for the evening. When we returned, the house was spotless. Every dish had been washed, every table and shelf dusted, all the floors freshly vacuumed.

We had expected Greg to be asleep, but he was still up, still cleaning. With a little prodding, he explained that he had been too frightened to sleep or even to sit and watch television.

He had crossed the living room toward the bathroom, he said, looked down the hallway, and saw a young, blond-haired woman in a peach-colored dress looking back at him.

I could not accept that she was a creature of my subconscious. She may have been a long-forgotten memory of this house or this land, but she was a memory that needed to be released, freed from whatever ties bound her to this place.

"I think she is buried here and can't leave until she is found," I told Ron.

He opened up the trapdoor that was in the bathroom when we moved in, and the crawl space below held confirmation of unusual activity there sometime in the past. We found a condom, a flyswatter, and the paper wrapper from an electric-saw blade.

Steven agreed to excavate that area the next day.

That night I dreamed of the spot beneath the floor and I saw a young woman, murdered, sexually violated, dismembered, and buried; I saw a man pouring concrete over the surface of a fresh grave.

Ron left early for work and Steven went to work with his shovel. I said nothing to him about my dream. About midday, he abandoned the project. A couple of feet down, he said, he had struck a hard surface and was unable to go any farther.

To continue probably would have required bringing in heavy equipment and doing greater damage to the house, which already looked like a disaster zone.

We closed the floor back up and left the secrets buried there.

*   *   *

When we moved back into the house, we were convinced that the worst of our ordeal was behind us. Consulting with Dr. Roll had given me a renewed confidence that it was only a matter of time until everything was sorted out and we could live normal lives again. But within two months, the stress began to mount again.

Grandpa got sick and had to come and live with us. Our financial burden still pressed down on us and, at times, the poltergeists seemed as mischievous as ever, tapping on walls, slamming doors, and whispering in the shadows.

I began to have vivid, horrible dreams, and I was convinced they were clairvoyant. Many were frighteningly accurate and prophetic and others were like soft lenses into the past—someone else's past, not mine. For weeks, those dreams were my reality and in them I slid back and forth through time.

I dreamed of a train wreck in England and described it in detail to Ron, who told me I was nuts. The next day, we watched a newscast about a train wreck near London.

Another dream was so perplexing that I related it to Georgia Jefferies. It took place in my house, but I wasn't a character in it. Rather, I was on the outside looking in.

"There were two men and a woman," I told Georgia. "The woman didn't dress like me and she had different mannerisms, but for some reason I felt she was me. She looked like me . . . her face and eyes . . . but she had blond hair. There was a fight in the living room, over jealousy or a love triangle. She ran out the door with one of the men and the other guy was lying on the floor. He wasn't dead, just beat up real bad. The woman and the other man ran into a restaurant with a long counter and a lot of people crowded around. Then it wasn't a restaurant. It was a pharmacy. They talked back and forth to another man and he handed them some pills. The woman opened her hand and there were two big, white pills. The man told her to take them. She did and I got the definite impression I was taking the pills and after I swallowed them it would be over; that would be the end of me."

Georgia said, "That was Beth. She was a tenant here before us. She was married, but she ran off with her husband's best friend. They were pretty rough characters, dealt drugs and the like. You know, when Greg and I first met you we talked about how much you look like Beth—except for your dark hair."

Just before Christmas, I woke up from a nightmare, went into the living room, and cried so hard that Grandpa came in to see what was wrong.

"I just had a dream and I thought Steven was dead."

It was one of those dreams that was not going to go away. Later in the morning, Ashley and I attended the annual Breakfast with Santa at St. Michael's School. When I sat down with Georgia and some other women, I was still shaking. Kellie came in with her daughters.

"What's wrong with you?" she asked.

"I had a nightmare and can't seem to shake it off," I said. "It was about some boys killed in a car wreck. I received a phone call telling me my son had sneaked out of his room and had been killed along with some other boys. Ron and I drove into a wooded area where we were asked to identify the bodies. They were covered with blankets. When we pulled them back, Steven wasn't dead. He wasn't even hurt. I didn't know any of the other kids, but one of them was wearing a flannel shirt."

"Hon, get over it," Georgia said. "It was just a dream."

We received a call that afternoon from one of Ron's coworkers. He told us there had been a car wreck the night before and three teenagers were killed. One of them was a young man named Jason, one of Steven's best friends. Jason was spending the night with a friend and they had gone riding with two other boys. Their car left the road and crashed into a wooded area. One, I learned later, was wearing a flannel shirt.

Bedeviled by guilt (did my dreams contribute to the tragedies played out in them?), uncomfortable with the growing conviction that I possessed psychic abilities I did not understand, and fearful that I would never conquer my demons, I began to slide back into depression. The emotional progress I had made from my sessions with Dr. Roll was quickly eroding. I was powerless against these forces and could not find my way out of the swamp.

Dr. Roll came back to Madison and we tried a few psychic experiments. Earlier, alone and at ease, I had concentrated on a matchstick to see if I could move it with sheer mental power. I had told Dr. Roll by telephone that I was certain the match had moved. In his presence, though, I was unable to duplicate the feat and wondered if I had imagined the earlier success.

"The other time you did it, you were playing at it," he said. "This time it is serious business. I come all the way from Georgia and . . ."

"Yeah, I felt pressure. All of a sudden, it was work."

"It's kind of hard not to make it serious," he said. "The innocence about it, the playfulness—can that be recaptured?"

"I don't know. You see, it's like two different sides to the same coin. Part of me thinks it's fun but another part gets really afraid. That part says, 'You don't understand this stuff enough to know where it can lead. If you get mad at your husband, are you going to cause something bad to happen?' "

"You're saying that if you prove you have the psychic stuff, it would be a great thing. And, if you prove you have it, it would be . . ."

"It would be a bad thing," I said.

"Well, we could decide not to do anything at all, just leave it alone and let things develop as they may," Dr. Roll said. "Or there may be some things that are okay to try. The person to ask is you, on that deeper level. You have to be the one to decide what to do."

"How much control do you have when you get into this?" I said.

"You have knowledge . . . and you may have more access to your wisdom. You are in that state when people channel, and channeling, as far as I know, is letting your higher self talk. So your higher self, or your guardian angel or whatever we call it, would be your guide."

Such psychic exploration, he said, has its perils. It may lead into closed rooms where the pain of the past is boarded up.

"Is this the time to open those windows or doors?" he said. "Again, you can choose. Is this the time to take one step, and another step some other time? It is up to you. The thing is, if something is pressed down, it builds up pressure. It is fairly common knowledge. And then it comes out in other ways, ways that are not controlled."

"I'd like to know if my moods are the cause of the happenings or the effects of them. The other night, I went to bed tired and anxious after doing some experiments and there was a presence here. I felt it . . . an old man. I saw a shadow outside the door and heard a dog barking frantically. Did I feel anxious because the presence was here or was it here because of the way I felt? That's what I want to know."

"These psychic disturbances—the dreams, the things you interpret as poltergeist activity, the apparitions—are manifestations of the pressure that has built up in you somewhere. You may have a locked room in your mind where suppressed memories are rattling around. If you let some light into it, the light of consciousness, perhaps . . ."

"I guess my worst fear is honesty," I said. "If I open the door and look into that room, then I may be left inside to deal with whatever is there. I know there is a lot of pain in there, a lot of damage."

"The light of consciousness can help you deal with it," he said.

What, I wondered, is in that locked room? I had spent most of my adult life coping with childhood memories that came to me in flashbacks during fights with my husband, in therapy sessions with my sister, in nightmares and visions. What else could the room possibly hold? How would I unlock the door?

"We could try hypnotic regression," Dr. Roll suggested. "Under hypnosis, perhaps, your subconscious will tell your conscious mind things it had shut out, things it has not wanted to deal with. You can then deal with them and put them behind you."

"I'll think about it."

Winter came to southern Indiana that year like an icy plague. As the nights lengthened and the winds broadcast snow across the farms and forests, I retreated farther into the burrow that was the house on Clifty Drive. Grandpa's health got worse and I stayed with him constantly, nursing him with undoubtable futility. His breathing became harsh and labored as the life slowly drained from him.

We brought a respirator into the house and set it in the hallway outside of Ashley's bedroom and he spent his last days there, his hair and beard growing long and white. Watching him struggle for breath one afternoon, I had another flashback, this time of a sound and a vision. A year ago I had heard raspy breathing and the wheeze of a respirator coming from that same spot in the hallway and had seen the specter of an old man reclining in a chair there, an old man with flowing white hair and a white beard.

That was no place memory. My psychic receptors had not tuned into the history of this house. That was something far different, I knew. I had heard my grandfather's death rattle long before he fell ill.

My relationship with Ron, which had improved once he began seeing the apparitions and experiencing the poltergeists, once again deteriorated as we both became convinced that my psychic powers were entwined with the events of the past few years. During that period when we could hold demons and ghostly intruders culpable for our plight, Ron and I were tentative allies. The poltergeists still had not departed and the blame was mine. Doors still slammed in the night and the ghost of the little girl was almost always with us. The disturbances were neither as robust nor as malevolent as they had been in the past, but they lingered as wicked reminders of unresolved conflict. Perhaps now Ron truly believed I was crazy. At the very least, he believed the problem was mine to fix and, in that regard, I had fared poorly.

When I was upset, which was frequently, things we now attributed to *psychokinesis* were common.

Ron came home one day and Ashley ran to meet him, shouting, "Daddy, Daddy, the candle had wings and it flew across the room."

He looked at me, somber as a mortician, and his expression seemed to say, "Is this ever going to end?" That afternoon, I had reached for a candle in a glass globe sitting on the stove. Before my hand touched it, the candle rose into the air and, as Ashley and I watched, it moved across the room and shattered on the floor near the table.

At such times, the internal conflict was ferocious. I could not have caused the candle to move; there must be a spirit present. If I did cause it, why? Was my subconscious taunting me, trying to demonstrate that it, not me—not the conscious me—was in control? Ever since we returned to the house, I had struggled to wrest control from the demons, even if they were of my own creation. All the strength and will I could muster would not accomplish that.

Dr. Roll had scheduled one more trip to Madison that winter, and I came to a decision. With his help I would try to pry open the locked room and see what the sunlight revealed.

Chapter 29

"The first thing I'm going to suggest, Doretta, is that we go back, we go to a situation in your life that may be relevant to some of the things that you are experiencing in this house," Dr. Roll began. "We'll go back to a time that you choose and you'll experience these things as if you are watching a scene unfold, images unfold on television."

It was late morning but the living room was dark, illuminated only by light that leaked in around the drawn curtains. I had reclined on the sofa and concentrated on relaxing every muscle in my body, closing out all thoughts and sounds except for the soft monotone of his voice. What I know of that session comes more from Dr. Roll's tape recording of it than from my own memory.

"Relax. Relax," he said. "You are in front of a TV and you have the remote control in your hand. You are going to click on the TV and you are going to choose a channel that has a story, a story from the life of a woman, a girl, named Doretta. The situations may or may not be emotionally intense, but they are going to be played on the television. You're going to experience those emotions from a distance, so they will be less intense to you.

"You're very relaxed. You really want to discover. You want to find out about this house, to put the pieces together, to understand the things that contributed to the things that have happened in this place. You're going to watch a program. It's called 'Playhouse of the Mind.' You are in control. You can turn it on, you can turn it off. You can do whatever you want. I will count to four and at four you will turn on the TV. You're going to see a story unfold."

He counted slowly and a picture came into focus.

A little girl. I feel that she is me but I'm not sure. She's frightened and hitting out at something. I can't see what she's hitting at.

"Look closely. See what she's hitting at," Dr. Roll said.

Her stepdad. Danny Daines. He's screaming and yelling and scaring her.

"How old is she?"

She's five and she trying to hide but Danny is holding her by the arm. He's hitting her with a belt. Her mother is there, watching her being beaten. She doesn't stop it. She won't help her. Nobody will help her.

"Why is he angry?"

"Because I wasn't supposed to go to the store. Nobody was supposed to know. Mom sent me. She made me go."

The images faded in and out like a weak radio signal. I struggled to fix on something . . . something about Danny Daines. I was like a child rummaging through a toy box looking for a lost crayon. Maybe it wasn't about Danny. . . .

> *The little girl is lying in bed, just waking up. Danny Daines is sitting beside her, slumping over with his elbows on his knees. He has tears in his eyes and sadness in his face. "Your mother left us," he is saying. The little girl gets out of bed and walks through the empty apartment. All of the closets are bare, except for the one where her few clothes are hanging. Her mother's clothes are gone; Marilee's clothes are gone; Nancy's clothes are gone. "Get dressed," she hears Danny say. He puts her things in a paper bag and calls a taxi. She's confused. Her mother packed up and moved away and left her behind. What did she do wrong? "I can't keep you," she hears Danny say. "I have to go away for a while." The cab bounces along and then stops at her grandparents' house. She looks at it through the car windows. It is quiet and deserted. Her grandparents have moved, too. What did she do wrong?*

"Your mother moved away and left you with a man who had hurt you?"

"She was scared of him and she left me with him. She hated me."

"Why?"

"I don't know."

"Did something else happen? Something you haven't seen yet?"

For an instant I saw the torn stuffed animal lying on the hospital floor and a little girl with fury in her eyes gripping the bars of the crib. Then time rolled backward.

"What is happening?" Dr. Roll asked.

"I'm kicking and screaming."

"Why?"

"He is holding my arms."

"How old are you?"

"Two."

"Who is the one holding your arms? Is it Danny?"

"No."

"Another man? A woman?"

"A man. I can't see him."

"Look up. You know who it is. Look up at his face. Who is it? You don't want to tell?"

I began to cough and cry.

"Just let yourself see what the scene is. Can you see the man?"

"Yes."

"Can you see the little girl?"

"Yes."

"What does the little girl feel?"

"She wants her mommy."

"What does the man want? Does he want to beat up the girl or does he want to do something else?"

"She doesn't like him."

"Is he a family member?"

"Stepdad."

"Another stepdad?"

Of all the stepfathers I had, of all the men my mother took up with, Jimmy Mikos was the one I knew least about. I was two years old when I went to live with my mother and him and prepare for open-heart surgery. Grandma had told me only that I was frail and needed to gather strength for the operation and that she felt inadequate to the task of nursing me along. Mother and Jimmy Mikos were better able to care for me.

"Is there something that's so unpleasant it's difficult to watch?" Dr. Roll said.

I'm wearing panties and a bra—odd that a two-year-old would wear a bra—and sitting on Jimmy Mikos's lap. Someone takes our picture. He hugs me and breathes in my face, the hot, sour breath of whiskey and meanness. I kick my legs and scream for my mother. Where is my mother? She's in the room, standing to the side, watching. There's a pain between my legs and I push my hands down to cover myself. A huge fist pulls my hands away and holds my arms behind me. Something tears at the flesh between my legs and scalding, piercing pain explodes in my stomach. . . .

"Did you know before now that he had done this?" Dr. Roll asked.

"No. She never talked. You could never tell."

"You could never tell what happened?"

"Never. Anybody."

"It had to be a secret. Well, now the secret is out, isn't it? What do you think happens to demons when their secret is out? I don't think they're as strong anymore. What do you think?"

"My mother had a demon. I thought I killed her."

"You must have really felt so angry and full of hate. Do you feel it was your angry intention? Do you secretly think your angry intention did her in?"

"She made me . . ."

"Made you do what?"

"He did it to me in front of her."

"Was that something she got from her parents? Was she hurt when she was a child, do you think? You think she was hurt?"

"She had a hard time . . . she gave all her kids away."

"Look at the little girl again. Take her in your arms. Hold her. You're strong and you can protect her. That little girl . . . Doretta . . . is no longer abandoned. She is no longer hurting. You've seen lightness. You understand things better. If you understand the hurt it becomes healing."

For a long time, I lay still and the injury I had felt dissipated like dew in the sunlight. Dr. Roll slowly counted to ten, then instructed me to return to the present and remember everything I had seen.

Memories continued to spill out of the locked room over the next couple of weeks, and some were so bizarre that I was suspicious of their authenticity. Jimmy Mikos had done more than just rape me; he had violated me in grotesque ways. I had memories of him sticking things into my vagina—sharp objects, sticks or something.

I wrote to Indiana University Hospital and requested copies of my medical records. When I received them, I became furious. They revealed that when I checked in for the heart surgery, the doctor who conducted the initial physical examination had noted that a foreign object was found in my cervix. The doctors must have told someone. My mother would have known. My grandmother must have known. Yet no one did anything. Damn them! How could anyone allow a child to be so vilely abused and say nothing?

What else, I wondered, is still in the locked room, still to be dragged into the light? Did I really have to know it all to gain control over the psychic tremors that followed me? The more I learned of my life, the more fearful I became of the powers I apparently possessed.

I have read that stress and trauma, such as violence and abuse, will alter brain chemistry and may cause permanent changes in brain function. If that were combined with a congenital brain configuration known as psychic sensitivity, might not the consequences be catastrophic? With only a thin understanding of physiology and parapsychology, I began to build in my mind fragile links between the mental and physical worlds that had been created for me and by me. Those two worlds could meld, Dr. Roll had said.

Perhaps months of abuse by a stepfather rendered a three-year-old psychic-sensitive child capable of invoking this thing called *psychokinesis* to destroy a teddy bear that was taken from her. Perhaps years of violence, abuse, and abandonment accumulated in the brain of a fourteen-year-old girl and empowered her to will her mother's agonizing death. Perhaps the guilt over an abortion compelled that same brain to project images of God and a dead child onto the window of a microwave oven. Such a brain might also project its demons into the environs of a house with its own tormented history.

What else was it capable of? Steven's car wreck and Ashley's hanging gnawed at me with beaver teeth. Could that brain harbor, in hidden layers and insurgent molecules, so great an obscenity? My worst nightmare was coming to pass. I had opened the locked room and looked inside and found scraps of myself, and I would have to live with them.

In February of 1993, I spent a week at Patricia Hayes's Delphi School of Inner Sense Development in McCaysville, Georgia. Given our financial circumstances, the tuition was prohibitive, but Dr. Roll believed it was so important for me to come to terms with my psychic abilities that he arranged for me to attend as a sort of scholarship student. Patricia was readily accommodating, both for my sake and for whatever contribution I might make to the other students whose psychic experiences had not been as intense as mine.

I went expecting to gain little more than a better understanding of how psychic sensitivity works, but I acquired far more than knowledge. I discovered a world of honesty, love, and growth—a world where psychic gifts are used to create happy lives.

The others who attended the seminar not only accepted me with open arms, they made me feel valued. There, I wasn't an oddity. No one feared me. No one doubted me. No one blamed me.

While a great deal of time was devoted to psychic demonstration—trying to sense the history of an object, such as a rock, or opening one's self to channeling—there also were large doses of clinical psychology, of sharing feelings, talking about the past, releasing inner pain and replacing it with love and understanding. And forgiving. Forgiving others. Forgiving oneself.

In group sessions, I shared deep, personal matters I had never discussed with anyone. I talked about my marriage and blamed my husband for the coldness and isolation and emptiness our lives together had become.

"He has told me he doesn't know how to love," I said.

"Some people are incapable of loving others because they have not reached that point in their emotional growth," Patricia said. "We are not to judge but we must strive for our own happiness. You deserve to be loved and you must surround yourself with people who are positive."

She helped me understand that there was no good reason for remaining unhappy. I would have to release those who were a negative force in my life. It is okay to say good-bye. Divorce my husband? The thought had occurred to me often in the past three years, but it was not a step I relished.

By the end of my week at Delphi, I felt like a new person: strong, peaceful, in control. I left a lifetime of guilt and hurt in those Georgia woods and returned to Madison eagerly anticipating my new life. That life included my husband. If I could change so radically in such a short time, surely he could do the same.

I related the details of my week at Delphi to him and he seemed pleased by the changes in me—my enthusiasm, directness, even my brashness. When I told him, as gently and lovingly as possible, that he could no longer control my life, he registered no complaint.

As the days passed, though, he began to find fault and criticize my new behavior. He was resentful of my openness with other people and my assertiveness with him. I felt myself being drawn back into the same mire. He still kept his feelings caged up, incapable, though he tried, to give the love I was determined to have. When I broached the subject of divorce, he reacted as he always did.

"That's not what I want, Doe," he said. "I want to experience the feelings you have, but I just don't know how. I want to do whatever I can to make you happy, but something seems to get in the way. I can never seem to pull it off."

In a sense, I know his need for inner peace is as great as mine. Maybe he is carrying his own demons. Why doesn't he know how to show love? At Delphi, I had looked into my heart as hard as I had explored the locked rooms of my mind. Ron needed the same searching, the same discovery. I loved him, but in a different way than I had before. I wanted him to have a good life, but I would no longer sacrifice my own happiness to that end.

Scraping together the money for him to attend Patricia Hayes's school would not be easy, but it might be the only way to save our marriage.

We talked every night by phone while he was gone, and each time I was encouraged by the changes I detected in him. He seemed to be discovering the world of love and self, and nearly each night he said, "We have a lot to talk about when I get home."

Ron changed as much as I had hoped. He was affectionate. He held me just for the sake of holding me. He laughed with me. He bought gifts for me and left cards and love notes where I could find them. We held hands and kissed in public.

I don't remember ever being so happy, and that euphoria seemed to flow through the house and seep into the land. For the first time, flowers grew in our yard. I planted shrubs, lilies, and rosebushes, and they grew. Four years earlier, we had planted three small pine trees and had barely managed to keep them alive. In the spring of 1993, they doubled in size. The lawn grew thick and green and houseplants multiplied.

Ashley was no longer afraid to sleep alone in her room or to sit up alone watching television late at night. Steven had come to terms with the fatal car wreck and was doing well in school.

As Ron had promised, we had much to talk about. Maybe too much.

In the beginning, his candor was refreshing and cleansing. He told me he honestly did not believe he loved me the entire eleven years of our marriage, that he only fell in love with me after he came back from Delphi. He confessed to lies and betrayals I had long suspected. When the poltergeist activity began, he truly thought I was crazy, he said. Even when he experienced the haunting himself, he would not defend me against his mother's suggestions that I was imagining everything.

In time, the frankness bordered on cruelty. For years I had longed for him to open up to me, to be honest and feeling and vulnerable, and at long last he was doing just that. He was baring his soul and his heart and I wanted to scream for him to stop.

When he finally confessed to an affair with a coworker, the anger built up inside of me like heat in a radiator and I made no attempt to hold it in. I swung and hit him with all the force I could muster.

"I've changed," he pleaded.

"How can I ever believe you again?"

Forgiveness may be crucial to the healing, as Patricia Hayes proclaimed, but at that moment it was beyond my reach.

The bout with Ron had left me emotionally and spiritually debilitated. *God, will it ever end?* I wondered. The next day, while he was at work and the children were in school, I moped through the routine housework and then drew a tub of hot water to soak away the misery.

I lay back in the tub, closed my eyes, and heard someone banging on the back door. I slipped out of the tub and, without drying, pulled on a robe and walked to the sunroom, where I could see through the door window. The banging continued but I could see no one. Summoned by the persistent knocking, I stepped carefully toward a window and looked outside.

No one was there. As I turned back toward the bathroom, I noticed that the door to one of the vacant motel rooms was standing open. We always kept those doors locked. For a minute, maybe two, I peered through the curtain at the black hole of that room. *I should go outside and lock it.*

I reached for the doorknob and stopped. The damp robe felt like cold rain against my skin and a shiver ran from my heels to my shoulders. I went back to the bathroom, slid into the warm water, back into the womb, back into the long night, all the way back to the beginning.

Epilogue

Journal entry, January 10, 1995:

For a long time, divorce seemed like the only resolution to the problems between Ron and me. I filed the court papers and asked him to move out. But as the weeks passed, my perspective changed. Ron felt that he really had changed and was being punished for his newfound openness and candor. He suggested that after the divorce is final we remarry and start over without the baggage of our old lives.

That was absurd. My heart ached constantly from the pain he had caused me.

Why, then, did I stop the clock and put the divorce on hold? With time to reflect, it seemed unfair to blame him entirely for the destruction of our marriage. We each brought to the union our own histories, our own weaknesses, our own burdens, our own demons. His external indifference and my internal turbulence were beyond reconciliation, but was the fault all his? I coveted the life he represented, the middle-class equilibrium, the safety, the promise. Was it reasonable for me to expect him to fully understand my childhood, with all its loathing, and the emotional burden that went with me into adulthood?

It seems I have spent my life loving people who couldn't love me back, and that may be because I couldn't love myself. I hated my childhood and hated myself for hating it. I hated my mother and hated myself for hating her.

With Dr. Roll's help, I picked up the little girl, the child Doretta, and held her in my arms and loved her. Now I am trying to find a way to love the little girl who grew up. Forgiveness is a part of maturing. I forgive myself. I am trying to forgive the man who says he loves me. . . .

*   *   *

In these pages I have tried to make some sense of the last eight years, perhaps of the last thirty-five years. If I have faltered in the explanation, it is because I have faltered in my own understanding. These are matters of the mind and the spirit and in those dimensions, the truth has many disguises.

Having entered the locked room, I'm still trying to clean it out, but I believe hard memories are still in there. As I discover them, one by one, I feel stronger and better able to control what goes on around me, better able to constrain the poltergeists. Still, I wonder if the noisy ghosts are of my own making. Most of the time I feel they are apart from me, beings unto themselves. Perhaps I'll never be absolutely certain which is the case.

This house still rebels against my presence. For no reason that I can discern, doors still slam without provocation and curtains flutter when the air is motionless. I strain to control my emotions, but anguished voices still come from the attic and cold spots move through the rooms like wayward moths. Sometimes, I still sense the presence of something that does not belong here.

And what of the visions, the holograms that are supposed to be memories held by this house? I now believe I possess a psychic gift that might enable me to perceive, with the psychic eye, things that may have happened here. But I also believe there are bodies—perhaps a blond woman and a little girl—buried on this land and their souls cannot rest until they are discovered.

One question that nagged me from the beginning concerned Ashley. Why did the haunting reside closest to her? She was the first to speak of the little girl, the people in the attic, the mean old man intent upon burning the house down. She was in the bathtub the first time I saw the image of a woman facedown in the water. It was in her room where the talking doll spoke without batteries, where we first felt the cold and found the scent of roses, where the noises in the attic were loudest.

The only answer I have is that psychic sensitivity is passed down through the genes, that it came to me from my grandmother through my mother and I have passed it on to my daughter. Several months ago, before Ron and I had separated, she told us she had a dream that two men, one of whom had dark hair, were going to break into our house.

For two weeks she insisted it would happen, but there was no burglary. Then, we received a call from the police. They had arrested two men for burglarizing a house and among the materials found on them was a list of targeted residences. Our house was among them.

Steven is an adult now and, outwardly, he seems to have put the last eight years behind him. Ashley sometimes wakes up crying, thinking something is after her, but most of the time she is happy and outgoing. She still talks about the little girl and is still protective of her.

I still watch both my children as carefully as ever and will until I know for certain this thing has ended. Each time a light flickers or a door slams or the wind brushes a branch against a window screen, my heart races a bit and I say a silent prayer. *God, don't let it start again.*